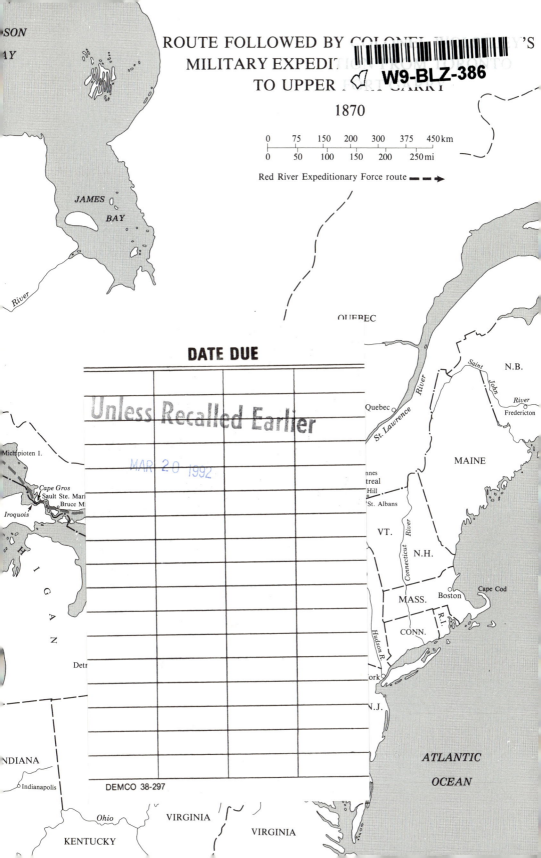

ROUTE FOLLOWED BY COLONEL ~~~~~~~~~ 'S
MILITARY EXPEDI~~~~ ~~~~~ ~~~~ ~~~~
TO UPPER ~~~~ ~~~~~~
1870

W9-BLZ-386

| 0 | 75 | 150 | 200 | 300 | 375 | 450 km |
| 0 | 50 | 100 | 150 | 200 | 250 mi |

Red River Expeditionary Force route ▪ ▪ ▪ ➤

JAMES BAY

River

QUEBEC

Michipioten I.

Cape Gros
Sault Ste. Mari
Bruce M
Iroquois

M I C H I G A N

Detr

NDIANA

Indianapolis

Ohio

KENTUCKY

VIRGINIA

VIRGINIA

Quebec

St. Lawrence River

Saint

N.B.

River
Fredericton

MAINE

nnes
treal
Hill
St. Albans

VT.

Connecticut River

N.H.

MASS. Boston

Cape Cod

R.I.

CONN.

Hudson R.

ork

N.J.

ATLANTIC OCEAN

GEORGE F.G. STANLEY

TOIL & TROUBLE

MILITARY EXPEDITIONS TO RED RIVER

DUNDURN PRESS
Toronto & Oxford
1989

Copy editor: Boyd Holmes
Design and Production: Andy Tong
Printing and Binding: Gagné Printing Ltd., Louiseville, Quebec, Canada

Dundurn Press Limited wishes to acknowledge the generous assistance and ongoing support of The Canada Council, The Book Publishing Industry Development Programme of the Department of Communications, and The Ontario Arts Council.

Care has been taken to trace the ownership of copyright material used in the text (including the illustrations). The author and publisher welcome any information enabling them to rectify any reference or credit in subsequent editions.

In the writing of this book the inferences drawn and the opinions expressed are those of the author himself, and the National Museums of Canada are in no way responsible for his presentation of the facts as stated.

J. Kirk Howard, Publisher

Canadian Cataloguing in Publication Data

Stanley, George F. G., 1907 -
   Toil and Trouble

Co-published by the Canadian War Museum.
Includes bibliographical references.
ISBN 1-55002-059-5

1. Red River Expedition, 1870.* 2. Canada. Canadian Army. 3. Manitoba - History, Military. 4. Manitoba - Militia - History. 5. Red River Settlement. 6. Manitoba - History - 1870-1918.* I. Canadian War Museum. II. Title.

FC3373.S87 1989   971.27'02   C89-095249-3
F1063.S87 1989

Dundurn Press Limited

in collaboration with

Canadian War Museum
Canadian Museum of Civilization
National Museums of Canada

Dundurn Press Limited
2181 Queen Street East, Suite 301
Toronto, M4E 1E5
Canada

Dundurn Distribution Limited
73 Lime Walk
Headington, Oxford 0X3 7AD
England

GEORGE F.G. STANLEY

TOIL & TROUBLE

MILITARY EXPEDITIONS TO RED RIVER

Canadian War Museum Publication No. 25

Canadian War Museum Historical Publications

Series editor: Fred Gaffen

Previous Titles in the Series

[1] Canada and the First World War, by John Swettenham. Canadian War Museum, Ottawa, 1968, Bilingual. OUT OF PRINT.

[2] D-Day, by John Swettenham. Canadian War Museum, Ottawa, 1969. Bilingual. OUT OF PRINT.

[3] Canada and the First World War, by John Swettenham. Based on the Fiftieth Anniversary Armistice Display at the Canadian War Museum. Ryerson, Toronto, 1969. Published in paperback. McGraw-Hill Ryerson, 1973. OUT OF PRINT.

[4] Canadian Military Aircraft, by J. A. Griffin, Queen's Printer, Ottawa, 1969. Bilingual. OUT OF PRINT.

5. The Last War Drum: The North West Campaign of 1885, by Desmond Morton. Hakkert, Toronto, 1972.

6. The Evening of Chivalry, by John Swettenham. National Museums of Canada, Ottawa, 1972. French edition available.

7. Valiant Men: Canada's Victoria Cross and George Cross Winners, ed. by John Swettenham. Hakkert, Toronto, 1973. OUT OF PRINT.

8. Canada Invaded, 1775-1776, by George F. G. Stanley, Hakkert, Toronto, 1973. French edition available.

9. The Canadian General, Sir William Otter, by Desmond Morton. Hakkert, Toronto, 1974. Bilingual.

10. Silent Witnesses, by John Swettenham and Herbert F. Wood, Hakkert, Toronto, 1974. French edition available.

11. Broadcast from the Front: Canadian Radio Overseas in the Second World War, by A. E. Powley. Hakkert, Toronto, 1975.

12. Canada's Fighting Ships, by K. R. Macpherson. Samuel Stevens Hakkert, Toronto, 1975.

13. Canada's Nursing Sisters, by G. W. L. Nicholson. Samuel Stevens Hakkert, Toronto, 1975. Bilingual. OUT OF PRINT.

14. RCAF: Squadron Histories and Aircraft, 1924-1968, by Samuel Kostenuk and John Griffin. Samuel Stevens Hakkert, Toronto, 1975. Bilingual. OUT OF PRINT.

15. Canada's Guns: An Illustrated History of Artillery, by Leslie W. C. S. Barnes. National Museums of Canada, Ottawa, 1979. French edition available.

16. Military Uniforms in Canada 1665-1970, by Jack L. Summers and René Chartrand, and illustrated by R. J. Marrion. National Museums of Canada, Ottawa, 1981. French edition available.

17. Canada at Dieppe, by T. Murray Hunter. Balmuir, Ottawa, 1982. French edition available.

18. The War of 1812: Land Operations, by George F.G. Stanley. Macmillan of Canada, Toronto, 1983. French edition available.

19. 1944 The Canadians in Normandy, by Reginald H. Roy. Macmillan of Canada, Toronto, 1984. French edition available.

20. Redcoats and Patriotes: The Rebellions in Lower Canada, 1837-38, by Elinor Kyte Senior. Canada's Wings, Stittsville, Ontario, 1985. French edition available.

21. Sam Hughes: The Public Career of a Controversial Canadian, by Ronald G. Haycock,. Wilfrid Laurier University Press, Waterloo, Ontario, 1986.

22. General Sir Arthur Currie: A Military Biography, by A. M. J. Hyatt. University of Toronto Press, Toronto, 1987.

23. Volunteers and Redcoats — Rebels and Raiders: A Military History of the Rebellions in Upper Canada, by Mary Beacock Fryer. Dundurn Press, Toronto and Oxford, 1987.

24. Guarding the Goldfields: The Story of the Yukon Field Force, ed. by Brereton Greenhous. Dundurn Press, Toronto and Oxford, 1987.

For further information on these titles, please write to the Canadian War Museum, Canadian Museum of Civilization, National Museums of Canada, Ottawa, Canada K1A 0M8.

DEDICATION

LE MORAN SPEIS DO M'MHNAOI
RUTH LYNETTE 'IC SHEASACHAN
A CHAIDH AIR A CEUD TURUS DO'N
ABHAINN RUADH ANN AN CARBAD OLA
TRI FICHEAD 'S A SEACHD BLIADHN' DEUG
AN DEIH DO KATE ST. JOHN A DHOL AIR ANN
TURUS CEUDNA ANN AN CURACH INNSEANACH

The god of soldiers,
With the consent of supreme Jove, inform
Thy thoughts with nobleness, that thou mayst prove
To shame unvulnerable, and stick 'i the wars
Like a great sea-mark, standing every flaw
And saving those that eye thee!

CORIOLANUS ACT V, SCENE III

ACKNOWLEDGEMENTS

This book is a work of traditional history. It tells the story of several military expeditions to the Red River Settlement, later Manitoba, exploits without carnage or moral involvement; exploits triggered by political flaccidity, but still, nevertheless of considerable note in the time and space of over a century ago. The several Red River Expeditions took place in an age when the people of Canada were becoming conscious of themselves as Canadians, not blind to the weakness of imperial Britain nor yet bedazzled by the imperial expansion of the United States.

In preparing this work I am indebted to many individuals: to those who provided me with source materials, in particular, the directors and staffs of the Canadian War Museum, the library of the Royal Military College of Canada, the Bell Library of Mount Allison University, the Saint John (N.B.) Public Library, the Cambridge Military Library (Halifax, N.S.), the Dalhousie University Library, the Queen's University Library, the National Archives of Canada, the Public Archives of Manitoba, the Glenbow Alberta Museum, and La Bibliothèque de la Burgergemeinde (Bern, Switzerland). To all of them I express my sincere gratitude.

I also acknowledge my indebtedness to His Honour Dr. George Johnson, Lieutenant-Governor of Manitoba, Miss Karen Smith, Mr. Hugh Dempsey, Mr. John Blackwell, Dr. Eileen Travis, Monsieur Guy de Meuron of Basel, Switzerland and Dr. William Rodney of Royal Roads Military College. I also express my thanks to Dr. Allan Ronaghan and Dr. Henry Best for the loan of their unpublished theses on Colonel Garnet Wolseley and Sir George Cartier, respectively. To the institutions and individuals who provided the illustrations, I am also greatly obligated. Pictures help explain the text and, I hope, add to the readers' pleasure.

For critical advice, I offer a special word of thanks to Mr. Fred Gaffen of the Canadian War Museum, and to Dr. Desmond Morton, Lieutenant-Colonel Daniel S.C. MacKay, Dr. Ruth Stanley and Dr. Laurie Stanley-Blackwell. For historical errors, solecisms or misspellings, I have only myself to blame.

The heavy responsibility of typing and preparing the manuscript for the publisher was assumed by Ruth Stanley and Gilda Cuming. The Reverend Sister Margaret McDonnell prepared the dedication. The maps were the work of William Constable of the Historical Section of the Department of National Defence; his artistry adds clarification to this book.

George F. G. Stanley

Sackville, New Brunswick
St. Crispin's Day, 1989.

CONTENTS

PROLOGUE
Fort Garry, 24 August 1870

Some time during the afternoon or evening of 24 August 1870, Redvers Henry Buller — a captain in Her Majesty's 60th Rifles (Royal Americans)[1] — took time from his military duties to write a letter to his sister, Henrietta.[2] Buller had just completed the journey from Thunder Bay on Lake Superior, to Fort Garry, as a member of Colonel Wolseley's Red River Expeditionary Force. It had been a strenuous journey, one that had lasted 39 days. Buller outlined some of the problems he had encountered as a junior captain and some of the hardships and dangers he had endured since embarking in unfamiliar watercraft on the unfamiliar waters of Shebandowan Lake on 16 July. After five and a half weeks struggling through the rocky, watery wilderness between Prince Arthur's Landing and Fort Garry, where even the silence seemed menacing, Wolseley's troops, Buller among them, finally drew up in battle array and advanced slowly to the expected assault. Here is how Buller described the capture of Fort Garry to his sister:

> Reveillé sounded at 3 but it was raining so hard that we did not get off till about 7 & then we had no breakfast as the rain beat us all in our attempts to make fires. We rowed to within 1 1/2 miles [2.4 km] of the fort & then all landed & in the pitiless rain marched to the attack; B Company skirmishing in front, H behind, the remainder, Guns Staff and foot in the middle up to our knees in thick, sticky, slippery black mud, we splashed our way; cutting through the corner of the town of Winnipeg, a scattering collection of indifferent wooden houses on a muddy road where we were enthusiastically greeted by a half naked Indian very drunk. We marched across half a mile of prairie and reached the back door of Fort Garry just as Riel & O'Donoghue his secretary walked out of the front door. Finding the back door open, we formed line, fired 21 guns, presented arms, gave three cheers for the Queen and stood at ease in the rain and so ended the attack & capture of Fort Garry. Just at this moment a supposed loyal citizen showed me two men standing on the opposite

*side of the river whom he informed me were Riel &
O'Donoghue, they were looking at us & in about 10 minutes
mounted their horses and rode off leisurely. (From what I
have since heard I have no doubt that it was really them.)*

*Well we took the fort & marched in the band playing the
Regimental Quick-Step & the men were given quarters in
some of the H.B. Store houses which Riel and his gang had
left pretty empty, and the officers went into Riel's house
which we incontinently proceeded to loot. He evidently was
rather hurried in his departure as we found his breakfast
served on the table still warm & only half eaten, we finished
it having had none ourselves, turned the house upside down,
found nothing worth taking unless perhaps this elegant
paper of sorts on which I am writing. Having cleaned out the
House we went into the good town of Winnipeg where we got
a very good dinner as much beer as we could drink for 2/6.[3]
I fancy we rather frightened the men with our capacity for
beer. Since that I have been wandering about, conversing
[with] enlightened citizens loyal & disloyal. And the more I
hear the more I am convinced what an utter farce this is that
we have come so far to take part in. Riel it appears was
originally incited to his rebellion by the H.B. Co. who put
him up to embarrass the Canadian authorities and to keep
back the settlement of the question, but he got too strong for
them, took possession of the Fort and pillaged them to such
an extent that they had to ask for assistance to turn him out.
I think if they were to hang a few priests up here it would
probably have a good effect; but I imagine the whole business
is a political job of that scoundrel Cartier's[4] and that everybody will be pardoned.*

*Fort Garry itself is an enclosure of about 4 acres [1.6
hectares] the front & half each side wall being stone, the back
and the other half of the side walls wood, there are 10 stone
bastions —4 corner ones two to each gate & one in the centre
of each side.*

*It is a strong structure and as Riel had plenty of guns rifles
and ammunition he might have made a very considerable*

12

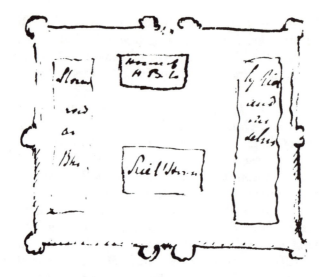

[sic] within it. I wish he had. It does so disgust one to have come all this way for the band to play God Save the Queen.

We leave this on Tuesday the 30th and shall be I suppose in Toronto about the middle of October. I hear we are to winter in Quebec; I should much myself have preferred Halifax or Montreal.

We hear distant rumours of great wars and the French being licked,[5] we also hear that the Army is to be increased; will you ask Jim if that is really true to write to H. Milligan and to ask him to try and get me in the event of the 4th Bttn being augmented transferred to it; tell him to tell Harry that I am going to write to him or the Col. as soon as I can but I expect that will not be before I get back. Mind and remember about the transfer.[6]

I am very well as this sort of work always agrees with me. I can not think of anything more to say so with my best love I am

Redvers Buller

MAJOR-GENERAL SIR REDVERS H. BULLER, V.C., K.C.M.G., C.B.

Redvers Buller

Colonel Garnet Wolseley, commander Red River Expedition, 1870.

CHAPTER ONE

The Soldier Explorers
1685-1816

I

When Canadians think about the first white men to establish a European presence in western Canada, it is the priest, the Christian missionary, who first comes to mind, followed by the fur trader. Few think of the military men, the soldiers of the state rather than soldiers of the cross. And yet the historical fact is that the western part of our country was first penetrated by young men who, for the most part, were soldiers, officers commissioned in the service of our first monarchs, the Kings of France. It was these men who pushed the Capetian flag beyond the limits of the "Western Sea," as Lake Superior was then known, through the Laurentian Shield and into the black-loamed prairies.[1]

There was, for instance, Daniel Greysolon Du Lhut, an officer who had served in Europe under Louis de Bourbon, "the Great Condé", the eminent and talented military officer who fought against Dutch William, later William III of England. Returning to Canada in 1675, Du Lhut established the French Canadian presence in the west by building posts on Lake Nipigon and on the Kaministikwia river in 1685. The latter, Fort Caministigoyan as it was originally called, was designed to attract the Indians southwards, away from the English Hudson's Bay Company posts on Hudson Bay. After Du Lhut came Zacharie Robutel, Sieur de la Noue, another young Canadian officer, who, along with Pierre Le Moyne d'Iberville, had taken part in the Chevalier de Troyes's destructive raid on the Hudson's Bay Company's posts in 1686. Some years later, in an effort to find a feasible overland route leading to the western ocean, la Noue came across Du Lhut's fort. It was in ruins. He therefore constructed a new one, on the opposite bank of the Kaministikwia.

Hard on la Noue's heels came the greatest of all early Canadian explorers of the eighteenth century, Pierre Gaultier de Varennes, Sieur de la Vérendrye. Like his precursors, Vérendrye came from a military background. His father had initially come to Canada as a member of the Carignan-Salières Regiment. Pierre, too, served as an officer in a French regular regiment, the Régiment de la Bretagne. He saw active service in Europe, taking part in the battle of Malplaquet, that "very murderous battle," as Marlborough called it, fought near Valenciennes in northern France in 1709. Returning to Canada, Vérendrye, carrying a commission as ensign, was sent as second-in-command to the Poste du Nord (Lake Nipigon), with responsibilities covering the north shore of Lake Superior. Fascinated by the vast, relatively unknown regions beyond his post, Vérendrye asked for and received permission to do some exploring.

During the next fifteen years he travelled widely, using the water routes so familiar to later generations of Montrealers. In the course of his journeys, he established a number of posts, or "forts" as they were called, including one at the mouth of the Pigeon River (Grand Portage) south of la Noue's old position on the Kaministikwia. Others were erected on the shores of Rainy Lake (Fort St. Pierre), Lake of the Woods (Fort St. Louis), at the mouth of the Red River (Fort Maurepas) and Forts Rouge (Winnipeg) and La Reine (Portage La Prairie) on the Assiniboine.

Following the establishment of the Canadian North West Company in 1783, a new post was constructed on Lake Superior, near the site of la Noue's post on the Kaministikwia. It was called Fort William, after William McGillivray, the principal director of the Company. Once it became clear the Grand Portage was in American territory, according to the treaty that brought the American Revolutionary War to an end, Fort William became the principal Canadian post on Lake Superior. Reconstructed in 1811, it became the western headquarters of the North West Company. Gabriel Franchère, who saw it in 1814, described it as follows:[2]

> Fort William has really the appearance of a fort, with its palisade fifteen feet [4.5 m] high, and that of a pretty village, from the number of edifices it encloses. In the middle of a spacious square rises a large building elegantly constructed, though of wood, with a long piazza or portico raised about five feet from the ground and surmounted by a balcony extending along the whole front. In the centre is a saloon or hall sixty feet in length by thirty in width [18 m x 9 m] decorated with several pieces of painting and some portraits of the

leading partners. It is in this hall that the agents, partners, clerks, interpreters, and guides take their meals together at different tables. At each extremity of the apartment are two rooms; two of these are destined for the two principal agents; the other two to the steward and his department. The kitchen and the servants' rooms are in the basement. On either side of this edifice is another of the same extent, but of less elevation; they are each divided by a corridor running through its length and contain each a dozen pretty bedrooms. One is destined for the wintering partners, the other for the clerks. On the east of the square is another building similar to the last two and intended for the same use, and a warehouse, where the furs are inspected and repacked for shipment. In the rear of these are the lodginghouse of the guides, another fur-warehouse, and finally, a powder magazine. The last is of stone and has a roof covered with tin. At the angle is a sort of bastion or lookout place commanding a view of the lake. On the west side is seen a range of buildings, some of which serve for stores and others for workshops; there is one for the equipment of the men, another for the fitting out of the canoes, one for the retail of goods, and another where they sell liquors,

Lord Selkirk's sketch of Fort William, 1816.

> bread, pork, butter etc., and where a treat is given to the travellers who arrive. This consists in a white loaf, half a pound [.227 gms] of butter, and a gill [1/4 pint — .284 litres] of rum. The voyageurs give this tavern the name of *Cantine salope*.[3] Behind all this is another range, where we find the counting-house, a fine square building, and well-lighted; another storehouse of stone, tin-roofed; and a jail, not less necessary than the rest. The voyageurs give it the name of *pot au beurre* — the butter-tub.

The *cantine salope* was an ideal spot for newly arrived voyageurs to consume their quart of rum, or more if they so desired. If and when they became inebriated, they were carried off to jail — half a pound of butter in hand — to spend the night in the "butter-tub."[4]

Once a year, during the summer months, Fort William was the scene of a general rendezvous of the Montreal partners and the partners who wintered in the west. They assembled for the purpose of discussing the general business of the Company, and determining the policy to be followed. Then, in the summer of 1816, strangers came to Fort William. They had not been invited. They were soldiers — in unfamiliar uniforms.

CHAPTER TWO

The First Red River Expedition 1816

I

The events of 24 August 1870, as described by Redvers Buller, were, in many ways, simply a continuation of the bloody encounters arising from the bitter competition between the two fur companies that dominated western Canadian history during the early years of the nineteenth century, and from the efforts of Thomas Douglas, fifth Earl of Selkirk, to solve social problems in Scotland and Ireland by encouraging emigration from the British Isles to North America. Not to the United States — indeed, part of Selkirk's purpose was to divert the stream of British emigrants moving to that country, by offering a feasible alternative within the territories of the British Empire. His original colonies in Prince Edward Island and Upper Canada proved less successful than he had hoped. However, after marrying into an influential Hudson's Bay Company family, the Wedderburns, Selkirk focussed his attention on the Company's territories as a possible location for his philanthropic efforts. Hoping for assistance from the Company, he began to purchase Hudson's Bay Company shares with a view to obtaining a Company directorship. His fellow directors, hard-nosed businessmen all of them, were, however, more interested in profits than philanthropy. Selkirk failed to arouse any real interest in or concern for the indigent people of Scotland and Ireland; but he did succeed in obtaining from the Company a grant of 30 million hectares (116,000 square miles) of land in what is now southern Manitoba and northern Minnesota. It was, in area, at least five times that of his native country, Scotland.[1] The Hudson's Bay Company was not interested. If Selkirk was intent upon starting another colony, it would be his responsibility. In no way discouraged, the Scottish nobleman went ahead with his plans, enlisting the services of a Canadian Scot, Miles Macdonell of Glengarry, to lead the first band of hopeful Scots, Orkneymen and Irishmen to the promised land of Red River.[2]

Thomas Douglas, Fifth Earl of Selkirk, 1771-1820.

Miles Macdonell ("Captain Cartouche").

Selkirk, however, had given little thought to the fact that his land grant and his proposed colony were located astride the overland route from Canada to the North West used by the Hudson's Bay Company's rival in the fur trade, the North West Company; and located, too, in a region favoured by that Company's buffalo hunters, the mixed blood Métis, who kept the interior posts furnished with pemmican, the staple food of the fur trade. The London-based Hudson's Bay Company always used the Bay route to reach the interior of the country; the Montreal-based Nor'Westers relied on the overland canoe route, originally used by the early French explorers and missionaries. That meant travelling over the Great Lakes, and along the intricate line of island-studded lakes and brawling rivers lying between the western shore of Lake Superior and the valley of the Red River of the North. Thus, when Miles Macdonell led the advance party of Lord Selkirk's settlers from York Factory on Hudson Bay, to Red River, he was entering a region the Montrealers regarded as peculiarly their own, if not by actual title from the Crown, at least by prior occupation. It did not help matters that Selkirk's settlers arrived at a time when the North West Company's supply of beaver skins was declining and when trade rivalry with the Hudson's Bay Company was assuming a rough and bitter character. And here was this unrealistic philanthropist, Lord Selkirk, about to establish an agricultural colony in the heartland of the buffalo country! Agriculture and hunting made uncomfortable bedfellows in the most favourable circumstances; and the circumstances were not favourable in 1812. If the colony survived, it was to be expected that the buffalo might not.

Selkirk's colony struggled along, receiving reinforcements in 1813 and 1814. But the growing numbers and dogged persistence of the colonists only aggravated the problem of finding food in quantities sufficient to satisfy the demands of both the fur traders and the colonists. Realizing the problem, "Captaine Cartouche" — the name given to Miles Macdonell by the French Métis — despite instructions from the Earl to use caution, issued a proclamation prohibiting the export of pemmican from the Red River region. His proclamation was dated 8 January 1814. It was an order of questionable legality, and although a temporary accommodation was arrived at with the Nor'Westers, the latter were more than ever convinced that Selkirk's colony was really part of a deep-seated plot on the part of the Hudson's Bay Company to cripple their trading rivals, at a time when the Nor'Westers were struggling to revive their economic fortunes. When, later in the year, Macdonell ordered the Nor'Westers to vacate their posts at Fort Gibraltar and Fort Dauphin, on the grounds that the land on which these forts stood belonged to the Earl of Selkirk, the Nor'Westers decided to take positive action. It was plainly, as the bourgeois saw it, a matter of economic survival.[3]

The tactics adopted by the Nor'Westers constituted a combination of "soft sodder," to use Sam Slick's familiar words, and the iron fist. Perhaps the settlers might be lured away from Red River with promises of better lands in Upper Canada and assistance to get themselves re-established. That was to be the responsibility of Duncan Cameron, who had served in the War of 1812 with the North West Company's Voyageur Corps, wearing, not his own captain's but a major's uniform, complete with sword borrowed for the occasion! Especially the sword, the symbol of military rank and authority. As for those stubborn souls who resisted, they would be compelled to leave. Force would be applied by the "freeman," the voyageurs, the Métis, the men trained to the North West Company's discipline; "a daring and numerous race," William McGillivray called them, "who considered themselves the possessors of the country and lords of the soil."[4] As far as Macdonell and his spurious "sheriff," John Spencer, were concerned, they were to be arrested on Canadian warrants and sent to Montreal for trial. "I hope that things will go better now," said the Nor'Wester, Charles McKenzie, "since the colony is gone to the Devil."[5] Whether they realized it or not, the Nor'Westers, by stimulating Métis nationalism were sowing the dragon's teeth.

Lord Selkirk's settlers generally proved to be men and women of tough fibre. The colony did not go to "the Devil," as McKenzie had predicted. Some of the settlers did, admittedly, go to Canada; but the rest went no farther than Lake Winnipeg. Despite the action of the North West Company in deporting Miles Macdonell, a new contingent of colonists, under the leadership of Robert Semple, arrived in Red River. Selkirk, too, hurried to Canada to take issue with the Canadian authorities over their failure to do anything about the illegal and high-handed actions of the North West Company. He wanted military protection for his colony. Sir Gordon Drummond (then acting as provincial administrator in Upper Canada) was, however, reluctant to send troops to Red River without positive instructions from London. He would look more deeply into the matter. But official investigations rarely moved with alacrity; and as far as Selkirk was concerned, time was of the essence.

The situation in Red River was daily becoming more explosive. Resettled on their farms with the help of Colin Robertson, a former Nor'Wester, now turned Hudson's Bay Company man, Selkirk's

Fort Gibraltar, c. 1804, sketch by H.J . Robertson.

settlers resumed their farming activities. Then, Robertson seized the North West Company post, Fort Gibraltar, with its field pieces and stands of arms, and placed several of his former associates under arrest. No blood was shed; but tempers were running hot. Nothing deterred Robertson. Fort Gibraltar was dismantled and what could be used to strengthen the Hudson's Bay Company post at Point Douglas was rafted along the river. The shell of Fort Gibraltar was then burned to the ground. To the Selkirk settlers, the Fort had been a symbol of oppression; but to the North West Company, it had stood as a symbol of their presence in the Red River valley. Were they going to accept Semple's action without a word or act of protest?

The Nor'Westers' response came quickly. Not from the fur traders themselves, but from their employees, the Métis. How far the Nor'Westers are to be held responsible for what subsequently happened may be a matter of argument. According to one man, John Pritchard, a former Nor'Wester who, out of favour with the Company, had become a settler, the blame could rightly be attributed to his former associates. During the early months of 1816 reports were constantly reaching the settlement that the Métis were assembling "for the purpose of driving us away"; and the nearer the spring approached, "the more prevalent these reports grew and letters received from different posts confirmed the same." On 19 June, a man in the watch-house at Fort Douglas cried out "the Half-Breeds are coming!" Semple, seeing for himself that this was no false alarm, said, "We must go out and meet these people; let twenty men follow me."[6] Caution advised that he should have remained behind the walls of the fort; for the Métis were not equipped to assault a fortified position. As the Métis appeared on horseback, about a kilometre away, Semple realized that his party was outnumbered. At that point he ordered forward a field-piece from the fort. But it was already too late. When the Métis rode up, more than sixty strong, some with faces painted in the Indian style, they formed a half-moon in front of Semple's men, partly surrounding them. Addressing Semple, one of the horsemen cried, "What do you want?" "What do *you* want?" was the governor's sharp reply. "We want our fort," came the answer. At this point Semple made the foolish gesture of trying to seize his questioner's musket. According to John Pritchard, who was present with Semple, "almost immediately a general discharge of firearms took place; but whether it began on our side or that of the enemy, it is impossible to distinguish."[7] The outcome was short and bloody. Semple had no chance. Within minutes, twenty of his companions were dead or dying, their bodies stripped and mutilated and their corpses left on the plain to rot. A sudden burst of passion and both Cuthbert Grant, the Métis leader, and Seven Oaks, where the skirmish occurred, became unforgotten names in Manitoba's history.[8]

II

Back in Canada, Selkirk was bombarding the acting Governor, Sir Gordon Drummond, with petitions to send a military force as soon as possible to protect the beleaguered settlers of Red River. While Drummond procrastinated, arguing that he could not act until he received "further and more specific instructions" from His Majesty's Government in London,[9] Selkirk looked elsewhere for help. There it was in Canada, ready and available: ex-soldiers, discharged from two Swiss regiments that had served on the British side against the Americans during the late war. Here were men who could fight and might be persuaded to remain in the west as settlers. Selkirk therefore engaged some 80 veteran soldiers from de Meuron's Regiment, together with four of their officers.[10] In addition, another 20 from de Watteville's Regiment and a few Glengarry Fencibles signed the engagement forms. They were to be employed and paid, not as soldiers but as civilians, at fixed rates, to navigate Selkirk's boats en route to Red River. On arrival in the Colony, each man would be given free land according to his rank. Although no longer technically soldiers, these men were allowed

Private soldier (Régiment de Meuron), watercolour by G.A. Embleton.

to retain their uniforms; and Selkirk provided them with firearms. There was nothing illegal about these engagements and the Canadian authorities were well apprized of what Selkirk was doing. With approximately 100 experienced soldiers, the Earl left Montreal on 4 June. Travelling by water, ten to twelve soldiers and three or four Canadians to a boat, Selkirk's flotilla passed York (Toronto) on 30 June, and then, travelling overland to Georgian Bay, they reached Sault Ste Marie by water on 29 July.[11]

Up to this point it had been Selkirk's intention to bypass the North West Company's headquarters at Fort William, travelling, instead, along the south shore of Lake Superior to the Grand Portage. He had no desire to provoke a confrontation or physical collision with the Nor'Westers. Then, at Sault Ste Marie, he was made aware of the events at Seven Oaks, the dispersal of his colony and the arrest of his colonists. At once he changed his plans; now he would go directly to Fort William, challenge the Nor'Westers face to face, and demand the release of those settlers being held in custody. To Sir John Sherbrooke, Governor of Canada, he wrote:

> It is with feelings of the most anxious concern, that I have to add the information recently received here of the success which has this season attended the unprincipled machinations of the North-West Company, who have again effected the destruction of the settlement on Red River, with the massacre of about twenty of the settlers and servants of the Hudson's Bay Company. The circumstances attending this catastrophe, and those which immediately led to it, have, as yet, reached me only in a very imperfect manner, and through channels which cannot fully be depended upon. I have no doubt that the North-West Company are in possession of more accurate information, but the interest they have to misrepresent the facts, must be too evident to require any comment. Of this I am confident, that Mr. Semple was not a man likely to act in a violent or illegal manner, so as to give any just ground for such an attack as appears to have been made. I trust that, in the course of a few days, I may obtain more complete information on this subject, at Fort William, where are now assembled many persons who must have direct knowledge of the facts, and on whom I propose, as a magistrate, to call for information.[12]

Captain Protais Odet-d'Orsonnens
(Régiment de Meuron).

Selkirk went on to point out that he would have preferred to use "some other magistrate" than himself, but since none was readily available, he was "reduced to the alternative of acting alone, or of allowing an audacious crime to pass unpunished." He continued, "I cannot doubt that it is my duty to act, though I am not without apprehension that the law may be openly resisted by a set of men who have become accustomed to consider force as the only criterion of right."[13]

Therein lies the explanation of Selkirk's change of course from Fond du Lac to Fort William. On 10 August, his boats entered Thunder Bay. Two days later they moved up the Kaministikwia River to the point above the North West Company fort. The soldiers disembarked and Selkirk set up his camp. William McGillivray, the principal partner of the North West Company, watched the whole proceeding through his telescope, unsure of what it portended, until a letter was placed in his hands by Captain Protais Odet-d'Orsonnens, demanding that the Nor'Westers free such Hudson's Bay Company employees as were being held in custody at Fort William. The letter bore Selkirk's signature as a Justice of the Peace of Upper Canada. Four of the prisoners were promptly released, including John Pritchard, who had survived the killings at Seven Oaks. Of the remainder, McGillivray told Selkirk that two of them had come to Fort William of their own accord; two others were on their way to Montreal "charged with felony."[14]

Meanwhile the Swiss, directed by two of their officers, Matthey and Graffenried, took possession of McGillivray's fort, encountering only minimal resistance. Graffenried described the episode in these words:

> Suddenly I heard bugle calls. Thinking that help was needed I got hold of my weapons and jumped into a boat where already several soldiers were present. We advanced towards the Fort in good formation with Matthey in front. In passing by, I admonished the North West Canadians to remain calm. With the remaining men we entered the Fort and took two small cannon and posted guards everywhere.
>
> Because the soldiers were dressed half in uniform and half in civilian clothes, and the officers wore short jackets, armed with swords and pistols, we resembled a band of robbers. At first it appeared that the men of the North West Company were going to resist. They locked the gates, as the constables approached under

Fort William, 1812.

cover; our men, however, were in no mood to fool around and broke down the gate. After a brief scuffle the fort was taken. The bugle call had been a sign of victory and not a call for help. Fortunately no shot was fired, otherwise we could not have restrained our men from plundering, and in all likelihood blood would have been spilled.[15]

This action was followed by the arrest of the old Nor'Wester himself and the detention of other North West Company leaders. All of them were unceremoniously bundled off to York and then to Montreal, under an escort commanded by Captain de Lorimier of the Canadian Indian Service and Lieutenant Fauche of the de Meurons. But, unfortunately for Selkirk, not before the Nor'Westers had succeeded in destroying much of the incriminating documentary evidence upon which the Earl was expecting to base his legal action against them.

With the Nor'Westers humbled and leaderless for the moment Selkirk was free to give thought to the restoration of his colony. For some months he had wanted to visit the Red River settlers, give them his personal encouragement and rebuild their morale. But that meant clearing the approaches. Accordingly he sent Captain Orsonnens, with a company of 30 de Meurons and a few Canadians, to seize the North West Company post at Lac la Pluie. Selkirk originally thought of sending two cannon with them; but when he discovered it would be difficult to manhandle the guns over the first portage, he left them at Fort William.

It was late in the season. The water level in the rivers was low and ice was forming, and only with great difficulty did the Swiss manage to reach Rainy Lake post safely on 3 October.[16] Orsonnens encountered no resistance here, and he readily accepted the assurances of the Nor'Westers that they would abstain from all hostile action. The Swiss officer had been given authority by Selkirk either to remain at Rainy Lake for the winter or to go on to Red River. The decision would be his. D'Orsonnens appears to have been uncertain which course of action to take. But when he was joined by Miles Macdonell, the Glengarrian who had overseen the beginning of the Red River Settlement, the Swiss officer decided to push on to the prairie country. Despite the lateness of the season, Orsonnens and Macdonell, with a mixed bag of de Meurons, de Wattevilles and Glengarry Fencibles, set off for Red River on 10 December, dragging two brass field pieces mounted on

Summer view of the environs of Fort Douglas, 1822, watercolour by Peter Rindisbacher.

runners with them. Because he did not altogether trust the Nor'Westers, Orsonnens sent several Nor'Westers ahead, telling them to follow the traditional route to Red River by way of the Winnipeg River. But not to forget that he would be following sharp on their heels.

This threat was only a *ruse de guerre*. Instead of making the journey by way of the Winnipeg River, Orsonnens and Macdonell followed the North West Company party through the dark and sombre woods, only as far as Lake of the Woods. Here they changed direction. They abandoned the frozen waterway and cut westwards through the bush and over the snow-covered prairie towards Fort Daer, a flimsy stockade near Pembina, which had been chosen by Macdonell some years previously as a suitable site for a stockade owing to its proximity to the pasture grounds of the buffalo. The weather was bitterly cold, the strong winds and biting blizzards forcing delays and taxing the endurance of both Swiss and Canadians alike. Nevertheless the soldiers reached Fort Daer safely and, after a few days warming their stomachs and their bodies and strengthening their resolve, Orsonnens and Macdonell pushed northwards towards Fort Douglas. Leaving Fort Daer on 2 January, the Swiss-Canadian force finally reached the junction of the Red and the Assiniboine Rivers on 10 January 1817.[17] Here, in the heart of Lord Selkirk's colony, they learned that Fort Douglas — that dreary little Hudson's Bay Company post — was still occupied by a garrison of Nor'Westers, but that the garrison numbered no more than 15 men. The decision was taken to attempt a night assault. Obtaining several ladders from the local Red River settlers, the Swiss and Canadians advanced slowly upon the unsuspecting garrison. Under cover of darkness, they placed their ladders against the wooden stockade. In complete silence several soldiers mounted the rungs, jumped into the interior of the fort and rushed to throw open the gates. It was all over in a matter of minutes. According to Macdonell's report to Selkirk, the operation was a complete surprise. The Nor'Westers were captured "before they had time to slip on their pants."[18] What a source of satisfaction it must have been to Macdonell at least, to see the tables turned on the men who had so unceremoniously bundled him out of the country several years before. The whole operation was the kind that succeeded, not as a result of careful, logistical planning, but because of individual initiative displayed by the Swiss and Canadians alike, men familiar with the problems of winter travel and accustomed to improvisation. But the soldiers were not wholly untrained. They had practised marching on snowshoes before leaving Rainy Lake and found it comparatively easy to follow the frozen rivers and lakes that were part of the old North West route. Their ration bags had been filled at Rainy Lake and there were always plenty of trout to be obtained, fishing through the ice. They had, moreover, taken the precaution of bringing a few horses and oxen with them.

Orsonnens and Macdonell were followed, some weeks afterwards, by another force comprising 18 Swiss soldiers and 3 Canadians, among them a sixty-five year old man who "knew the country thoroughly." This party was under the command of Frédéric von Graffenried. It left Fort William at ten o'clock on the morning of 31 December,[19] accompanied during the first few hours by Lord Selkirk and some townspeople. Four horsedrawn sleighs hauled the luggage. Towards evening the horses and the escort returned to the fort and the Graffenried's party was left on its own to continue with sleighs, each drawn by three dogs. According to the commander's account, he had some difficulty "in keeping the men quiet since they were all more or less drunk from numerous farewell toasts." About midnight he awoke. This is what he saw:

> In the flickering light of the three fires the men resembled in their various positions and unusual clothes,

a band of robbers taking a rest. The encircling sleighs serving as protection, and the rifles leaning against the trees completed the picturesque scene which was animated by the distant howls of wolves.[20]

Then he began to think about the past, about the New Year's festivities in his own country, and how, one year ago, he had been singing with his friends in Montreal and joining a sleigh riding party with "fifteen torch lit sleighs." Now, here he was, in a northern forest, anticipating dangers and difficulties that were "not without a certain attraction."[21]

On 1 January the Swiss party began their march in earnest. They followed the Kaministikwia River, travelling on the ice, taking to the "brush-covered banks" when the current made the ice unsafe; then following the Matawin River. Their guide walked ahead followed by his dog-team. Immediately behind him came Lieutenant Graffenried with his team, all richly ornamented with red cloth, silken ribbons and sleigh bells. They had a difficult climb over the portage, bypassing Kakabeka Falls, and finally establishing their camp above the falls. On the second day, they set off early, reaching the mouth of the Matawin River, continuing on the next and succeeding days, to Lake Matawin and Lac des Mille Lacs.

Every day the weather seemed to grow colder. The pipe-stems froze to the men's lips and their "rum ration took on the consistency of honey", and even though he wore "two jackets, two hoods and a fur cap," Graffenried still felt the cold chill of the wind. Each man in the expedition was equipped with a hooded blanket coat in the traditional western style, a fur cap, flannel shirts, blanket material to cover the feet and six pairs of moccasins. Each man also wore fur gloves and carried a buffalo hide and blanket for the night. All marched on snowshoes.

About 12 January, several of the Canadians returned to Fort William, but Graffenried and his men kept on going, frequently sinking deep in the soft snow. The Swiss officer had some difficulty in managing his snowshoes; but, in his journal, he expressed thankfulness at having practised diligently at Fort William in walking on these long (1.5 m x .6 m) cumbersome footwear. By 15 January, Graffenried's party reached Sturgeon Lake, camping near the mouth of the Maligne River. Two days later, he recorded that three of his men collapsed from exhaustion. A fire was started, "with great effort," and the men were revived; but two of them had to be carried the next day because of frozen feet. One serious mishap occurred on 20 January, when Graffenried's sleigh plunged through the ice. That he survived was due only to the fact that his musket, suspended by a strap from his shoulder, became lodged cross-ways on the ice and his men were able to pull him out. Before arriving at the post at Rainy Lake, the little band of men ran short of rations and the Swiss commander became depressed, not only by the cold, but by the fear that he was leading his men to their deaths. It was, in fact, a near thing. Fortunately, Rainy Lake was not far distant; but when he finally arrived there, so emaciated did Graffenried appear, that a grenadier from his own regiment failed to recognize the thin gaunt face of his officer. In his diary, Graffenried wrote:

> It was only then I realized how much hunger and misery had changed my appearance. I was so weak that frequently my voice failed me. I entered the apartment of two of the clerks, Chatelain and MacPherson, who lived here with their wives, a little métisse and a Canadian. . . . They hastened to offer me food, but although I was hungry, I was overcome with such feeling of nausea, that it was impossible for me to touch anything. I threw myself on a straw bed and fell at once into a deep sleep. Towards evening all the other stragglers arrived, one of whom was swollen all over.[22]

Graffenried was in no condition to continue his journey, physically or psychologically. He had had enough of travelling in the Canadian winter. However, on 25 March news arrived at Rainy Lake that Captain d'Orsonnens had reached Pembina and captured Fort Douglas by a *coup de main*, and now required Graffenried's reinforcement. Three days later, the Swiss officer set out again. At this time of the year Graffenried and his men had to contend less with the cold than with problems arising from melting ice. The choice was one of wading "up to our knees in the river" or "in the soft snow along the bank." In his account Graffenried wrote:

> My carelessness in not having changed clothes after falling into the water, resulted in my suffering the consequences of bad rheumatism that bothered me a long time and which was only eased by applying hot compresses with pine needle tea. A heavy downpour was added to all this, extinguishing the fire at night which had been drying our clothes and forcing us to be in slush.[23]

In the end he concluded that further travel was just not feasible. He therefore remained at Rainy Lake until 12 May, when he felt ready to resume his journey to Red River by canoe. From Rainy Lake he went on to the Lake of the Woods and to the Winnipeg River — the route subsequently followed by Wolseley in 1870 — reaching Lake Winnipeg on 20 May. Two days later he met up with Orsonnens and went with him to Fort Douglas where they were subsequently joined by Lord Selkirk himself.[24]

Selkirk remained in the Red River Settlement until August, visiting and encouraging his settlers. But to stay indefinitely was impossible. Reluctantly the Earl accepted the fact that he could not absent himself from the court proceedings in Montreal where the North West Company had taken the initiative by laying countercharges against him. He would have liked Captain Matthey to remain in Red River as commander; but he, too, was involved in the legal proceedings and his return to Montreal with the Earl was imperative. At least the rank and file de Meurons were free to remain and to take up land as settlers. Their presence would be a guarantee of stability.

Colonists in Red River (including Swiss settlers and children, a Meuron soldier, Scottish settler and French Canadian), pen drawing by Peter Rindisbacher.

III

Peace had been brought to Red River by military action. Its continuance was ensured by the absorption of the North West Company by its rival, the Hudson's Bay Company, in 1821; and, above all, by the deaths of the two principal antagonists, Selkirk and McGillivray, the former dying in France on 8 April 1820, and the other in England on 16 October 1825. During the years that followed, most of the old provocative names and the symbols disappeared. Fort William, however, remained undisturbed on the banks of the Kaministikwia; so, too, did the fort on the shore of Rainy River. These were both taken over and occupied by Bay men. However, the old canoe route, used for years by the North West Company fur traders as their highway to the outside world declined in importance and became little more than a local trail from Fort William to the Red River. The principal outlet from Red River to the centres of commerce and civilization in Europe was, during the next generation, by way of Hudson Bay and the north Atlantic to Great Britain. Memories of the old days were erased by the disappearance of Fort Gibraltar and Fort Douglas and by the erection of two new forts on the Red River, both bearing the name of Nicholas Garry. Strengthened by the retirement of many former and now redundant employees of the North West Company, and the older and less aggressive members of the Hudson's Bay Company, the Red River Settlement grew slowly in numbers, extending along the river banks, in English and Gaelic-speaking parishes from St. Peter's and St. Clement's in the north to the French-speaking parishes of St. Norbert and Ste. Agathe in the south; and west, along the Assiniboine River, from the forks to Baie St. Paul, High Bluff and Poplar Point. Technically still the property of the Douglas Estate, the Settlement finally reverted to the Hudson's Bay Company in 1834. Nominally the settlers were governed by a local governor and an appointed council. But behind all the local officials was the dominating figure of the senior Hudson's Bay Company officer, the Governor of Rupert's Land, Sir George Simpson.

Looking back to the days of his father in the Red River Settlement during those mid-century years, the historian, R. G. MacBeth, nostalgically referred to the post-Seven Oaks Red River Settlement as the "Western Arcadia."[25]

CHAPTER THREE

The Defence of the Red River Settlement 1840s - 1860s

I

Just as the Arcadians of the ancient world found themselves exposed to outside aggression from the Spartans, the Arcadians of the Red River found themselves compelled to contend with pressures from beyond their frontiers. Ever since 1775, when Richard Montgomery and Benedict Arnold had led their troops into Canada to bring the "Fourteenth Colony" into the American rebellion against King George III, Americans had hoped to achieve a continental union under American control. The invading forces failed at Quebec. So too did Jonathan Eddy at Fort Cumberland.[1] But the failures of the 1770s did not remove the threat imposed upon the British Colonies by the United States. The ambition to acquire Canada and the traditional rivalry with Great Britain were major motives in the second effort of the United States to seize Canada by force of arms in 1812. Again the military attempt failed, largely as a result of the British military presence in North America — but only after three years of bitter fighting.

Following the second setback, the American imperial drive was diverted from the north to the south and to the west. Deprived by the Treaty of Ghent of the assistance from Great Britain upon which they had previously relied, the Indian nations were never able to offer much in the way of consistent and concerted resistance to American expansion. "Old America seems to be breaking up and moving westward," wrote Morris Birbeck in 1818.[2] During the mid-nineteenth century, territorial expansion was the American dream; the West was the new land of promise. The Reverend Henry Ward Beecher, the great American anti-slavery preacher, wrote of the western frontier in apocalyptic terms:

The West is a young empire of the mind, and power, and wealth, and free institutions, rushing up to a giant manhood, with a rapidity and power never before witnessed below the sun. And if she carries with her the elements of her preservation, the experiment will be glorious,— the joy of the nation ,— and the joy of the whole earth, as she rises in the majesty of her intelligence and benevolence, and enterprise, for the emancipation of the world.[3]

Land, and more land, was what the Americans wanted and what they were determined to get. No Indian nation or foreign fur company was going to stop them. Expansion was part of the divine plan. "Manifest Destiny" it was called. Did "Manifest Destiny" include the Red River of the North? Norman Kittson and his associates in the American Fur Company thought so. So too did Henry Sibley, the American fur trader soon to become Governor of Minnesota. How else does one explain the construction of the military post at Pembina, only 80 kilometres south of the Red River Settlement; or the posting of American cavalry there; or the despatch of the spy, J. W. Taylor, to report to Washington on the country between the Red, the Saskatchewan and the Fraser Rivers; or the introduction of that presumptuous Bill into the United States Senate, proposing that the United States Government offer ten million dollars to the Hudson's Bay Company "in full discharge of all claims to territory or jurisdiction in North America?"[4] In 1845 John Peter Pruden, who was with the Métis hunters when they were stopped at the frontier by the American cavalry and told they could no longer hunt on American lands unless they became American citizens, reported his concern to Governor Pelly of the Hudson's Bay Company that "If a war ensues there is no doubt what side the half-breeds will take. The Soldiers boasted they were now strong enough to thrash daddy England."[5] No good American liked the idea of the British monarchy being firmly established in what he regarded as his own republican backyard.

The threat inherent in American western expansion was not lost upon the British military authorities. In 1845 two military officers, Lieutenants Henry James Warre and Mervin Vavasour, were sent on a special mission by the officer commanding the British forces in Canada, following instructions received from the British Foreign Secretary, Lord Aberdeen. They were disguised as travellers; but their real purpose was to examine and report how British territories might be defended in the event of war with the United States, and upon the practicability of sending troops to the West via the Great Lakes and Fort William — the old North West canoe route used in 1816 by Orsonnens, Macdonell and Graffenried. They concluded that it could be done, but that heavy ordnance would have to move through Fort York on Hudson Bay. Among other things, they suggested that a body of cavalry and artillery would be most useful. Both would provide a core around which a local force of Métis might be built.[6]

Unaware of the Warre-Vavasour mission, two other British officers made suggestions. Captain M. H. Synge, Royal Engineers, stationed in Canada, deeply impressed with the depth of American hostility towards Great Britain, published a pamphlet, *Canada in 1848*, stressing the urgency and the advisability of building a transcontinental railway across British North America as the only means by which British troops might be moved quickly to any threatened area in the West. At the same time — there was no collaboration between them — another British officer, Major Robert Carmichael-Smythe, was thinking and writing along the same lines, urging the establishment of connecting trans-Atlantic and trans-Pacific steamship lines. He laid great stress upon the commercial advantages of such an arrangement; but it is clear that defence was uppermost in his mind.[7]

A more immediately practical response to the threat implied in American expansion to the southern frontier of the Hudson's Bay Company territories was the despatch of British troops to the threatened area. On 23 February, Lord Cathcart, commander of the British forces in North America and administrator in Canada during the illness of Sir Charles Metcalfe, wrote to Sir George Simpson, the Governor of Rupert's Land, putting several questions to him about sending troops to Red River. He was wondering about the possibility of using Métis volunteers. "What proportion," he asked, "should consist of cavalry and what of infantry?" Simpson replied:

> The inhabitants of Red River . . . would be effective either as Cavalry or Infantry. They are excellent horsemen, and quite remarkable for their activity on foot; and from the constant use of the snow shoe in winter, could, during that season, when the employment of horses would be impracticable, on account of the depth of snow, perform journeys on foot which Whites would be unequal to.[8]

Obviously, there was little doubt in Simpson's mind of the loyalty of the Half-Breed population. Otherwise, he would hardly have been prepared to use the local inhabitants to support British regulars, should they be sent to the North West. Cathcart was also anxious to know if the Company would assist a British garrison by providing accommodation for the troops. Simpson was quite agreeable. But he did point out that the Lower Fort, "square, of 800 feet [243 m] with stone walls 14 feet [4 1/4 m] high" and "four corner bastions", was unfinished. It could, however, be readily completed with some assistance from the troops themselves. Sir George exaggerated the height of the walls; but it was clear that the Company was anxious to be cooperative.[9]

A subsequent letter from Cathcart to the British Secretary for War is of particular interest. While the official explanation for any movement of troops to the West would be the need to secure "the allegiance of British subjects along the United States Frontier" and to maintain British interests on Rupert's Land, the real reason was "the important bearing of such a measure prospectively in influencing the success of a War with the United States." Cathcart continued:

> By thus creating a nucleus for a formation of a Native Corps of considerable amount composed of a warlike and hardy race in a situation which would necessarily occasion the greatest possible annoyance and embarrassment to the enemy from its having been unforeseen and unprovided for. The appearance of such a Force on that Frontier of the United States would likewise in all probability determine the greater part if not the whole of the Indians tribes residing in their territory to revolt, it being well known that they cherish a deadly hatred towards the Americans.[10]

Cathcart even went on to suggest that if British instructors trained the Indian and Métis levies, they might well be "more to be depended upon than British soldiers, who would be strangers to the country and might fall into habits of Drunkenness and Irregularity."

The scheme was alarming to the Duke of Wellington. He opposed sending British regular soldiers to Red River. He believed that the Americans would react by attacking at once, if only to "acquire a little military reputation for the United States Army,"[11] at the expense of British regulars. His suggestion was that if the Settlement had to be

Portage on the route between Hudson Bay and Fort Garry, watercolour (outlined in ink) by Peter Rindisbacher.

garrisoned, then strong fortifications should be constructed on the banks of the Red River, a suggestion that had little appeal to the British Treasury. In consequence, the Duke — now a generation past his glory days of Waterloo — wondered if the whole project of sending British troops to Red River ought to be cancelled. "If we are to lose the Country," he wrote, "it would be preferable to lose it undefended; and without disgrace to Her Majesty's Troops."[12]

Regardless of the Duke's doom and gloom opinion, the proposal to send British troops to Red River went ahead. On 1 May 1846 it was officially announced that a detachment of the 6th Foot would be sent to the Red River Settlement under the command of Major John ffolliott Crofton. Crofton's force consisted of 347 infantrymen, gunners and sappers, accompanied by 17 women and 19 children, in all 383 individuals, young and old. Along with them they carried three 6-pounder cannon and one 8-pounder gun. Unlike earlier soldiers sent to Red River, Crofton's men did not use the route through Canada. They travelled over the route traditionally used by the Hudson's Bay Company men; that is, by way of Hudson Bay, Fort York, the Hayes River and Lake Winnipeg, and up the Red River to

Fort Garry. It was a distance totalling over 1100 kilometres. The settlers knew why the soldiers were there. Alexander Ross, a local trader and magistrate, wrote, in his history of the Settlement that the appearance of the troops was the outcome of "the unmeaning fuss and gasconnade of the Americans about the Oregon question, for we were not aware of any inducement but the protection of the frontiers, that could have moved our government to send out troops to this isolated quarter."[13]

The Hudson's Bay Company may have been considering its own interests when it expressed alarm at the establishment of Norman Kittson's post at Pembina on the northern Minnesota frontier in 1844; but the willingness of the British government to send troops to the remote area of Red River was clearly inspired by a genuine concern about American flag waving in the northwestern regions of the continent. The President's Message to Congress in 1846 may well have contained more sound than substance; but no British government could overlook the fact that Polk's Democratic party had come to power with a mandate to support American expansion and the integration of occupied lands into the United States.[14] Driving the Indians and the fur-bearing animals before them and bringing their flag and government with them, the Americans came, moving inexorably towards the long, tenuous surveyor's line that separated those regions under the control of the Hudson's Bay Company from those under the jurisdiction of the United States. Pierre Parrant's bootleg liquor post at Pig's Eye quickly developed into the thriving town of St. Paul, and by 1849, the lands lying between the Missouri and Rupert's Land assumed new political significance as the Territory of Minnesota.[15]

Crofton's command did not include one of the better known British regiments. The 6th Royal Warwickshires were a modest outfit, respectable and exemplary in conduct, but still too good a regiment in the mind of the Commander-in-Chief to be isolated in the middle of the North American wastelands, an indefensible country, lacking fixed defences and convenient sources of supplies. At least this was the Duke of Wellington's opinion, when he ordered them back to Great Britain in 1847.

To fill the place vacated by the Warwickshires in Red River, came an indifferent group of British military pensioners, comprising 56 men, 42 women and 57 children. These people were given plots of land, in the anticipation that they would settle down, make their homes in the Settlement and, at the same time, provide it with a corpus

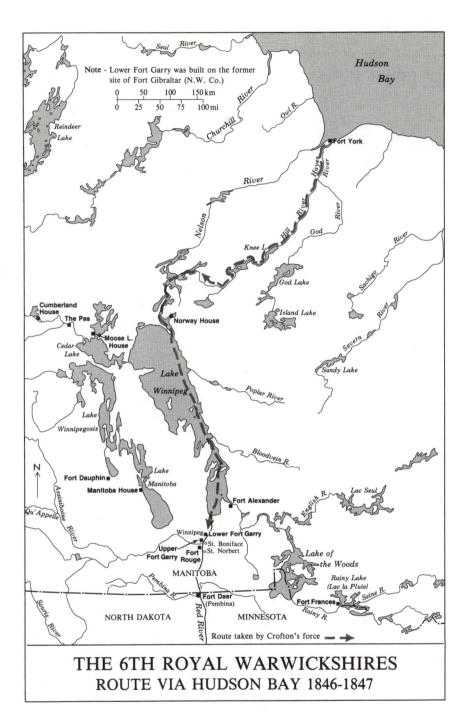

Note - Lower Fort Garry was built on the former
site of Fort Gibraltar (N.W. Co.)

0   50   100   150 km
0   25   50   75   100 mi

Hudson
Bay

Seal River

Reindeer
Lake

Churchill River

Owl R.

Fort York

Nelson River

Hayes River

Hill River

God River

Knee L.

God

Sachigo River

God Lake

Island Lake

Cumberland
House

The Pas

Norway House

Severn River

Sandy Lake

Moose L.
House

Cedar
Lake

Lake
Winnipeg

Poplar River

Lake
Winnipegosis

Bloodvein R.

N

Fort Dauphin

Lake
Manitoba

Manitoba House

Lac Seul

Fort Alexander

English R.

Qu'Appelle

Assiniboine River

Winnipeg Lower Fort Garry

St. Boniface
St. Norbert

Upper
Fort Garry   Fort
             Rouge

Lake of
the Woods

MANITOBA

Rainy Lake
(Lac la Pluie)

Pembina R.

Seine R.

Souris River

Red River

Fort Daer
(Pembina)

Fort Frances

Rainy R.

NORTH DAKOTA   MINNESOTA

Route taken by Crofton's force   ➡

THE 6TH ROYAL WARWICKSHIRES
ROUTE VIA HUDSON BAY 1846-1847

British soldiers in winter dress at Fort Garry, 1846, drawing by George Finlay.

of military expertise. Unfortunately, the pensioners turned out to be a useless lot, lazy and indifferent. And their commanding officer, Major William Caldwell, proved, at his best, to be "destitute of business habits and of the art to govern," and at his worst, "an elderly, dull-witted giant, punctilious with respect to his own dignity and comfort, but incapable of maintaining the one or of ensuring the other."[16] Like the de Meurons, the pensioners were townsmen, unsuited to country living. They won few, if any, friends in Red River, and Alexander Ross, who was a contemporary, wrote about them in these words, "If people on the arrival of the 6th were ready to chant a *Te Deum*, they were no less ready, on seeing the conduct of the pensioners, 'to hang their harps on the willows' and sing a requiem."[17]

The next group to come to Red River were soldiers. They came in 1857, a hundred or more officers and men of the Royal Canadian Rifles, an old soldier regiment composed of veterans with long military experience, all of whom were approaching retirement.[18] Like the 6th Warwickshires, the Royal Canadians were sent to Red River as a direct response to the threat implied in the appearance of American cavalry on the southern frontier of the Settlement. Although it has been suggested that the cavalry was present to protect American citizens against the Sioux, Jefferson Davis, the American Secretary of

War, was probably nearer the truth when he said in 1856 that they were there for the purpose of "acquiring information respecting the region."[19] Certainly to station troops on the northern frontier of Minnesota seemed an odd way of defending Minnesotans against the Sioux, an enemy located not north, but south, of the frontier.

The Royal Canadian Rifles, under their commanding officer, Major George Seton, sailed from Montreal on 23 June. They headed north along the Labrador coast, arriving at their destination at York Factory at the end of August. By 19 October, they reached the mouth of the Winnipeg River; three days later they were in barracks at Fort Garry. The journey up the Hayes River at low water levels was an arduous one, involving frequent portages. Some barrels of sugar were damaged and a considerable number of the bottled medical supplies were broken; and, horror of horrors, the port wine bottles were so poorly corked that all the wine leaked out on the journey from York Factory to Fort Garry! The Enfield rifles were so carelessly packed on embarkation that they had to be repacked at York Factory. And, to the embarrassment of the officers, there were no field officers' marquees and a scarcity of tents.[20] Fortunately there were no casualties, other than the death of the infant daughter of Colour-Sergeant McDonald and his wife. The baby was buried on the shore of Lake Winnipeg "in the presence of its weeping mother."[21]

Fort Garry, 19 March 1858, watercolour by George Seton.

After three years' service in the Red River Settlement, the Colonial Office concluded that there was no further requirement for the Royal Canadians, and the troops were, therefore, ordered to return to Canada. It was true that they had not been needed, either to defend the colony against the Americans or to preserve order within the boundaries of the Settlement; but their very presence provided a stabilizing influence, an insurance against invasion or disorder. The Hudson's Bay Company had no wish to see the soldiers leave. It even offered to provide free quarters and rations for the troops and to pay the officers' allowances, if only the regiment were permitted to remain. The Royal Canadians, however, packed up and poled away, leaving Fort Garry on 6 August 1861. They arrived at York Factory on the 23rd and sailed for Canada on the 30th.[22]

The settlers were sorry to see these troops leave the Settlement. When various bands of Sioux Indians, led by Little Crow, Standing Buffalo and Little Six, refugees from the bitter fighting with the Americans in Minnesota, made their way to safety in Red River and its environs, the local people could not but wish that the British soldiers were back again. Petitions were sent to London by the Governor and Council of Assiniboia, all of them begging the Colonial Office for military protection. The British government was, however, adamant. If the Settlement needed troops, then that was a matter for the Hudson's Bay Company, not for the people of Great Britain. "Form a militia of your own," was the recommendation of the Duke of Newcastle, the Colonial Secretary in William Gladstone's administration.[23] His Grace, like his Prime Minister, was not an imperialist. Talk of "Empire" was an irrelevance. Imperialism, so vigorously exploited a few years later by Gladstone's rival, Benjamin Disraeli, had barely begun to fire the imaginations of the British public or the members of Parliament, who followed rather than led public opinion.[24] That is why there were no soldiers of any kind in Red River when the Hudson's Bay Company was finally compelled by the British government to sell the western country and its inhabitants to Canada in 1869.

II

Most British politicians might not yet be imperially-minded, but Canadian politicians had begun to respond to their own brand of imperialism and to look acquisitively upon the territories administered by the Hudson's Bay Company. They were prepared to challenge the right of any commercial company to maintain a vast monopoly in the continental North West. And how very convenient to link the idea of free enterprise, as propounded by the British classical economists, with Canada's growing sense of nationalism. There were good historical arguments. Had it not been Canadians, the Nor'Westers, who had pushed the British frontier to the Arctic and to the Pacific Ocean? What were those western plains waiting for, but exploitation by British and Canadian farmers? George Brown, the spokesman for those who thought in these terms, seldom lost an opportunity to argue his case against the Hudson's Bay Company monopoly, and to press for political action by Great Britain and Canada before the grasping Americans should step in and get a grip upon a country that economically and historically belonged both to Great Britain and to Canada. Mining men and railway promoters also got into the argument, talking about the prairies as a future market and source of supply for Canadian business. This was not the kind of talk that politicians would or could afford to ignore, even though John A. Macdonald always seemed a bit hesitant about adopting any course of action that might bring the English and French elements of Canada's population into a conflict of opinion and interest. It was clear to him that the agitation in favour of taking over the North West and throwing the Bay men out was essentially an Upper Canadian, not a Lower Canadian movement. With the Reform Party insisting that the acquisition of the West should be part of their party platform, Macdonald, while he might drag his heels, could not afford, politically, to offer much resistance to Brown's expansionist arguments.[25] Many votes were to be gained by some kind of an accommodation with the Hudson's Bay Company. Good arguments also existed for moving quickly rather than slowly. The transportation revolution in the United States had already brought the railway to the Mississippi and freight was now moving to and from St. Paul with ease and rapidity. How could York Factory, the Hudson's Bay route and the Company's York boats ever hope to compete successfully? The acquisition of the North West and the construction of a Canadian transcontinental railway would have to go hand-in-hand and the Canadian government would have to act quickly.

The British, too, were becoming interested in opening the North West to colonization. Not just because it was good politics or good military strategy, or even because money was to be made in trade, but because public attitudes in Great Britain towards colonial possessions were undergoing profound changes. Thomas Clarkson, William

Wilberforce and the Evangelicals of the Clapham Sect had pointed the way towards a new British colonial policy. Slavery had been abolished, self-government was now considered the popular panacea for colonial political troubles and the Colonial Office in London was under the direction of the "deeply religious, sensitive, introspective," Sir James Stephen, a man described by his son as possessing "a morbidly vivid perception of possible evils and remote dangers."[26] Even that reckless extrovert, Lord Palmerston, was beginning to have doubts about commercialism as the sole justification for imperialism. Civilization and peace — "to render mankind happier, wiser, better" — might be a more legitimate and politically convincing argument for keeping colonies.[27]

With the drums of western civilization sounding loudly, both in England and in Canada, the Imperial government decided to appoint a special Parliamentary Committee "to consider the state of those British Possessions in North America, which are under the administration of the Hudson's Bay Company, or over which they possess a Licence to trade." The members numbered nineteen, among them some of the most distinguished men of their day: Sir John Packington, Secretary of State for War and for the Colonies in Lord Derby's government; Lord John Russell, who had been Prime Minister from 1840 to 1851; Lord Edward Stanley, a member of Parliament for nearly thirty years; William Ewart Gladstone, a former Colonial Secretary, Chancellor of the Exchequer and Prime Minister-to-be; Viscount Sherbrooke, a Chancellor in the making; and John Roebuck, the radical lawyer and friend of the economist, John Stuart Mill. The chairman was the Rt. Hon. Henry Labouchere. From February to July 1857, the Committee held its meetings, examining 25 witnesses and filling 550 pages with evidence from soldiers, sailors, settlers, fur traders, sea captains, explorers, clergymen and businessmen.[28]

The Reform Party in Canada was delighted at the news of the appointment of the Parliamentary Committee and even more delighted when they learned that Canada had been invited to send a representative to London to express the views of the Canadian government. Here, at last, was Canada's chance to argue its case and, hopefully, to secure possession of the Company's territories at no cost to the Canadian treasury. John A. Macdonald was rather less enthusiastic. Neither Macdonald nor Cartier wanted to inject a controversial issue into Canadian politics; and neither wished to commit himself to heavy financial outlays to acquire the Company's territories. That was why Canada's representative at the meetings in London, Chief Justice William Henry Draper, when asked to present his views, skillfully avoided binding his country to any positive policy of acquiring the North West. The interests of a trading company, he suggested, were not compatible with those of a local government. He favoured the establishment of a British Colonial regime, with, of course, Canadian cooperation; to which he added his conviction that the Company should continue to hold the Indian territories, if only to preserve the peace. These were the answers of a cautious man, controlled, non-controversial, avoiding all extravagant statements.

Despite the numerous prevarications of Sir George Simpson, the Company's Governor, the man whom everyone called "The Little Emperor," the Commission's final report was short. It contained less than one thousand words. It recognized the "just and reasonable wishes of Canada," leaving it to "Her Majesty's Government to consider . . . its details . . . before an Act of Parliament is prepared," and suggested that in those regions "where there was no reasonable prospect" of settlement for many years, and where there were Indian rights to be considered, the Company should "continue to enjoy" the privileges of exclusive trade.[29] The British government would, for the moment, offer no challenge to the anachronistic Charter of 1670. In a sentence, the Select Committee, while drafting the epitaph of the Company of Adventurers Trading into Hudson's Bay, was not yet prepared to assume responsibility for its early demise.

The next move was up to Canada. However, Macdonald had other and more immediate problems confronting him. For the present, he had no time for further arguments with the Hudson's Bay Company. There was a civil war going on in the United States, one that, from time to time, threatened to spill into Canada. And there was that urgent matter of a Canadian interprovincial union. Much too busy to concern himself further about the shareholders of the Hudson's Bay Company, Macdonald devoted his time and energies to the task of completing the federal union of the four original provinces; and then, immediately afterwards, he addressed himself to the even more critical task of pacifying the anti-Confederates in Nova Scotia. Not that he forgot the North West: the Americans would not let him. The purchase of Alaska from the Russians by the United States was a sharp reminder of the covetous interest Americans had always displayed in the northern regions of the continent. That is why he felt compelled to give some attention to the future of Rupert's Land and why he acquiesced in the Hon. William McDougall's resolutions introduced into the House of Commons, praying Her Majesty to unite Rupert's

Land and the North Western Territory with Canada. Speaking to McDougall's motion, the Prime Minister asserted,

> It is imperative to find a broad country for the expansion of our adventurous youth, who are not satisfied to look here and there for an isolated tract fit for settlement. It has consequently always been a political cry in Western Canada[30] that this country must be obtained; no sentimental cry either, but one eminently practical — a cry expressive of both principle and interest. If this country is to remain British, it is only by being included in the British North America scheme.[31]

Introducing his resolutions, McDougall made no reference to the Hudson's Bay Company Charter of 1670. Canadians had never been prepared to take it to court; since they could not get around it, they simply ignored it. A somewhat useless and offensive tactic, since, to the British, the Charter was a valid document and would remain so until set aside by the courts. The British therefore insisted that if the Canadians wanted the North West, they must compensate the Company for it. The Canadian delegation despatched to London to talk to the Governor of the Company, comprised Sir George Cartier and William McDougall. The negotiations were stiff and might have been prolonged had not Great Britain been anxious to get the whole matter out of the way. Applying pressure first on one party and then upon the other, the British tactfully succeeded in forcing both contestants to come to an agreement. The Canadians would have liked to see Great Britain take over the region and set up its own colony. But the British refused to entertain the idea: Canada would have to accept its destiny willingly, or unwillingly. In the end, Canada obtained a bargain. For a cash payment of £300,000, and a substantial land grant to the Company within the fertile belt south of the Saskatchewan River, and small blocks of land around existing Company trading posts, Canada obtained legal title to the whole of Rupert's Land, an area claimed and occupied by the Hudson's Bay Company for two hundred years.

The Deed of Surrender was signed on 19 November 1869. It was understood that the business transaction would be completed and formal possession of their new territory taken by the Canadian government on 1 December following.[32] For his services — and perhaps to get an awkward politician out of the way — Macdonald recommended that William McDougall be named Lieutenant-Governor of the new Territory. It seemed a logical choice. For a long time,

McDougall had been interested in western expansion and had taken an active role in the negotiations with the Company. Meanwhile, the Canadian Parliament ratified the deal Cartier and McDougall had made and prepared the way for the takeover of the Hudson's Bay Company Territories, by passing an "Act for the Temporary Government of Rupert's Land." This Act provided for the government of the newly acquired territory by a governor and an appointed council.

To encourage Canadian immigration, and, incidentally, provide jobs for the people of the Red River Settlement, the Canadian government asked the Company's permission to build a road from Lake of the Woods to Fort Garry, and to commence work on a survey which would, in due course, extend to the whole of the North West Territories. Macdonald wrote to his friend Colonel Gray of Prince Edward Island:

> We are in a happy state of ignorance as to the system of government that obtains there under the regime of the Hudson's Bay Company, and until McDougall has time to look about him and report, we desire to make no appointments lest they might jar with the prejudices and feelings of the people of the North West.[33]

Not a little concerned about McDougall's rigidity of mind, the Prime Minister wrote to his new Lieutenant-Governor Designate on 20 November, counselling patience and moderation and reminding him, "The circumstances will vary from day to day, and we think that we had better leave you to make such arrangements as you think best, having every confidence in your prudence and tact."[34]

III

Unfortunately for Canada, "prudence and tact" were qualities few Canadians, particularly those who knew him well, would have associated with the personality or career of William McDougall. As Minister of Public Works and principal protagonist of the annexation of the Hudson's Bay territories, he wholly overlooked the fact that, for over half a century, the inhabitants of the Red River Settlement, Scots, Irish and Métis, had developed their own peculiar pattern of life and their own distinctive identity. The Swiss had long since departed the country. Intimidated by the floods and grasshoppers, they had abandoned Red River after several years of failure in their efforts to succeed as farmers in the valley of the Red River. Essentially townsmen and not peasants, they lacked the skills and adaptability necessary to survive a frontier existence. The stubborn Selkirk men, however, had remained, weathering all storms, political and climatic. They were not men willing to uproot themselves because of the vagaries of the weather, even if a few of them, of lesser stamina or stomach, did pull up and move to Canada. The Métis, of course, were at home. The Red River valley was their country, their native land. Both groups, Selkirk men and Métis, therefore, survived, living in their own parishes, speaking their own tongues, worshipping the same God but doing so, each group in its own way and in its own churches. The Scots tended their little farms and the Métis worked for the fur company as voyageurs and buffalo hunters. There was little intercourse between them; but, no longer were there hostilities, nor would there be as long as each group recognized the sensitivities of the other.

Hon. William McDougall, Minister of Public Works, 1869.

Problems, when they did arise, developed out of the Hudson's Bay Company's heavy-handedness in trying to prevent the sale of furs by Métis settlers to American free-traders in Minnesota. It was just such a policy that had led to the trial of one Guillaume Sayer, a Red River Métis, who was charged in 1849 with illegally selling furs. [35]

For a short time it seemed as if there might be trouble; but when a mixed jury of Scots and Métis returned a verdict of guilty with a recommendation for mercy, the people generally were satisfied and the Company was wise enough not to try to assert its monopolistic rights again.

The most significant evidence of changing conditions, however was the arrival of immigrants from Canada. Some, such as A. K. Isbister and James Ross, were not really newcomers. They were local men who had received their education outside and returned to their homeland, with new ideas. They were not distrusted, because they were not outsiders. Real outsiders, however, began to make an appearance in the Settlement from the 1850s onwards. They included men, such as William Coldwell and William Buckingham, who started the newspaper *Nor'Wester* and proceeded to put forward new and disturbing political views, such as annexation to Canada: they included Dr. John Schultz, and his dentist friend, Dr. W. R. Bown, and the newspaper correspondent, Charles Mair, all from Upper Canada, and John Snow, the federal government road contractor. None of these people made any effort to conceal his sense of superiority and low opinion of the local inhabitants, particularly those who were Roman Catholic by faith and French by tongue. If aggressiveness and intolerance were characteristic of Upper Canadians, then people native to the Settlement or who had spent a great part of their lives there, were not going to be attracted by the possibilty of political union with Canada. Yet that is exactly what the newcomers were talking about; how much better off Red River would be once it came under Canadian jurisdiction. Small wonder that annexation to Canada held little appeal to local inhabitants when Canadian surveyors began driving stakes here and there in lands the Métis looked upon as their own. Certainly the Canadians who established themselves in Red River prior to the transfer brought small credit to their country, and even less credibility to the Hon. William McDougall. Was it not he who had negotiated the transfer? Was it not he, who, as Minister of Public Works, had authorized the unpopular surveys? Now, here he was, almost on the doorstep, prepared, as Lieutenant-Governor, to take over the administration of the colony from the Council of Assiniboia. Land was a particularly sensitive issue. To the Métis, the men who hunted the buffalo and carted the furs, land was not something to be measured, something to be fenced, something to be ticketed. It was not something to be owned, or to be accumulated for speculative purposes in the way Dr. Schultz seemed to be doing. Land was something to be lived on, with and by. Although he was never a supporter of the Métis, R. G. MacBeth, as the descendant of one of the

52

Selkirk settlers, understood the situation in the Settlement well enough to write,

> ... the Canadian authorities seem to have blundered by overlooking the fact that the new territory had a population of some ten thousand people, who ought at least to have been informed in some official way of the bargain that was being made, and of the steps being taken to secure and guard their rights and privileges.[36]

By the time McDougall, accompanied by his secretary, his assistant secretary and his chief of police, arrived at Pembina, it should have excited no surprise when he was met, not by a welcoming party, but by a group of Métis horsemen bearing a letter that read:

> Sir,
> The National Committee of the Red River Métis orders Mr. William McDougall not to enter the North-West Territory without the special authorization of this Committee.
>
> By order of the President, John Bruce
> Louis Riel, Secretary.
>
> Dated at St. Norbert, Red River, this 21st day of October, 1869.[37]

McDougall blustered; but to no effect. At least he had sense enough not to venture to force his way past the Métis delegation. He had, in fact, little choice but to comply with the National Committee's demand, and to withdraw to American territory. It was an embarrassing, even humiliating beginning to his term as governor. Especially when he had to endure the snickers of the Americans at Pembina and the subsequent amusement of his colleagues in Ottawa, who called him "Wandering Willie." But McDougall was nothing if not stubborn. He was determined to wait in Pembina until 1 December. Then he would return and proclaim the annexation of Rupert's Land to Canada and his appointment as Lieutenant-Governor and representative of Her Gracious Majesty, Queen Victoria. The Law would be on his side then. The Law would give him authority to bull his way into the Red River Settlement.

CHAPTER FOUR

The Métis Resistance 1869-1870

I

It is hardly surprising that it was the Métis who had taken steps to halt McDougall at the frontier. It was they who had taken the initiative at Seven Oaks in 1816, and again at the trial of Guillaume Sayer in 1849. Once again, in 1869, they seized the opportunity to oppose the intrusion of an outside jurisdiction into the North West. The initial encounter with Canadian authorities had occurred on the properties claimed by André Nault at St. Vital. Here, a party of Dennis's land surveyors was halted by eighteen unarmed Métis led by Louis Riel, whose father had been the leader of the anti-monopoly agitators at the Sayer trial. Highly educated in Montreal in philosophy, classics and law, the young Riel was an obvious choice as leader. For the moment it suited the purposes of the Red River Métis to use John Bruce as the figurehead. But it was Riel, not Bruce, who drafted the order blocking McDougall's entry into the territory; and it was Riel, with help from Father Noel Ritchot of St. Norbert, who was the motivating force behind the Métis National Committee. It would not be long before Bruce would be quietly dropped and the young Louis Riel would become the acknowledged leader of the Métis opposition to Canadian annexation.

Riel's initial success at Pembina encouraged him to make his next move; to take possession of Fort Garry. He was firmly convinced, and not without reason, that the Council of Assiniboia, the legally consti-tuted governing body, lacked the enterprise and initiative to offer any real opposition to Canada's plans to take over the Red River territory. In all probability it would supinely have allowed McDougall into the country; and that would have been the beginning of the end for the Métis people, at least in Riel's opinion. He believed that he would have to keep his band of Métis followers under arms, if only for the sake of maintaining peace within the settlement. The question was, where would they be housed, fed and provided for? The answer to what was basically a question of logistics, was to take possession of Fort Garry. The fort would provide Riel with the armoury, the accommodation and the food he needed. That is why the Métis occupied Fort Garry on 3 November.

It was easy enough to do. Riel and his men simply walked in. They encountered no opposition. The old order and the old alliance of the fur trade and the native population were breaking down. Attitudes were changing. Hudson's Bay men had been losing influence among

A Red River Métis, 1870.

the native population ever since the introduction of white women into the settlement made *mariage à la façon du pays* unacceptable. It is conceivable that William MacTavish, the Hudson's Bay Company governor, might have mustered some opposition to Riel, but he was too ill to make the effort; and his second in charge, Dr. William Cowan, lacked the intestinal fortitude to assume the responsibility; or, perhaps he just looked at the situation realistically. After all, since the withdrawal of the Royal Canadians, where could the company find a military force capable of dealing with Riel's tripmen and buffalo hunters? These latter were rough, tough men, unemployed during the winter months. They were not traders or farmers. They were as ready to follow Riel, as Cuthbert Grant's horsemen had been to follow him.

Even with Fort Garry's stone walls, stores and cannon at his disposal, Riel knew that he could not control the whole of the Red River Settlement. He needed a wider base of support than that provided by a handful of undisciplined Métis soldiers.[1] Above all, he required, if not the active, at least the moral support of the settlers, English or Gaelic-speaking as well as French-speaking; a union of minds in a common cause. That explains why he invited the English and Gaelic-speaking parishes to send twelve representatives to Fort Garry, to join twelve representatives from French-speaking parishes to discuss the future of the colony. The local settlers, generally, saw no harm in this suggestion. After all, Riel had taken no steps to overthrow the old Council of Assiniboia, or to interfere with the sittings of its courts. That is why, on 16 November, representatives of both English-speaking and French-speaking parishes met in the courthouse, for the purpose of talking over what course of action should be taken with regard to union with Canada. The leadership of the English-speaking group was assumed by James Ross, the half-breed son of the historian, Alexander Ross. The leader of the French-speaking settlers was Louis Riel. When the delegates arrived, they were welcomed by a *feu de joie* (ceremonial rifle salute) and a 24-cannon salute fired by Riel's soldiers. According to observers, these latter appeared to be reasonably well disciplined. When one of them attempted to desert, he was condemned to walk up and down carrying a tin of water in each hand. The "disgrace of the punishment was meant to serve as a warning for the future," was Alexander Begg's comment.[2]

Meanwhile, a miserable William McDougall, shivering in his primitive quarters in Pembina, Minnesota, was warning the Métis to lay down their arms or be considered in a state of rebellion against the Crown. This warning, which McDougall sent directly to Governor

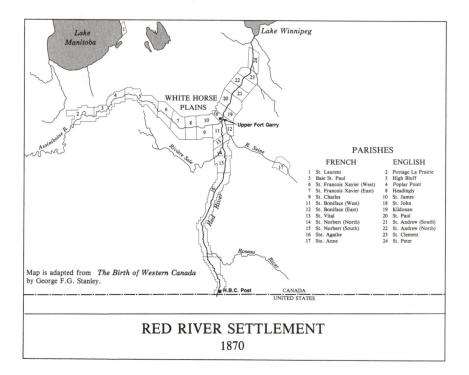

Map is adapted from *The Birth of Western Canada* by George F.G. Stanley.

PARISHES

FRENCH	ENGLISH
1 St. Laurent	2 Portage La Prairie
5 Baie St. Paul	3 High Bluff
6 St. Francois Xavier (West)	4 Poplar Point
7 St. Francois Xavier (East)	8 Headingly
9 St. Charles	10 St. James
11 St. Boniface (West)	18 St. John
12 St. Boniface (East)	19 Kildonan
13 St. Vital	20 St. Paul
14 St. Norbert (North)	21 St. Andrew (South)
15 St. Norbert (South)	22 St. Andrew (North)
16 Ste. Agathe	23 St. Clement
17 Ste. Anne	24 St. Peter

RED RIVER SETTLEMENT
1870

MacTavish, placed Riel in a compromising position and had the effect of raising doubts in the minds of some people about the legality of the meeting in Red River. In reply, Riel advanced the idea that the delegates of the people should form their own government, a provisional government, that could speak and act for the resident population of Red River. This was strong political medicine for many of the English-speaking delegates to the Convention. They demurred, suggesting that they had better take political soundings in their constituencies. The first Convention, therefore, adjourned until 1 December.

On that very day McDougall and his household staff shuffled across the frontier to the Hudson's Bay Company post on British territory. It was bitterly cold. But to McDougall it was a point of honour to issue his official announcement of the annexation of Rupert's Land by Canada, on Canadian, not upon American soil. With his handful of shivering companions standing by, he read to the wind what purported to be a Royal Proclamation announcing the transfer of the Hudson's Bay Company Territories to Canada; then he read a second Proclamation announcing his own appointment as Lieutenant-Governor. Despite the chill, he added a third Proclamation,

2nd Earl of Granville,
detail of drawing by F. Sargent.

addressed to the officer in charge of the Canadian surveyors, Lieutenant-Colonel J. Stoughton Dennis, appointing him "Lieutenant and conservator of the Peace," in and for the North West Territories, authorizing him:

> . . . to raise, organize, arm, equip and provision, a sufficient force within the said Territories, and with the said force, to attack, arrest, disarm, or disperse the same armed men so unlawfully assembled and disturbing the public peace; and for that purpose, and with the force aforesaid, to assault, fire upon, pull down, or break into any fort, house, stronghold, or other place in which the same armed men may be found. . . .[3]

This last document read like an official declaration of war but, in actual fact, it had no more validity than did the two other Proclamations. McDougall himself had his doubts when drafting these documents, admitting in a private letter to Joseph Howe, the Secretary of State, "I hope I am right in using the name of Her Majesty as prominently as I have done."[4] Both Howe and Macdonald had warned McDougall against headlong action. But caution was not a characteristic feature of McDougall's career. In fact, the significance of what he was doing was probably not very clear to him, although it might have been anticipated by a more adroit politician. It was grasped at once by the Prime Minister. As soon as he learned of McDougall's rejection at the frontier, Macdonald immediately backed away from the deal with the Hudson's Bay Company, instructing his agent in London, Sir John Rose, to hand over no monies to the Hudson's Bay Company, and to inform the Colonial Secretary, Lord Granville, that Canada would not accept the transfer of the North West Territories, "unless quiet possession can be given." That left the Colonial Office holding the unwanted child. Granville, however, did not want it either. He simply handed it back to the Hudson's Bay Company, together with complete responsibility for "the disorders which are to be expected when the prestige of a Government long known to be inadequate, is shaken by the knowledge that it is also expiring, and by the appearance, however well intended, of its successor."[5]

On 1 December, when Riel's Red River Convention met again, the delegates, uncertain of the exact status of McDougall's Proclamation and worried about Dennis's call to arms, wondered what they should do. Certainly the "List of Rights" the Métis leader submitted to the Convention contained nothing they considered to be unreasonable. The only point of contention was the Métis leader's continued refusal to admit McDougall into the Settlement or recognize him as the Queen's representative, until the "rights" claimed by the people of Red River were secured "by an Act of the Canadian Parliament." It was over this issue that the Convention finally broke up and the English-speaking members returned home. One week later, when Riel felt surer of his position, he issued a positive statement to the effect that since the Hudson's Bay Company had obviously ceased to function as a government, the people of Red River might be considered free to form a "provisional" government of their own, giving it visual significance by hoisting a distinctive flag over Fort Garry on 10 December. The flag consisted of a fleur de lys and shamrock on a white ground. On Friday, 10 December, Alexander Begg wrote in his diary, "Mr. Riel addressed the French at Fort Garry and in the course of his speech hoped his men were all loyal to the Queen. Thus was inaugurated the Provisional Government of Red River under Bruce and Riel. How long it will last remains to be proved."[6]

Dr. John Christian Schultz, 1870s.

Meanwhile Colonel Dennis's call to arms fell flat. After setting up his headquarters at Lower Fort Garry and enrolling a number of recruits, including fifty of Chief Prince's Indians, Dennis discovered that the martial enthusiasm of the pro-Canada group in the Settlement was waning rapidly. Accordingly, after several days, he called the whole thing off and returned to Canada. Only a handful of the "Friends of Canada" remained in Winnipeg, and a number of them met in Dr. John Schultz's house ready to defy Riel. Accepting the challenge, the Métis leader assembled his armed Métis supporters and, directing a 9-pounder gun at Schultz's building, demanded a surrender within fifteen minutes. He received it. The men who were with Schultz, about 40 in number, marched to Fort Garry as prisoners. Years later, Dr. J. H. O'Donnell, one of those involved, looked back at this episode in Manitoba's history, to remark that the gathering at Dr. Schultz's place had been, to say the least, imprudent. It had been, in fact, contrary to Dennis's advice to Schultz to "Shut up your premises and let the government property take its chance." That, of course, was exactly what Dennis himself did at the Lower Fort.[7]

II

Having refused to accept Rupert's Land into the Canadian Confederation while the western country was in a state of turmoil, and having recalled the embarrassing and embarrassed William McDougall to Ottawa, Sir John A. Macdonald looked about for someone who might be able to calm the excitement in Red River. Who were better qualified to do so than a Roman Catholic priest, a distinguished French Canadian military officer and, of course, a representative of the Hudson's Bay Company? Were not the Company and the clergy the very factions believed to be promoting the Red River troubles? Accordingly, the Prime Minister named Grand-Vicar Jean-Baptiste Thibault, who had ministered to the Métis and the Indians on the western plains for thirty-nine years, Colonel Charles de Salaberry, whose forbear had been the Canadian officer who defeated the Americans at Chateauguay in 1813, and Donald A. Smith, the senior officer of the Hudson's Bay Company in North America, as special emissaries of the federal government to clear up what Macdonald referred to in a letter to Sir John Rose on 31 December as "a most inglorious fiasco."[8] Smith suggested to Macdonald that George Stephen might accompany them as an independent businessman, unconnected with politics. Stephen declined but hinted that Colonel Garnet Wolseley, the Quartermaster-General of the Militia, was anxious to go to Red River. Macdonald, however, was opposed to sending "an officer high in rank in military service," if only because "he would be looked upon as having the olive branch in one hand and a revolver in the other."[9] Rather than a soldier, Macdonald preferred to enlist the support of Bishop Alexandre Taché of St. Boniface, then attending the Ecumenical Conference in Rome, who, while *en route* to Italy, had warned the federal authorities of the possibility of trouble in the Red River region. Taché had, in fact, indicated his willingness to return to Canada to lend his voice and influence in the cause of the Settlement's peaceful transition from Company to Canadian rule. Because the Bishop could not respond immediately, the other three emissaries set out at once. They arrived in Red River in the late days of December.

After some preliminary discussions with the president of the Provisional Government, Donald A. Smith, unquestionably the most astute and most effective of the federal government emissaries, proposed that a mass gathering of the people of the Settlement should be held at Fort Garry, to whom he could explain the Canadian point of view. Two large public meetings were held, one on 19 January and the other on the 20th. Both were held out of doors in weather well below the freezing mark. Despite the unfavourable conditions, there was a good attendance of settlers who, even if they shivered and stamped their feet, listened to what Smith and Riel had to say. The one to propose, and the other to dispose. In the end, it was agreed by mass vote, to elect a new Convention to meet in five days' time. When the delegates to the second Convention met in Fort Garry, they proceeded

Louis Riel, a sketch, 1870.

to draft a new List of Rights. Then came a startling proposal, advanced by Riel. Red River should enter the Canadian Confederation, not as a territory, but as a province! This suggestion was completely unexpected. Smith could hardly believe his ears and doused the idea with cold, cold water. In spite of Riel's appeals, the members of the Convention turned down his proposal by a vote of 24 to 15. He did, however, obtain what he wanted when the Convention agreed that a new Provisional Government should be formed, a suggestion which implied that the previous Provisional Government, formed in December, had possessed the elements of validity. At that point Smith invited the Settlement to send a delegation to Ottawa, where a final agreement might be translated into legislative action by the Canadian Parliament. Everybody was happy. Riel promised to release the prisoners from the cells of Fort Garry and, in Winnipeg, fireworks, originally intended to welcome William McDougall, blazed and guns boomed. "A regular drunk commenced," wrote Alexander Begg in his journal, "in which everyone seemed to join." Riel did not take an active part in the festivities; but, if Begg is to be believed, he did take "a good horn of brandy with Mr. Bannatyne when he released him."[10]

On 11 February, Louis Riel, with the Convention's concurrence, named the several delegates who were to go to Ottawa to negotiate the terms of union with the federal government in Ottawa. They included the priest, the Rev. J.-J. Ritchot from St. Norbert; John Black, the Recorder of Rupert's Land who had represented the parish of St. Andrews and presided over the Convention when it drew up the List of Rights; and Alfred H. Scott, an American bartender in Bob O'Lone's Red Saloon.[11] Scott's appointment was thoroughly absurd. He had nothing to contribute to the discussions in Ottawa; he can only have been chosen as a sop to appease the Americans in the Settlement, or to hold the threat of American annexation over the federal cabinet.

Prospects now looked bright for a peaceful and satisfactory conclusion to the problems of Red River. The only cloud on the horizon was the anti-Riel activity of several Canadians who had escaped from the cells at Fort Garry and were at large in the Settlement. Among them was Thomas Scott, one of the Ontarians recruited to work on the road John Snow had undertaken to build for the Department of Public Works, between Winnipeg and Lake of the Woods. Another escapee was the redoubtable Dr. Schultz. The latter had made his way northwards along the Red River to the Scottish parishes, seeking asylum in the English-speaking settlement at Portage la Prairie, whither a number of the road workers had previously fled. Indeed, Portage la Prairie had become the principal refuge for the Canadians. Hoping to enlist

Thomas Scott, 1869.

the support of the Red River Scots at Kildonan and St. Andrews (parishes which had, incidentally, sent delegates to the Convention at Fort Garry) Scott and his Portage associates, led somewhat reluctantly by a former officer of the 100th Regiment, Charles Boulton, set off for the Lower Fort in the hope of mustering support in the Scottish parishes for armed action against Riel. But neither Schultz nor Scott found many of the old Red River settlers ready to join forces with them, and after the unfortunate double-shooting of a young Scotsman, John Hugh Sutherland, and a mentally retarded Métis, Norbert Parisien,[12] the whole project collapsed. Schultz set out to make his way on foot to Ontario; Boulton elected to lead his people back to Portage la Prairie.

The fact is that Smith's mission and the cooperation achieved by the second Convention had pretty well erased any support for the use of armed force against Riel, even in the Protestant Scottish parishes. It was most unfortunate that Boulton's party, instead of returning individually or in small groups to Portage la Prairie, decided to travel in a body by way of Winnipeg. That meant, of course, passing close to Fort Garry. To the over-sensitive Métis it appeared to presage an assault upon the fort. There was, however, no fighting. Boulton's party readily surrendered to a band of mounted Métis, and promptly found themselves occupying the cells so recently vacated by the earlier prisoners. Boulton was charged with the serious offence of levying war against the Provisional Government. But when both Donald Smith and the grief-stricken Sutherlands interceded on Boulton's behalf, he was granted a reprieve.

Thomas Scott was not so fortunate. He lacked common sense enough to keep his mouth shut and to curb the verbal abuse he constantly hurled at his captors. This unfortunate inability to control tongue and temper proved fatal to Scott. The Métis guards demanded that this offensive fellow be brought before a Métis court martial. On 3 March 1870 he was tried and found guilty by a majority of an *ad hoc* court and sentenced to be shot. Appeals for his life by Donald A. Smith, and by members of the Protestant and Roman Catholic clergy alike, proved of no avail. The courtmartial made the decision; Riel would not intervene to change it. The sentence was therefore carried out. On 4 March the poor man was executed by a Métis firing party outside the walls of Fort Garry. Had Riel taken steps to prevent Scott's death, Canadian history might have followed an entirely different course. This refusal to grant a reprieve to his opponent, the Ontario Orangeman, Thomas Scott, was the one single act that was to deprive

Execution of Thomas Scott, 4 March 1870.

the Métis leader, in the minds of many people, Manitobans and Canadians alike, of the place he was well on the way to earning for himself as the father of his province.[13] Alexander Begg noted in his journal, "A deep gloom has settled over the settlement on account of this deed."[14]

Several days later Bishop Taché, who had hurried back from Rome at Macdonald's request, made a strong plea for moderation and unity within the boundaries of the Settlement. His appeal met with a favourable response. *The New Nation*, Riel's newspaper, dropped its strident tone and softened its anti-Canadianism. Riel responded by releasing the remaining prisoners. The Bishop's assurances that the Ottawa authorities had promised him that all the participants in the events in Red River during the past months would be covered by an amnesty, was believed and welcomed throughout the Settlement. Only in Riel's mind did there linger a small, nagging doubt that the Bishop might, perhaps, be promising more than Ottawa was prepared to deliver.

Meanwhile, with the aid of his principal supporters, Louis Schmidt, Thomas Bunn and William O'Donoghue, Riel carried on the government of the Settlement. A new List of Rights was drafted, including, not only land grants to the Métis as their share of the aboriginal title, but provision for official bilingualism and separate schools in the new province. These were, incidentally, new demands the Convention had not approved; but the delegates named to go to Ottawa raised no objections. Neither did they oppose the suggestion that the new province should be named Manitoba rather than Assiniboia.

On 22 March the Provisional Government delegates, Father Noel-Joseph Ritchot, John Black and Alfred Scott, set off for the Canadian capital. Although two of them were arrested on their arrival in Ontario on charge of complicity in the "murder" of Thomas Scott, they were quickly set free and were received by the representatives of the Federal Government, Macdonald, Cartier and Joseph Howe. After several days' sharp debate, the demands of the delegates, in particular, those of Ritchot and Black (their bibulous colleague, Scott, played little or no part in the discussions) were accepted by the Canadian government and embodied in a bill to be put before Parliament. On 12 May this bill, henceforth known as the Manitoba Act, 1870, became law. According to its terms, the old district of Assiniboia was to become a new province called Manitoba, with a constitution similar to that of other Canadian provinces, except that Manitoba would be bilingual and possess a separate school system. In addition, some 566,580 hectares of land would be set aside for the children of all Half-

Breed families. The vast area beyond the limits of the new postage-stamp province, would be administered as federal territory. The delegates were assured, or believed that they had been promised, that a general amnesty would be granted, and that a new Lieutenant-Governor (not McDougall) would be appointed as titular head of the new provincial administration. On 15 July 1870, Manitoba officially came into being, after the federal authorities had completed their long overdue financial deal with the head office of the Hudson's Bay Company in London. In Red River, politics ceased to be the one all-absorbing topic of conversation or activity. The Scots went back to their farms and the Métis to the plains to hunt buffalo; of course, those who had spent the winter months in pursuit of furs had little knowledge of what had happened in Red River during their absence.

Back in Fort Garry Riel's Provisional Government continued to function, enjoying *de facto* recognition by virtue of the acceptance of its delegates as representatives of the only effective administration in the Settlement. The last of the officials of the Hudson's Bay Company, William MacTavish and Dr. Cowan, returned to Great Britain. Norbert Gay, the strange French adventurer who appeared in the Settlement in January, ostensibly as a French newspaper correspondent, was still around trying to instill a knowledge of European cavalry tactics into the heads of the few

Norbert Gay, Riel's French cavalry officer.

native horsemen Riel was able to muster.[15] Money was plentiful and the Hudson's Bay Company continued to carry on its commercial transactions as it had always done. Most of the people of Red River seemed ready to accept the situation as they found it; although there were still a few who complained that the Manitoba Act had conceded too much to the French. However, efforts to promote controversy made little impact upon the majority who saw no reason to grow excited or to stir up trouble. "The winter was overpast and the summer had come, in more senses than one."[16]

Despite the fact that everything seemed to be going his way, Riel was worried. The promised amnesty still remained only a spoken promise. He had received nothing on paper, nothing really positive. Moreover, it was no secret that Ottawa was sending an armed force to Red River. Troops, British regulars and Canadian militia, were being assembled when Ritchot and his fellow delegates were in Ottawa. Riel had been assured through Father Ritchot that Sir George Cartier wanted him to carry on the local government until the new Lieutenant-Governor, the Hon. A. G. Archibald, should arrive in Red River. Moreover, the officer commanding the armed forces *en route* to the west, Colonel Garnet Wolseley, had sent a Proclamation to Red River stating, "Our mission is one of peace and the sole object of the expedition is to secure Her Majesty's sovereign authority." He had also promised that the "strictest order and discipline" would be maintained and that private property would "be carefully respected."[17] Riel had not only seen the Proclamation; he had asked the editor of *The New Nation* to publish it and had himself helped to set the type. The Proclamation seemed clear enough; although some local sceptics wondered if Wolseley's expedition was not just "another Col. Dennis affair."[18]

From time to time, Riel was urged to take the initiative in opposing Wolseley's troops. The Irish Americans, in particular O'Donoghue, O'Lone and Alfred H. Scott, pressed the Métis leader to send messengers to meet the troops at Lake Winnipeg and demand a written guarantee of an amnesty for all those who had taken part in the opposition to the Hudson's Bay Company; if the amnesty was not forthcoming, the troops should be warned to expect armed resistance. John Lennon, one of Winnipeg's several American saloon-keepers, who was a supporter of annexation, even proposed that Riel should be hanged "for having sold the Americans in the settlement."[19] He was probably consuming too much of his own stock. Others, more sober and less belligerently inclined, such as Auguste Harrison, a member of the Convention, suggested instead that Riel's government should plan a great bonfire and a guard of honour to greet Wolseley's men. Riel could not make up his mind; and because he could not, he prepared neither for a war nor for a welcome. Several years later he wrote the story of the last hours of the Provisional Government when Wolseley's troops were camping in the rain outside Fort Garry:

In the evening,[20] I summoned the Council; Girard, Royal, Dubuc, came to see us; I deferred the Council a quarter of an hour; during that time I made these gentlemen come in; they took their leave after about ten minutes spent with us; I went to see them to the traverse of the Grande Rivière. It was very dark; it was beginning to rain a little. At the end of a quarter of an hour of interruption, I was at the fort continuing the Council. It was two o'clock. I said to the councillors that our duty was not to leave the position until the troops took it; it was important that none of our men in the fort should go out without orders, that night more than ever; that I feared, however, that our enemies of the previous winter would avail themselves of the approach of the troops to attempt some assaults upon us, that we must not allow ourselves to be massacred by those people. As to the troops themselves, I said that I wanted to reconnoitre myself what they would do during the night, that, in consequence, two things were necessary: 1. That while continuing to rid the fort of the effects which belonged to us, it was necessary that the soldiers and all our people be very punctually on the watch. 2. That I required four horsemen to accompany me to Wolseley's camp by the west, to see whether there were any movements in that direction. We left in a drenching rain coming from the north; the weather was so dark that two men on horseback, holding each other's hand, hardly saw each other. We were armed from head to foot. We advanced with the greatest care, especially when we had to cross the bridge of some coulées, for the abundance of rain having raised the coulées, the apprehending also that parties were lying there in ambush, we dared not, in the midst of this darkness, venture near the bridges nor on them, since they unobstructed on the way out, might have been barricaded for the return; we would, therefore, reconnoitre the ground as much as possible. At last we sighted the glimmers of the fires; we pushed far enough to distinguish the fires themselves, but it was evident we were approaching the sentries' line and the outposts, and not caring to fall into their hands, we turned back. Our horses seemed to be on the alert, snorting considerably. The password having brought together the four guards, two on each side of me, we returned to the fort, always watching: Colonel Gay, Baptiste Nault, Francis St. Luc, and Pierre Champagne were the persons who accompanied me.

Gay, who had taken our interests to heart, was restless and would now and then break out against the English. Champagne played tricks; and the other two were very gay, especially St. Luc; but were wet to the skin. We re-entered the fort at about 1 o'clock a.m. I saw everybody, those who were on guard, the soldiers who were on watch at the barracks, and the representatives. O'Donoghue also returned, having discovered nothing. I took off my wet overcoat and my shoes, threw two heavy blankets on my back, wrapped myself up in them and went to bed; I slept for about three quarters of an hour. My chief papers had been sent away, Louis Schmidt working to save those of his department. When I got up, it was beginning to dawn. The rain had not abated. About eight o'clock a breakfast of cold meats was served to me. I was hungry: I ate well, but the cold and the lack of sleep had undoubtedly indisposed me too much; I felt it soon after my breakfast. [21]

At this point, one of Riel's councillors, James Stewart, arrived on horseback, shouting a warning to Riel that Wolseley's troops were less than three kilometres distant, and that all should run for their lives. The fort was quickly evacuated. Riel and O'Donoghue were the last to depart, leaving the gates open behind them. There would be no shooting; no bloodshed. That was why Wolseley's green-coated[22] soldiers entered the open gates of Fort Garry without opposition. But, if there was no opposition, neither was there a bonfire nor a guard of honour to welcome Wolseley's men.

CHAPTER FIVE

Mobilization
1869-1870

I

From the very outset of the Red River troubles, Macdonald hoped to avoid any action likely to lead to bloodshed. He kept in close touch with developments in the Red River Settlement through his two Cabinet colleagues, Joseph Howe and Charles Tupper, both of whom visited Fort Garry in the latter part of 1869. Repeatedly the Prime Minister urged McDougall to use discretion when approaching the Métis and to remember that he was only a private citizen, until he should officially receive notification of the transfer of the North West to Canada. Macdonald told McDougall:

> The point which you must never forget is that you are now approaching a foreign country, under the government of the Hudson's Bay Company. You are going there under the assumption that the Company's authorities assent to your entering upon their territory, and will protect you when there. You cannot force your way in.[1]

He warned him, too, that Stoughton Dennis, the head of the survey crew was "a very decent fellow, and a good surveyor and all that, but he has no head and is exceedingly fussy."[2] Later he repeated his warnings, "let me press upon you to remember the famous axiom of William Pitt, that the first, second, and third requisites for a statesman are *patience*."[3] Macdonald might as well have spared his ink. McDougall was ill-disposed towards patience and even less disposed towards accepting advice. He did everything he was not supposed to do and in doing so, made himself the laughing stock of the Americans in Minnesota and the Métis in Red River. Well might the Prime Minister write to his friend and confidant, Sir John Rose, "McDougall has made

Sir John A. Macdonald,
Prime Minister of Canada, 1871.

a most inglorious *fiasco* at Red River."[4] It was to pull Canada out of this "fiasco" that Macdonald sent three emissaries, Thibault, de Salaberry and Smith, to Red River to make a political deal with Riel's Provisional Government.

As soon as the Prime Minister was more fully acquainted with the misadventures of "Wandering Willie", he caused Lord Granville to be informed by telegram of what had taken place, and advised him that no immediate change should be made in the existing status of the Red River Settlement. Canada would not, under any circumstances, proceed with the transfer as long as the Settlement was in a state of turmoil. If the Hudson's Bay Company should insist upon surrendering its territories, then the British, not the Canadian, government would have to look after them and assume full responsibility for peace in Red River. At the same time, Macdonald issued positive instructions to Sir John Rose, his agent in London, to have no further dealings with the Company, and to withhold the £300,000 payment unless and until such time as the Company could guarantee peaceable possession. Neither Lord Granville nor the Company's Governor was happy about Canada's stiff-necked attitude. His Lordship was, to say the least, considerably annoyed at what he regarded as Canadian intransigence. Nevertheless, Macdonald remained firm. He noted in a letter to Sir John Rose:

> I cannot understand the desire of the Colonial Office, or the Company, to saddle the responsibility of the government on Canada just now. It would so completely throw the game into the hands of the insurgents and the Yankee wire-pullers, who are to some extent influencing and directing the movement from St. Paul, that we cannot forsee the consequences.[5]

At the same time, he wrote to William McDougall:

> My previous letter will have told you our action in England. It has stirred up the Hudson's Bay Company, and they have doubtless sent, and will continue to send, urgent messages to everybody under their influence, to act energetically in putting an end to this state of anarchy. From Rose's letters, it is obvious that both the Colonial Office and the Company would like to throw the whole responsibility on Canada, and, if we once accepted it, they would leave us to get out of the trouble the best way we could. By our positively declining to do so, and insisting upon getting peaceable possession, we shall, I have no doubt, secure the active co-operation of both; and if it be necessary, in the spring, to send a force by Fort William, it will be, I have little doubt, a combined force of regulars and volunteers.[6]

II

That an armed force of some description might be necessary to ensure the peaceful transfer of Rupert's Land was an idea never far from the minds of Canada's political leaders from the moment they agreed to take over responsibility for the future of the Hudson's Bay Company territories. Sir John A. Macdonald was well acquainted with the vast quantities of blood spilled by the American troops as they pushed their way aggressively into the Indian country to the west of the original Thirteen Colonies, and beyond the Mississippi. He did not see Canadians supporting a policy of expansion by force of arms; but he did see them giving their approval to an armed force that might resemble, not the sabre-wielding American cavalry, but rather a force of mounted police similar to the Royal Irish Constabulary; a force that would keep peace between the settlers and the Indians, and between the various Indian nations. Above all, he wanted to spare his own country the bloody episodes that stained the history of the United States.

The kind of police force the Prime Minister contemplated was a mixed English-French force, with a core of officers and men recruited in Canada and fleshed out with recruits enrolled in the Canadian West. That is why, when William McDougall set out for Red River in the latter part of 1869, he was accompanied by Captain Donald R. Cameron, son-in-law of his colleague, Charles Tupper, and cases of rifles with which the new territorial police force was to be equipped when its organization should be completed. Among his papers McDougall had a letter from Macdonald outlining the Prime Minister's scheme for a Mounted Police force.[7] Cameron, too, had a letter from the Prime Minister which read in part:

> It seems to me that the best Force would be Mounted Riflemen, trained to act as cavalry, but also instructed in the Rifle exercises. They should also be instructed, as certain of the Line are, in the use of artillery. This body should not be expressly military, but should be styled Police, and have the military bearing of the Irish Constabulary.[8]

Most British police forces were modelled upon the Metropolitan Police in London. But, because the community of Red River bore little resemblance to London, Macdonald took his cue from Ireland, where the Royal Irish Constabulary had developed against a background of religious and civil strife and social unrest, such as Macdonald feared might develop in the Canadian prairies between the whites and the native peoples, Métis and Indian.

Although Macdonald soon gave up on McDougall, he did not abandon his police project. On 4 February, while considering the possibility that the Smith-Thibault-de Salaberry mission might not succeed, the members of the Canadian Cabinet gave some thought to the despatch of an armed force to Red River. They had in mind a combined British-Canadian military force, not to replace the proposed mounted constabulary, but to give it a little more muscle.

That Macdonald's Cabinet even considered the possibility of a military force, arose from reports reaching Ottawa from Red River, to the effect that the Métis movement was developing a strong pro-American bias. Annexation to the United States was a threat that could not be ignored. It was the possibility of American intervention, more than anything else, that alarmed the members of the Canadian Cabinet. At a Cabinet meeting on 11 February it was agreed that any delegates coming to Ottawa on behalf of the people of Red River would be received "kindly" and with respect; should they be found inclined towards annexation to the United States, no discussion would be possible. On that point there would be no compromise:

> In such case . . . the Mission would fail of any satisfactory result. The consequence might then be, that the delegates, . . . smarting under the sense of failure would, unless confronted by a Military Force and a strengthened Government, make violent appeals to the people and raise a second insurrection on a more formidable basis.[9]

If there should be any real substance to the annexation business, then a military force would become a necessity.

But could Canada act alone? It was not likely. Canada did not have the military strength to engage the United States. There would have to be joint action with Great Britain. The Minute of Council of 11 February read:

> It is obvious that the Expedition must be undertaken, organized, commanded and carried through under the authority of Her Majesty's Government. Canada has no authority beyond her own limits, and no power whatever to send a Volunteer Force or to order her Militia on this, to her, a foreign service.[10]

There were other arguments in favour of a joint military operation. A combined Anglo-Canadian force would enjoy much greater political prestige and military expertise than a purely Canadian effort. The people supporting Riel might be hostile to Canada; they were considerably less so towards Great Britain. Besides British participation in a military force organized in Canada, might well discourage any American disposition to meddle in Red River. Joint British-Canadian action was therefore considered essential; so too was prompt action. Any military expedition should be mounted as early as possible, preferably in the spring and with the minimum of delay. The Cabinet Minute concluded with a request to His Excellency, the Governor General, to inform the Colonial Secretary, Lord Granville in London, of the Canadian government's wishes, in order that Her Majesty's government might "take the matter into consideration for the purpose of *immediate* action."[11] As the Canadian politicians saw it, any joint military force should be prepared and made ready for despatch to Fort William at the head of Lake Superior

> . . . immediately on the opening of navigation. In ordinary seasons the Sault Ste Marie Canal, through which the Steamers to be used in the transport of the Force must pass, opens about the 25th of April. Before that time every preparation as to men, transport, munitions of War, and supplies should be perfected, so that the Force may be assembled at Fort William by the 1st of May.[12]

At no time was Macdonald particularly enthusiastic about the idea of coercing the people of Red River into accepting the transfer of their country to Canada; neither was Lord Granville, who was not much of an imperialist. When he learned of the troubles in Red River, the Colonial Secretary limited himself to urging restraint and cabled Macdonald:

> The Queen has heard with surprise and regret that certain misguided persons have banded together to oppose by force the entry of the future Lieutenant Governor into Her Majesty's settlements on Red River. . . . She relies on your Government for using every effort to explain whatever is misunderstood, to ascertain the wants and to conciliate the goodwill of the Red River settlers. But meantime she authorizes you to signify to them the sorrow and displeasure with which she views their unreasonable and lawless proceedings. . . .[13]

There was more behind British policy than the Queen's "surprise" and "regret"; more even than her "sorrow and displeasure" over the "unreasonable" and "lawless proceedings" of the Métis settlers in Red River. The Empire was making too frequent demands on British pocketbooks, and William Ewart Gladstone's government had already decided upon a policy of withdrawing British troops from the self-governing colonies. Both Colonial Secretary Granville, and Secretary of State for War Edward Cardwell, had warned Macdonald and Cartier a year before the Riel troubles, that the British garrisons abroad were going to be reduced both in number and in strength. And this would apply to Canada.

Macdonald did a lot of thinking about what he should do about the Red River crisis. That he was inclined towards negotiation with Riel is apparent from his correspondence and his actions. At first he placed his confidence in the calming influence of the Bishop of St. Boniface, Mgr. Alexandre Taché. Writing to Sir John Rose, on 21 January 1870, the Prime Minister expressed his pleasure at Taché's willingness to return from Rome, adding, "Should all attempts at conciliation fail, we can then talk of sending a special commissioner to Red River; but we should not send an Englishman ignorant of the country."[14] A month later he was saying the same thing:

> Bishop Taché has been here and has left for the Red River, after exceedingly full and unreserved communication with him as to our policy and requirements, of all of which he approves. He is strongly opposed to the idea of an Imperial Commission, believing, as indeed, we all do, that to send out an overwashed Englishman, utterly ignorant of the country and full of crotchets, as all Englishmen are, would be a mistake.[15]

He also told Rose that a delegation from the Provisional Government in Red River was on its way to Ottawa. He even hoped that it might include, among its numbers, "the redoubtable Riel" himself. "If we once get him here," he wrote to Rose, "as you must know pretty well by this time, he is a gone coon. There is no place in the ministry for him to sit next to Howe, but perhaps we may make him a senator for the Territory!"[16]

Macdonald was disposed to use his familiar tactics of patronage or pressure when dealing with political crises, but there was a war party in Ottawa that favoured more direct and forceful methods when it came to dealing with Riel. Among them was the humiliated and unforgiving McDougall; and there was also the stiff-necked Anglo-Irish knight from Cavan in the south of Ulster in Ireland, who was living in Rideau Hall. He was Sir John Young, the Governor General, whose questionable conduct during the amnesty crisis suggests, if it does not explicitly reveal, his strong anti-Catholic, anti-French bias.

In any event, the issue of sending a police force, or a military expedition to Red River was settled, not by Macdonald, or by Cartier, or by Taché, or by Young, but by an outburst of political indignation in Ontario when the news broke of the execution of the Ontario surveyor and Orangeman, Thomas Scott, by a Métis firing squad. From the beginning of the Red River troubles, people in Ontario had generally shown no sympathy for, or understanding of, what motivated Riel and his Métis supporters. To many Ontarians, the name Riel meant one thing only: he was the individual responsible for opposing Canada's westward expansion, and for placing Ontario citizens in the cells of Fort Garry. Even more, he was responsible for executing one of them for no good reason whatsoever. The violence of vocal opinion was frightening. It was a bursting forth of pent-up prejudices of the loyal Protestant, anti-French, anti-Roman Catholic elements of Ontario's population, many of whom came from Northern Ireland and were dedicated members of the Orange Order. They were the people who read the Toronto *Globe*, who looked upon its editorials as Holy Writ and regarded its editor, George Brown, as a latter-day prophet.

At the outset of the Red River troubles, George Brown had adopted an attitude of lofty pity for the poor misguided Roman Catholic Métis who had opposed McDougall's entry into the Settlement. Then he turned to ridicule:

> It is altogether too much of a joke to think of a handful of people barring the way to the progress of British institutions and British people, on the pretense that the whole wide continent is theirs, and that they mean to treat it as such . . . the 'insurgents' have, it is said, in true French fashion organized a Provisional Government, and for the moment, probably, really believe that they are not so ridiculous as the rest of the world will declare them to be.[17]

Three weeks later the *Globe* resumed its traditional anti-Catholic stance:

There seems to have been some idea on the part of the French, that they were about to be overrun by Protestants from Canada; but it is only charitable to believe that few of them could have conceived the idea that they could withhold from settlement the fourth part of a continent, in order to keep them from the contamination of Protestantism. The French race on this continent is wonderfully exclusive in its ideas; but this is a touch beyond what even a Lower Canadian Frenchman ever conceived.[18]

In January the tone of the Toronto journal became threatening. The editor wrote, Canada "will not permit a handful of armed traitors to tyrannize over their unarmed brethren . . . either Riel or Canada must go down."[19] Then, a little over a month later: "These French insurgents, it would appear, were the most lamb-like personages one could think of; and if forced to kill some people, would simply have to be pitied and sympathized with."[20] Learning of the imprisonment of Boulton and the death of Thomas Scott, the *Globe* writers beat the editorial war drums constantly and vigorously during the months of March and April, calling for revenge and the punishment of the Red River rebels. Then, on 13 April, the *Globe* printed a resolution adopted by the Orange Order in Toronto:

> Whereas Brother Thomas Scott, a member of our Order, was cruelly murdered by the enemies of our Queen, country and religion, therefore be it resolved that while we sympathise with the relatives of our deceased Brother, we, the members of the L.O.L. No. 404 call upon the Government to avenge his death, pledging ourselves to assist in rescuing the Red River Territory from those who have turned it over to Popery, and bring to justice the murderers of our countrymen.[21]

In view of the strong stand taken by the *Globe*, it is interesting to observe that, with the exception of John Galt and Alexander Mackenzie and, of course, the embittered William McDougall, few members of Parliament ventured to open their mouths in the House of Commons in criticism of Macdonald or Cartier, the two leading government figures. Two or three wrathy outbursts were heard during the arguments on the Manitoba Bill but the debate in Parliament was comparatively quiet. To the government members the issue was simple, either the government "had to send an army to conquer" the Red River Métis, "or to consider their claims as put forward by the delegates."[22] Nevertheless, to have ignored the constant prodding of the Orange Order and the new *Canada First* movement would have shown a complete absence of political imagination on Macdonald's part; and Macdonald was ever sensitive to the winds of public opinion. Organized by the Ontarians, George Denison, Henry Morgan and William Foster, and the transplanted Nova Scotian, Robert Haliburton, and exploited to the full by Charles Mair and John Schultz, *Canada First* became the principal political instrument of the pro-expansionists, the pro-English and the pro-Protestant elements in Ontario. Here the "refugees" from the Red River were welcomed as guests in the homes and on the platforms of *Canada First*. With their tales of abuse, Schultz, Mair and others stirred the blood of Orange Ontarians and stimulated the desire to avenge the death of "Brother Scott." Protest meetings were held the length and breadth of the province, with monster meetings in Toronto, the heart of old Ontario. That there was a widespread, and obviously enthusiastic response to this agitation, confirmed Macdonald's earlier decision that troops would have to be sent to the West, not just to discourage the American annexationists, but also to appease Ontario expansionists. Macdonald admitted as much in a letter he sent to the Earl of Carnarvon on 14 April:

> Scott was known in Canada and has relatives here, and the blood of the people is at fever heat. They are calling for retribution upon Riel, and all connected with him. Indignation meetings have been held all over Canada, and the Government has been called upon by some of them to refuse to receive any delegates commissioned by Riel.
>
> I hope, however, that we shall be able to arrange matters so satisfactorily that the expedition which is now being prepared, and which *must* go, will be accepted, not as a hostile force, but as a friendly garrison.[23]

*Lieutenant-General
the Hon. James Lindsay, 1870.*

III

Up to this time slow progress had been made in organizing the Red River Expeditionary Force. On 23 February Sir John Macdonald informed his colleague Rose in London that he was "exceedingly glad" to learn that the British were sending Lieutenant-General Lindsay to Canada as the senior British officer. "He knows something of the country, and is a good soldier and a frank and ready man of business,"[24] was how Macdonald described him to Rose. However, when Lindsay arrived in Canada, he carried no precise instructions about putting together a force to march against the Métis of Red River. Even as late as 23 March, a note from the Colonial Office to the War Office did not go beyond warning Lindsay that the Governor General, Sir John Young, might require him to send a "detachment" not exceeding 200 infantry and a small number of artillery, to the Red River Territory, supported by a larger number of Canadians, "to maintain order in that settlement during the process of its annexation to Canada."[25] Other than that, however, Lindsay's instructions seemed clear enough. Should the Canadian government decide upon sending a force to Red River, then Lindsay must make it clear that "there is no intention that any part of the Imperial Force shall remain at Fort Garry during the winter."[26] That meant that the British troops would have to be back in Canada by the end of September. After that they would promptly return to England.

There were other stipulations laid down by the Colonial Secretary, Lord Granville. The Governor General alluded to them when he wrote to Sir John Macdonald on 10 April stating that the British government did not wish its troops to be used "to force the people to unite with Canada," or, as the Governor General sarcastically remarked, the troops were to be "of no use." Young was furious: he wrote, "Now if we accept the Country we are committed to its conquest. . . . We can't return the Country to Her Majesty or the H.B. Company." He even wondered "why should we agree to pay for Troops that may be ordered not to act when they get to Fort Garry?" He did his utmost to persuade Macdonald to tell Lord Granville that Canada would accept the transfer only "if regular troops are sent to be used if necessary to put down insurrection."[27] Macdonald had more political sense than his bellicose Governor General and, after some further discussions, Young agreed to omit from his telegram to London any reference to putting down "insurrection" and to seek agreement on distribution of the costs of the expedition between Canada and England. Like any good politician, Macdonald had his eye on the financial outlays involved. From his standpoint, this was essential. The British government was quite prepared to drive a hard bargain; they would pay only one fourth of the total cost. No more. Or, as Sir John Young put it, this was "the outside measure of the liability which the Ministers in England will be disposed to exercise."[28] Lindsay's first responsibility, as far as any Red River force was concerned, was to discuss with the Governor General, and then to pass on to the War Office, the name of the officer they both considered best qualified to command the expedition, keeping in mind the possibility that the Canadian government might wish to appoint him as "the first civil Lieutenant-Governor of the district." [29]

This stipulation appeared to present no problem. The choice seemed obvious; at least to the man who hoped and expected to be selected. He was the Quartermaster-General of the troops in Canada, Colonel Garnet Joseph Wolseley, an officer referred to by a later generation as "perhaps the most promising young officer of the British Empire, and probably the most cock-sure."[30] His military qualifications were impeccable. He was well known to the soldiers of

Sir John Young, later Lord Lisgar
Governor General of Canada, 1869-72.

the Canadian Militia as the officer who had commanded a military camp at La Prairie in 1865 and organized a militia concentration at Thorold, late in 1866, following the Fenian invasion of Ontario that year. Like the Governor General, he was a strong Anglo-Irish Protestant and a Freemason,[31] a fact Lindsay apparently overlooked. Had Lindsay been more sensitive to the racial-religious factor in Canadian political life he might have had some reservations about the suitability of a man of Wolseley's background as commander of any force being sent to Red River at a time when the French-English, Catholic-Protestant issue had reached a fever pitch following the shooting of the Orangeman, Thomas Scott. Neither did the racial-religious factor enter Wolseley's mind, so pleased was he with his appointment. He looked forward with happy anticipation, not only to his new command, but also to the possibility of becoming the new Lieutenant-Governor of Red River, and hurried to pass the good news to his brother Dick:

> I suppose you will have seen in the papers that I have been nominated to command the expedition to Red River. I have been busy for some weeks past drawing

up plans and proposed arrangements for such an operation. It is far from being an easy one as the whole route from Fort William on Lake Superior to Fort Garry on the Red River is a howling wilderness where nothing except some fish is to be had to eat. . . . I am in great hopes that I may be used in the double capacity of Commander and as provisional Governor. The whole of the arrangements have up to the moment been kept as profoundly secret as is possible to do so, but of course a little has leaked out, although when anyone asks me if the report of my going is true I always profess to know nothing beyond what appears in the papers.[32]

Because the Canadians were expecting Great Britain to contribute troops to the expeditionary force, Lindsay suggested to the Canadian government that perhaps they might like to see the Royal Canadian Rifles employed as the British component in the Red River Force.[33] To his surprise and disappointment, the Canadian response was a strong negative. The British general had believed that the Rifles, during their short stay in Red River between 1857 and 1861, had left a favourable impression on the people of the Settlement. Moreover, because the Royal Canadian Rifles included men nearing retirement, most of them might well wish to make their permanent home in the Red River region. This very fact provided the explanation of the curt rejection by Ottawa of Lindsay's proposal. What the Canadian government wished sent to Red River was not a collection of old sweats, counting the days to their retirement and their pensions — the earlier group of British military pensioners had been a useless lot. Canada wanted young, vigorous men willing to work hard, able to fight and anxious to carve a permanent niche for themselves in the western prairies. What was even more important, the government was determined that no one would be sent to Red River who had any tie or association with the Settlement, or with its past. This was, in fact, one of the requirements laid down for the enlistment of Canadians in the militia component of the Red River Expedition.

The Royal Canadian Rifles not being acceptable to Canada, Lindsay had little choice but to agree to the employment of the 60th Rifles. Raised originally in North America during the 1750s under the name of "The Royal Americans," the 60th wore dark green uniforms patterned after those of the Austrian Jaeger units. From the outset these troops had been armed with rifles, rather than the standard smooth bore muskets. They had also received special training based upon the ideas of the legendary Robert Rogers.[34] Supplementing the regular infantry, the British also undertook to contribute a handful of men belonging to the Royal Artillery, Royal Engineers, Army Service Corps and Army Hospital Corps to the Red River Expedition.

The original proposal was that Wolseley's force should number 1000 men, 250 of whom would be British regulars and the remainder Canadian militia. This coincided with London's insistence that the British share of the financial cost of the Red River Expedition would amount to no more than one quarter of the total sum. Canada would pay the remaining three quarters.

However, as time went on, Ottawa began to wonder if this number of troops was really adequate to deal with the military task facing them. The British, however, were adamant. They would contribute and pay the costs of 250 men. No more than that. Lindsay would have to keep his eye on the Canadians and make sure that they did not try to put something over the British by increasing their own contribution, thus augmenting the total cost and the share the British would be expected to pay. Perhaps that cost-sharing formula of 25 percent was too elastic. The War Office was nothing if not vigilant in defending the interests of the British taxpayer. Poor Lindsay! He must have grown weary of the battles over the financial arrangements, when he found himself, as late as 15 July, still arguing with the Secretary of State for War:

> The construction to be placed upon the telegrams that have passed is certainly open to argument, and Canada may contend that she has read them in a way more favourable to herself than I have done.
>
> I assume that Her Majesty's Government will be glad to avoid any discussion of this kind, if the interests with which it is charged, justify it in doing so.
>
> I venture therefore to express my belief that there would be no ground left for dispute if the Imperial Government engaged to pay one-fourth of the total of the general expenses of the whole force sent, instead of the share of 250 regulars only. Indeed, the Secretary of State for the Colonies is reported to have said in the House of Lords that England would pay one-third....
>
> The difference which either proportion would make in sum to be found by the Imperial Government is small, considering the object in view.[35]

It was not with the War Office alone that Lindsay had his troubles. Dealing with the Canadian Department of Militia appeared to him to be equally frustrating. Where the British were penny-pinching and obstinate, the Canadians were penny-pinching and dilatory. He saw the Canadians as apparently oblivious to the urgency of getting their troops ready. Canada was committed to a military operation of considerable difficulty and magnitude, considering the number of men involved, the rough nature of the country to be crossed and the short time available for training men for the tasks they were about to undertake. But did the Canadians act with despatch? Lindsay wrote petulantly:

> It was only on the 15th April, and after the receipt of my Memorandum of the 10th April, which was sent in within a few days of my arrival in this command, that the Adjutant-General of Militia submitted a plan for raising two regiments of Militia for service in the North-West.[36]

The most acute problem, as Lindsay saw it, was that, owing to the delays in getting organized, the troops would start serious training "only a short time" before they would have to move to Fort William *en route* to Red River. In all probability, these untrained soldiers would find themselves faced with the problems of coping with "insurgents" likely to be assisted by those "roving and lawless societies which are to be found in the United States."[37] By which, it may be assumed, he meant members of the Fenian Brotherhood.

IV

Despite, or perhaps because of Lindsay's worries, the logistical arrangements, transportation, and provisions for the Red River force were quickly taken in hand. Owing to the fact that the route the troops would follow on the journey to Red River would, in large measure, determine the nature of the transport requirements and the type of rations and supplies to be carried, it was necessary to obtain a firm decision as quickly as possible on how the troops would reach Red River.

One route was clearly out of the question. That was the railway through the United States to St. Paul, and the steamer down the Red River to Fort Garry. The ill-concealed hostility of the United States government to the expedition made it obvious that any request for permission to travel through that country would be refused. In any event, to use the St. Paul route, would underline the fact that the Americans had easier access to the western British territories than did Canada. That meant that troops would have to follow a route through British territory: either the northern route by way of Hudson Bay, the route traditionally used by the Hudson's Bay Company and followed by the 6th Warwickshires and the Royal Canadian Rifles in the mid-nineteenth century;[38] or the southern route, traditionally used by the North West Company, and in the early years of the century by Orsonnens and Selkirk. The arguments in favour of the northern route were obvious. It could be navigated by boats, whereas the southern route had always required canoes. No less an authority than the late Sir George Simpson — and no one could pretend to have had greater experience of navigating the inland waters of British North America — had always upheld the superiority of the northern route.

At the same time, however, serious objections existed to the Bay route in 1870. It would be virtually impossible for the British contingent, after reaching Fort Garry by way of York Factory, to return the same way to Montreal within a single season; and the British War Office had stated emphatically that permission would not be given for British troops to remain in North America for another year. Against the opinion of Sir George Simpson, was that of Simon Dawson, an engineer and road builder, who believed the southern route to be a practical one. After all, he had travelled the Lake Superior route and was already engaged in constructing a road over it.

Dawson had, in fact, been hired by the federal government in 1869. His task was to improve transportation facilities along the southern route, thus making it possible for prospective settlers to move to the prairies without having to travel through the United States, where they would be exposed to inducements to settle in the republic. During the autumn of 1869, Dawson had begun work, not only on a road from Lake of Woods to Fort Garry — his surveyors, incidentally, were those who had frightened and irritated the Métis — but also another road westward from Fort William to the Height of Land, making it possible, even practical, to travel most of the way to Lake of the Woods by boat, and then overland to the Red River. Dawson was disposed to play down the problems stressed by Simpson and the Hudson's Bay men. "They were," he said, "exaggerated." Those were words that both Lindsay and the Canadian Department of Militia wanted to hear; even though no one was very clear just how much progress Dawson had actually made with his road building. However, on 25 April 1870, he told the authorities:

Simon James Dawson, the civil engineer who opened communications from Lake Superior to Red River, 1869-70.

When the work of road making was brought to a close last fall, a section of 25 miles [40 km], reckoning from Thunder Bay, was practicable to waggons, with only one interruption at the Kaministikwia, which was then unbridged, and continuing on the line an additional section of ten miles [16 km] was cut out in such a way as to be practicable to oxen with sleds or carts.... At the same time instructions were sent to the officer in charge, to set all the available force to work on the road as soon as the snow should have so far cleared off, as to admit of operations thereon being resumed, so that about eighty men are by this time engaged on the unfinished section of the line.[39]

These words were sufficiently encouraging to convince both Lindsay and Wolseley that the southern route was, in fact, feasible for the movement of troops. The decision was therefore taken to send the Red River Expedition over the same route Orsonnens had used half a century earlier.

Throughout the month of April, Dawson was in close touch with the military authorities. Not only did he inform them that the work had started once more on the road, he told them that he would provide boats specially designed for use on the inland water system, with its lakes and rivers, and swift flowing rapids, and would undertake to hire men to man them; skilled voyageurs, boatmen with experience in navigating the inland waters of Canada and driving logs in rapid rivers. The number of men thus engaged would by summer total 800. To get the soldiers to the western shores of Lake Superior, Dawson chartered two steamers, *Chicora* and *Algoma*, both specifically adapted to carry troops and stores. These two vessels were scheduled to run continually all summer between Collingwood and Thunder Bay, sailing alternately, at five-day intervals, throughout the navigation season.

There is no doubt that, before he arrived at Thunder Bay, Colonel Wolseley was well aware that he would encounter serious problems using the route Dawson had mapped for him. He had the engineer's report on the incomplete state of the road leading to Shebandowan Lake. He was also in receipt of a report on the road from the North West Angle of Lake of the Woods to Fort Garry, indicating that, not only was the land in that region low and swampy, but that difficulties might be encountered when trying to obtain horses and waggons in a region sparsely settled, particularly from a scattered Métis population. It would be better to follow the water route all the way, using the Winnipeg River, Lake Winnipeg and the Red River. "In the one case," said Dawson, "the men would reach Fort Garry fatigued with a long march and hard work in road making, in the other they would arrive vigorous and fresh."[40] Wolseley's choice was as obvious as it was predictable.

V

While Dawson was arranging for the transportation of Wolseley's force, Matthew Bell Irvine and the officials of the Control Department were looking after the foodstuffs, forage, fuel, stores, hospital supplies, postal, pay and other problems attending the despatch of any body of troops.[41] All these were essential items and important for the maintenance of the morale of the troops and the success of the operation. According to *Standing Orders* dated 10 May 1870, the rations were to consist of one pound of biscuit, or one and a half pounds of bread, or one and a half pounds of flour; one pound of salt pork or one and a half pounds of fresh meat; one third of a pint of beans or one quarter of a pound of preserved potatoes; one thirty-sixth of an ounce of pepper, per man per day. If and when fresh vegetables were obtainable, one pound would be issued as a ration. These rations were those for men in camp. When the soldiers were obliged to do heavy road work or manhandle the boats, their rations would be increased in quantity, although not in variety. The biscuit was purchased in Quebec, at three and a quarter cents per pound. The controller reported after the expedition was over, that all the rations had been of good quality. One recommendation he did make for the future was, however, that supplies should be removed from the barrels in which they were shipped and be repacked in lighter canvas bags at Thunder Bay, owing to the added weight of the heavy barrels and the added labour of manhandling them over the many portages along the water route.

Fresh rations would have been preferable. But they were just not available in quantity, even at the Hudson's Bay Company posts along the way. There were, however, occasions when it was possible to serve fresh bread rather than stale biscuit. This proved to be the case at Prince Arthur's Landing, at Matawin Bridge, the Dam-Site and Fort Frances, and, of course, at Fort Garry. Anticipating this likelihood, the expedition was equipped with six field ovens, Aldershot style, distributed along the route — although, as was expected, there were brick ovens available both at Lower and Upper Fort Garry. The fresh bread, incidentally, was a very popular item, and according to contemporary accounts, "invariably beautifully baked."[42] The troops found it a pleasant change from hard biscuit. Owing to the summer heat the barrels of pork had constantly to be re-coopered and re-brined, but apparently kept well, with the exception of a number of barrels carried by the troops of the 1st (Ontario) Rifles. Some of the soldiers of this battalion, in order to lighten the loads they carried, released the brine, thus hastening the decay of the meat. For this little mishap the Battalion was obliged to forfeit the sum of $140.[43] Fresh beef was obtainable at Thunder Bay and along the route at Shebandowan Lake, and later at Fort Frances and Fort Alexander, but not on the return journey. The preserved potatoes, carried in hermetically sealed containers, proved to be a great success; with boiling water, only a few minutes were required to change them into an edible vegetable. They were transported in 25 kilo tins containing 224 rations. In addition to the foodstuffs, 1360 kilos of tobacco and 900 kilos of soap were carried on the expedition and issued to the troops on repayment. Spirits, incidentally, formed no part of the ration and nothing of this kind could be procured by the men *en route.* Tea only was available and, as Irvine reported, "every man returned in as good if not better health than when he left."[44]

In addition to the rations for the men, there were rations for the horses and cattle required to work on the road between Thunder Bay and Shebandowan Lake. Hay, oats and ox feed, all obtained under government contract at Collingwood and Owen Sound, in Ontario, were transported by boat to Prince Arthur's Landing. The ration, in this instance, was four and a half kilos of oats and five and a half kilos of hay per animal—a quantity which proved quite inadequate, owing to the exceptionally heavy work the animals were required to do.

The waggons used by the expeditionary force were, for the most part, built at Markham, near Toronto. They proved to be most useful. According to Irvine, "They were well and strongly built, required but little repair, and were all in fair serviceable condition at the termination of the Expedition."[45] These vehicles were used for the conveyance of stores and supplies and also to carry the boats over the road to Shebandowan Lake at the beginning of the inland water system. One of the few complaints that Irvine had to make in his report concerned the constant wear on the horse collars and the consequent loss of time while they were being repaired. He suggested that, in future, should any similar expedition be undertaken, it would be advisable to keep a certain number of breast harnesses in reserve, to be available for use while the horse collars were undergoing repair.

Although he was generally satisfied with the items supplied by the contractors, Irvine was not so enthusiastic about some of the civilian employees with whom he had to contend. The civilian establishment included not only a veterinary surgeon who was less then competent, but a number of teamsters, blacksmiths and collar makers of varying ability. All of them drew better pay than the soldiers and were not amenable to military discipline. According to Irvine's report, two teamsters had to be brought before the Magistrate at Sault Ste Marie, where they were committed for several days in the local jail because they insisted, against orders, in "driving furiously" on the road way. In this context it should be noted that a representative of the Society for the Prevention of Cruelty to Animals accompanied the expedition to the lakehead. It was he who laid the charges![46] The best teamsters were men who were farmers. They, at least, had some concern for their animals.

VI

The Canadian component of the Red River Force included two battalions of militia riflemen, each consisting of 21 officers and 350 non-commissioned officers and men, raised in the provinces of Quebec and Ontario, and engaged for one year service "or for such longer period as the government may require, but not exceeding two years in all."[47] Each battalion comprised seven companies, each of 50 men, commanded by a captain, supported by a lieutenant and an ensign. The battalions would be raised by voluntary enlistment, hopefully from existing militia units in both provinces. The pay rates were to be 20 dollars a month for a sergeant-major and quartermaster-sergeant, and 18 dollars for the paymaster's clerk, hospital-sergeant, armourer-sergeant and colour-sergeant. Ordinary sergeants would receive 15 dollars, corporals and buglers 13 dollars and private soldiers 12 dollars monthly. All non-commissioned officers and men would, of course, draw free rations, clothing and lodging. Men volunteering for the two battalions were required to be between the ages of 18 and 45, be "of good character" and "sober habits" and have had no association whatever with the events that had taken place in Red River during the preceding months. They had to prove that they were "physically fit for service" and be willing to undergo a final medical examination just prior to departure for the west. Initially the various Adjutants-General recommended the officers. They would be drawn from militiamen who were considered "best qualified" to act as Captains, Lieutenants and Ensigns. Their names were to be submitted by 2 May and were published in *Militia General Orders* on 12 May. Among them were some well known persons and others who would become well known. The most experienced soldier among them was Lieutenant-Colonel Louis Adolphe Casault, the officer commanding the 2nd (Quebec) Rifles, who fifteen years earlier had enlisted in the French army as a private to serve in Crimea and later in Algeria and who accepted a commission in the 100th Regiment of Foot, a Canadian unit raised by voluntary enlistment for service with the British Army.[48] Then there was Major Thomas Scott who, a year later, would command another battalion of militia sent to Manitoba to fight the Fenians. There was Hugh John Macdonald, the Prime Minister's son who always wanted to be a soldier rather than the lawyer or politician his father had set his heart on his being. Hugh John made it into the 1st (Ontario) Rifles with the help of Sir George Cartier, while his father was ill, and he always regretted that the Red River force had not remained in existence to become "the nucleus of the Canadian Army in which he might have served permanently."[49] There were Charles Bell and Daniel McMillan, both of whom were to make their homes in Manitoba, the one to become a historian and receive an honorary doctorate; and the other to receive a knighthood and become Lieutenant-Governor of the province. And there was also Sam Steele, who, despite his commission in the 31st Grey Battalion of Infantry, chose to enlist as a private soldier, but who finished his military career as a Major-General. "I was better off without chevrons," he wrote years later, and "learned how to appreciate the trials of other men to an extent that I should never have been able to do had I been promoted."[50]

There was no lack of recruits as far as the Ontario Battalion was concerned. *Canada First* saw to that. So too did the Toronto *Globe*. But in Quebec the response was slower and less enthusiastic. There was, in fact, little inducement for young French Roman Catholics to offer their services in an expedition which, as both the Quebec and Ontario press indicated, was directed against francophone Catholics in Red River. What other conclusions could be drawn from George Brown's remark that "Donald Smith's chicken broth has failed to cure his Winnipeg disorder, so suppose we try to effect a steel tonic?"[51] Sir George Cartier and other French Conservatives in Ottawa might natter about Wolseley's force being sent on "a mission of peace," but there were others who saw the expedition, just as many Roman Catholic priests and French language editorial writers saw it, as an anti-Catholic crusade.

There was another factor that tended to discourage recruiting in Quebec for the western expedition. That was the threat of renewed armed activity by the Fenian Brotherhood at the province's back door. Throughout the spring of 1870 rumours constantly circulated in the province that the Irish Republican Army was planning another invasion of Canada, probably via Montreal. These rumours became reality on 24 May, the Queen's birthday, when the Fenians crossed the frontier, from their base at St. Alban's, Vermont, into Quebec. The local Missisquoi Militia, supported by other militiamen from Montreal, succeeded in defeating the invaders at Eccles Hill, pushing them back into the United States. The conclusion drawn from this episode was obvious to Quebeckers. Was it not better to stay home and protect it against a real enemy, than to indulge in some fanciful gesture far away from Quebec? That this explanation has some validity seems to emerge from the fact that in response to Eccles Hill and the continued Fenian threat, several thousand officers and men of the volunteer militia were mobilized during the next few weeks for defence duties along the United States-Canada border.[52]

Lieutenant-Colonel Louis Adolphe Casault, 2nd (Quebec) Rifles. *Captain (later Lieutenant-Governor of Manitoba) Daniel H. McMillan.*

Following enlistment at their local headquarters, the Red River recruits, regardless of their place of origin, were sent to Toronto where they were housed in the Crystal Palace,[53] a large glass structure which had, at an earlier date, been the scene of the brilliant ball offered in honour of the Prince of Wales (later Edward VII) on the occasion of his visit to Ontario. Here, the men were told off into companies and presented with their short Snider-Enfield breech-loading rifles and other items of their kit. Here, too, they met the regimental barber. Much to the annoyance of the press, reporters were excluded from the daily Orderly Room and forbidden to obtain information from junior officers. Even so, they were able to entertain their readers with accounts, more or less accurate, of the gradual transformation of what they initially referred to as "an awkward booby squad" into "a regiment of soldier-like looking men who already appeared to be used to their harness and marched with a steadiness which would do credit to a Battalion of the Line."[54] There was some good, honest reporting too. According to one newspaper man:

94

The bare and not over clean floor with the row of badly stuffed straw beds placed along the walls, and the general idea of untidiness, conveyed by the variety of garments, arms, accoutrements and other parapha- nalia of a military life, strewed about it in what appears to be an inextricable confusion, is not at all calculated to impress one with a desire for military honours, leaving out the question altogether of the monotony of the nearly constant drill to which the men were sub- jected, and which has already considerably dampened the ardour of several who volunteered without the remotest idea of what they would have to go through.[55]

That was probably not far from the truth. In the two or three weeks the soldiers were in Toronto, they learned a good deal about the dull monotony of military routine, the repetitive sameness of reveillé, orderly room, drill, more drill and lights out. And they were all awaiting the expected order to move.

On 24 May, the day the Fenians crossed the frontier south of Montreal, the militia troops in Toronto paraded for inspection. These part-time militiamen, now become full-time soldiers, "acquitted them- selves most creditably" according to Colonel Fielden,[56] the command- ing officer of the 60th Rifles, who inspected them. After the inspection, each man was presented with a "handsomely bound Bible", by the

Red River Volunteers drilling in front of the Crystal Palace, Toronto, 1870.

representative of the Upper Canada Bible Society; and then, with high hopes, boarded the waiting coaches of the Northern Railway Company. The soldiers were ministered to by their regimental Chaplains, the Reverend R. Stewart Patterson of Stratford (Ontario Rifles) and the Révérend Père Marie Joseph Royer (Quebec Rifles). Their destination, some 145 kilometres distant, was the port of embarkation, Collingwood, a small town located on Georgian Bay.

They were not, however, the first men to leave for the North West. While the volunteers were still undergoing basic training in Toronto, some 140 workmen and voyageurs, including Iroquois Indians from Kahnawake near Montreal, had set out for Thunder Bay. They were accompanied by the supplies necessary to set up the base camp on the lake shore near Fort William.[57]

CHAPTER SIX

Collingwood to Shebandowan Lake May - July 1870

I

The first troopship to leave Collingwood was the steamer *Algoma*. She set sail 3 May, heavily laden, according to observers, with barrels, barrows, spades and a chaos of military stores. As she moved from her moorings, she was loudly acclaimed by a crowd of spectators. Some of the French Canadians on board responded with songs, one of which was about dying "pour la patrie." A little "out of tune," wrote the *Globe* reporter, somewhat acidly, "each one chose his own key," supplying "his own version of the words." He added, "the singers, it is hoped, will not die for their country, but rather live to complete the Dawson Road, the greater part of which, from all I can learn, has yet to be built."[1] On board *Algoma* were S. J. Dawson and Wemyss M. Simpson, the Member of Parliament for Algoma, the Rev. Mr. Hill of Manitoulin, several Toronto newsmen and half a dozen more "waifs."[2] The weather was favourable and the vessel made good time, passing Owen Sound during the night, tying up briefly at Killarney, and then continuing past Bruce Mines to arrive safely at Sault Ste Marie. Presenting herself at the entrance to the canal and locks on the American side of the frontier, *Algoma* slipped quietly through. She continued the voyage to Michipicoten Island and, after an uneventful voyage, arrived at Fort William. Here the men on board were greeted with shouts and cheers from a number of Dawson's workmen who had elected to remain at Fort William during the winter rather than return to Ontario and Quebec.

Meanwhile, at Collingwood, *Chicora*, a vessel that had acquired a sinister reputation among the Americans as a blockade runner during their Civil War,[3] was taking on her cargo of military stores. She, too, carried some 120 workmen and voyageurs and a small number of soldiers belonging to the advance party. Accompanied by the usual

Troopship Chicora *1870.*

cheers, songs and waving of flags, appropriate music was supplied by the 32nd Bruce Militia band. Meanwhile, according to one newspaper reporter, "an old lady with a large parcel of oranges was busy distributing them to the troops."[4]

The principal concern of those on board was whether the American authorities would allow *Chicora* to pass through the American locks at the Sault as readily as *Algoma* had done. To be on the safe side, it was decided that *Chicora* should discharge her military stores and passengers on the Canadian side of the frontier, and then continue into American waters to pass through the canal. Once on Lake Superior, *Chicora* could return to Canadian waters and everything could be loaded on board again. There was some reason to hope that the American authorities would not look too closely at *Chicora*. After all, the Canadians had allowed American vessels during the Civil War to pass unchallenged through the locks, including the Welland Canal, and American troops had been transported on Canadian railways. But still, the doubts remained. That is why it was planned to unload *Chicora* at the Canadian Sault and allow here to pass through the United States waters light. Some politically-minded Canadians were disposed to mutter something about Canada building her own locks, and the *Globe* editorialist wrote menacingly that, should *Chicora* be refused passage, "There can be only one course for our Government to pursue."[5] But he did not specify just what that course should be.

To avoid any trouble, *Chicora* dropped her army personnel and her obvious military material on the Canadian side of the St. Mary's River, and then sailed into American waters. At the entrance to the United States canal, American officers carried out an inspection, discovering certain large boxes labelled "hardware," together with stocks of provisions and wooden boards. They then reported that the vessel was "obviously" carrying military supplies. *Chicora*'s captain was therefore informed that his vessel would not be permitted to pass. The American canal master stated, "Until further instructions, I cannot permit you to pass through the St. Mary's Falls Ship Canal with the *Chicora*."[6] The document bore the signature of Edward H. Carleton.

Hoping that a personal appeal might help the situation, Lieutenant-Colonel W. F. Bolton,[7] the senior British officer at the Sault, wearing civilian clothes, paid a courtesy call upon the Brigadier-General commanding the 100-man American garrison stationed there. However, Bolton's explanations and protests carried no weight. The American general, while receiving the British officer with courtesy, simply replied, "My instructions are absolute. Nothing whatever connected with the Red River expedition can pass the canal. I must, therefore, absolutely refuse to allow the *Chicora* to pass through."[8]

The American commander was telling the truth. His instructions were precise. As early as 3 May, when the news broke that the Canadian government was going to send a military force to Red River, Governor H. P. Baldwin of Michigan wrote to Washington to determine the President's reaction to the possibility of Canadian troops using the Sault Canal. "Is it your wish," he wrote, "that I direct the Superintendent of the Canal not to allow its use for that purpose without positive instructions from Washington?" Hamilton Fish, the Secretary of State, replied the same day:

> The President desires me to say that the granting of transit through or over any part of the United States to the military force of foreign Power, is wholly within the control and direction of the Federal Government. . . . He desires, therefore, that no military expedition of any foreign Power, whether of troops or of boats intended for the purpose of taking part in any military or warlike expedition or of warlike material, be allowed to pass through Sault Ste Marie canal without

*Hamilton Fish, U.S.
Secretary of State who ordered the
stopping of Chicora.*

express instructions to that effect from the Government at Washington.[9]

The American action in stopping *Chicora* was followed by an
outburst of indignation in Canada, both from the troops and from the
press. Scorn and curses were the very natural reaction of those who
realized that any serious delays resulting from the action of the United
States authorities might well imperil the success of Wolseley's expedition. The editor of the *Globe* mingled scorn with anger and injured
innocence, pointing out that:

> ... there is no question of belligerency, or of neutrality
> in the matter. There is nobody in question whose rights
> and interests the Washington Government was bound
> to protect save the owners of the *Chicora* and her
> shippers and passengers. There is no war in Manitoba;
> no rebels even; all that has been settled. But the Ameri-
> can Government are so eager to show their sympathy
> with the abandoned insurrection that they try to stop

the progress of the garrison designed to secure the peace of the lately disturbed district.

Still, he suggested, there was a lesson to be learned from this experience:

> We shall gain nothing from Americans or anyone else, by tame submission to wrong and insult. If the Americans choose to shut out our vessels from their single little canal, in order to put difficulties in the way of our North-Western progress, we must close our larger works to them. We can live quite as well without them as they without us.[10]

Learning from Ottawa of the problems presented by the uncooperative policy adopted by Washington, the British Ambassador, Sir Edward Thornton, on 16 May requested President Grant to change his mind and to authorize the free passage of *Chicora*, expressing hope that the canal

> ... shall remain on the same footing as regards Canadian vessels as the Welland Canal is with regard to vessels of the United States, there being no intention to send through the canal any ammunitions of war for the expedition which is about to proceed to the Red River Settlement, and that the *Chicora* and other vessels of that class be allowed to pass through.[11]

He added that the Canadian government had received delegates from the Settlement and with their assistance had prepared an Act of Parliament establishing a Canadian province in the western region, to the joy and content of the people of the region. He wrote, "The expedition, therefore, which is now being sent to that Settlement is in no way to bear a hostile character. It will be a peaceful expedition, with the object of maintaining good order in that district and of insuring the regular and harmonious establishment of the new Government."[12]

On 16 May Bancroft Davis, the Acting Secretary of State, told Governor Baldwin that since the difficulties in the Red River country had, in fact, been "amicably" settled and the military expedition was only "a peaceful one," President Grant "does not desire to oppose the passage of the *Chicora* and other vessels of that class, through the canal in the jurisdiction of the United States, so long as they do not carry troops and munitions of war."[13] No sooner were Thornton's message and Grant's instructions revealed to the press, than the *Globe* directed its editorial wrath on this occasion, towards Sir Edward Thornton, demanding to know why he should have thought it "proper to humiliate himself and his country" by offering a "pitiful explanation" of the situation in Red River to the President of the United States. "How could Mr. Thornton go down on his knees in this miserable fashion," the editor asked, and explain "as if to a Suzerain, all the outs and ins of the dealings of the British Government with a handful of British subjects."[14]

II

Once the *Chicora* affair had become past history, the build-up of Wolseley's force absorbed the attention of both government and press. The Canadian government chartered additional steamers, including *Waubuno, Shickluna* and *Frances Smith,* and these, along with the *Chicora,* maintained a steady shuttle service between Collingwood and Sault Ste Marie. According to one newspaper correspondent, the "dreary quiet" of Collingwood was replaced with "bustle and activity," and the town, enjoying its great moment in Canadian history, was "galvanized" into temporary life. The *Globe* writer even went so far as to call Collingwood "a miniature Chicago," filled with excitement and activity in which the townspeople rejoiced.[15]

There was, of course, equal activity at Sault Ste Marie. The voyageurs and workmen went to work building the Portage Road. At the same time a small wharf was run out at the head of the rapids and a scow brought from Collingwood was used to convey troops and stores from the wharf, where the water was shallow, to the head of the Sault Ste Marie rapids. Steadily the stock of men and materials grew larger: soldiers, horses, barrels of pork, flour, preserved potatoes and sugar, and bales of hay and oats, together with carts, boats and camp equipage. Dull the work of road building over the five kilometre portage at the Sault may have been, and the unloading and reloading of the vessels too, but an atmosphere of excitement prevailed.

For a while the soldiers regarded the Sault experience with greater favour than the routine drill that had occupied their time in Toronto. The expedition to the North West was beginning to take on the air of a glorified camping trip. Here, at Sault Ste Marie the men were under canvas, not in the draughty glass structure in which they had spent

Landing at Sault Ste. Marie, watercolour and gouache by William Armstrong, 1870.

their previous weeks in routine military training. At Sault Ste Marie, it was possible to catch a few speckled trout from the wharf, near the Hudson's Bay post; and what a welcome change fresh fish provided from a steady salt pork diet! Of course, as soldiers, the volunteers had to follow the customary military routine, reveillé at 0400 hrs, breakfast at 0700, fatigues and guards, short drill sessions, retreat at sunset, tattoo at 2130 and lights out at 2200 hrs. For the sake of protection, a garrison was organized, consisting of four companies of the 1st (Ontario) Militia Rifles. The duties of the garrison were not only to guard the troops and supplies moving from Lake Huron to Lake Superior, where *Algoma* and *Brooklyn*, the latter an American vessel on Lake Superior, were carrying on the shuttle service to Fort William, but also to keep a sharp lookout for spies and saboteurs. Throughout the whole expedition there was talk about the Fenians and what they were up to: spying on the movements of Wolseley's troops; watching the build-up of Canadian troops from across the Sault Canal; chartering a fast tug to tow a schooner-load of saboteurs to seize *Algoma*. One report had it that Irish-American groups in Duluth and Marquette were planning to move against Dawson's road builders in Fort William. Fenian spy stories of every kind circulated among the men at the Sault, but the *Globe* reporter probably came nearest the truth when he wrote, "The Fenians, judging from the conversations I have had with likely-looking 'cusses' on the American side, are considerably dispirited by the actions of the American authorities, and feel less secure in the carrying out of their plans than heretofore."[16] Most, if not all of the spies and saboteurs were more imaginary than real. But they did produce some excitement at Sault Ste Marie. According to Captain Harman of the Ontario Rifles, a civilian clergyman who was travelling with the troops in order to reach his charge in Fort William, was spotted by an over-zealous sentry while the cleric was sketching the camp. Believing him to be a Fenian spy, the guard not only threatened the poor man with his rifle, but raised an alarm "which brought out nearly the entire camp."[17] On another occasion, threatening noises at night led to a turn-out of the garrison. It was very dark and as the members of the guard skirmished through the thick underbrush, they heard sounds nearby and promptly fired their rifles. According to Bugler Tennant, the victims of the guards' earnest approach to their duties, were not dead Fenians, but "a few dead hogs, the property of the Hudson's Bay Company."[18] Perhaps the most sensible (and obviously, most experienced) men were those who, instead of worrying about imaginary enemies, spent their time preparing for real ones, fabricating gauze veils for use against the mosquitoes they were already encountering at the Sault and with which they would have to contend in greater hordes after reaching Fort William.

On 23 May *Chicora* once more presented herself at the entrance to the Sault Canal. The way having been cleared by Sir Edward Thornton's intervention, no problem arose and the side-wheeler moved to the

Military camp at Sault Ste Marie, 1870.

dock at the Lake Superior terminus of the five kilometre portage road that had been constructed by Dawson's men at Sault Ste Marie. After the celebrations of the 24th — a *feu de joie* and a royal salute, and 21 shots fired by one of the residents of the Sault from his revolver — a number of the troops embarked in a "downpour of steady sleet." During the next few weeks, vessels moved constantly between Collingwood and the Sault, and between the Sault and Thunder Bay carrying supplies, troops, and civilian workmen .

Meanwhile, Colonel Wolseley and his staff had landed at the Canadian Sault and marched to the Lake Superior shore while the vessels passed through the American canal. Then they re-embarked. Rounding Point aux Pins and steaming past Capes Gros and Iroquois, "the portals of Lake Superior," as Agassiz called them,[19] the Canadian vessels moved into the waters of that great freshwater sea, Lake Superior. They passed Michipicoten Island and Nipigon Bay along the rocky north shore and, after a short stop at Silver Islet, entered the sheltered waters of Thunder Bay, guarded on one side by the huge basalt promontory of Thunder Cape and on the other by McKay's Mountain. It was an impressive sight. Paul Kane, the artist, who saw it in 1846, wrote "Seeing it, as I then did, for the first time, by the glare of the almost incessant flashes of lightning, it presented one of the grandest and most terrific spectacles I had ever witnessed."[20] Wolseley, however, had little to say about it. His eyes, like his mind, were on the shore-line. He wrote "There was but a small clearance in the woods when we landed, where a few wooden shanties had been erected, and all around the prospect was extremely desolate."[21] One of his staff officers, Captain G. L. Huyshe, carefully wrote, no doubt for the eyes of the historian, that Colonel Wolseley landed on the shores of Thunder Bay on a "bright and beautiful day" — it was 1000 hrs on 25 May, — and that he gave the place the name of "Prince Arthur's Landing," in honour of the third son of Queen Victoria who, as a recently gazetted lieutenant in the Royal Engineers, was serving in Canada with the Royal Engineers.[22] Once ashore, Wolseley's staff selected a site for the military camp and put the soldiers to work, unloading waggons, horses and stores of all kinds, and erecting tents. By 2200 hours the landing was complete and the troops turned in for a sound sleep.

III

Of the men who were part of or attached to Wolseley's force, only one was thoroughly familiar with the terrain. He was Simon Dawson.

Thirteen years previously, Dawson had made his way to the North West at the request of the Canadian government, for the purpose of surveying the region between Lake Superior and the Settlement with a view to ascertaining the best route for a roadway between Canada and the territories of the Hudson's Bay Company. He looked first at the Grand Portage route, reporting adversely upon it; in his opinion it was suitable only for light canoes. Instead he argued in favour of the river-lake waterway west of Fort William, by way of Dog Lake and Shebandowan Lake. He proposed that a waggon road should be built to Dog Lake, and that the entire water route westwards be improved by means of dams and short stretches of road built over the most difficult portages. He also recommended that carts or waggons be used at the various portages and that ultimately steamers be placed on the lakes. This report was submitted to the Canadian government in 1857. But nothing emerged from that body in the form of enabling legislation.

Yet there was obviously considerable Canadian interest in the western region. Not only were there several official exploring parties led by such people as George Gladman and Henry Youle Hind, and John Palliser, but there were also those curious travellers such as Paul Kane, Viscount Milton and Dr. Cheadle, and the Earl of Southesk. All of these were pre-Confederation expeditions. Once the union of the four initial provinces became a political fact, the Canadian government decided to expand the federal union by acquiring the western territories of the Hudson's Bay Company and building a new "Dominion" *a mare usque ad mare.* In its expansive mood it was logical for the federal government to take another look at Dawson's suggestions. He was, therefore, commissioned to build an immigrants' road from Thunder Bay to the Red River Settlement.

The first steps were taken to realize the road-building project during the summer of 1869. Despite the fact that it encountered some opposition within the Red River Settlement during the autumn, Dawson was directed by the federal authorities to continue his project. In January 1870, he was authorized to increase the size of his work force at the Thunder Bay end "so as to have the larger bridges completed and other necessary preparations made, before the opening of navigation." Lindsay Russell was therefore sent to Thunder Bay to take charge of the work. He travelled through the United States during the winter months, completing the last 320 kilometres of his journey on snowshoes. Actually, there was little that Russell could do. He reported, however, that he had been able to complete 40 kilometres

American canal at Sault Ste Marie, showing Chicora *passing through the canal.*

Algoma *passing Thunder Cape, 1870, engraving by William Armstrong.*

of the road to Shebandowan Lake, and to do some preparatory work on the portages between Shebandowan Lake and Lac des Mille Lacs. In making his report he indicated a need for more stables, blacksmiths and teamsters. He made no effort to exaggerate the state of the road one way or the other. When Wolseley inspected the road after his arrival, he admitted that it was "as good as I expected to find it, and quite equal to what the country roads in Canada usually are."[23]

Early in May 1870 Molyneux St. John, the correspondent of the Toronto *Globe*, travelled to Thunder Bay to cover the arrival of the troops.[24] Owing to the obvious fact that Wolseley's expedition would depend, in large measure, upon the condition of the Dawson Road, St. John asked for and obtained Lindsay Russell's permission to travel with him on a journey of inspection along the road Colonel Wolseley might be expected to follow. Early in May the two men set out, travelling as far as the Oskondagee, a stream intersecting the line of march some distance from Thunder Bay. St. John noted the changes in the soil, the nature of the gradients and the general character of the countryside. In his report, later published in the *Globe*, [25] he pointed out that the initial climb from the beach up "the Sandhill" would be unpleasant for heavily-laden waggons carrying provisions and stores, whether drawn by horses or oxen. He did not think it would present real problems for marching troops. "A nuisance," he called it, "that may be got rid of," if the road were to become "a permanent institution."[26] He found no serious problem in the region that extended to Strawberry Creek and the range of hills beyond. This section he described as a succession of level stretches of easy gradations of ascent and descent. From Strawberry Creek there was a long ascending hill with a corresponding declivity into the valley of the Kaministikwia. Here was located the first station on the road. It was about 34 kilometres from Thunder Bay. In this section of the road, the character of the country changed several times, from rocks to sand, then a marly section, followed by heavy clay-like soil. In the succeeding stretch of rocks and light soil it had been necessary to cut down a number of trees and to level stumps with occasional blasting, earth excavated from the ditches being used as a covering for the road. In some instances corduroy was used as the foundation, with an earth covering.

As far as the troops were concerned, the road builders estimated that a march from Thunder Bay to the Kaministikwia, between breakfast and supper, would present the soldiers with no difficulty. There were, after all, several streams with fresh, cold, potable water, which would be a great help to the marching men. There was also a good wooden bridge over the Kaministikwia River.

From this point the road continued over a long red marl in a northwesterly direction to the junction of the Shebandowan and Kaministikwia Rivers. There was a bridge over the Kaministikwia (Matawin) and another over Sunshine Creek about one and a half kilometres further along the way. The road was fairly level at this point, passing over soft, marshy soil. A working party was engaged at the time the report was written, constructing a corduroy base over the marshy sections. At Sunshine Creek there was a temporary bridge which was soon to be replaced with something more substantial, higher up the stream. From Sunshine Creek the road was cut through the woods for 18 kilometres to Oskondagee where it terminated. "Of these . . . ," wrote the reporter, some sections are good, "and some are as yet in the first stages."[27] There were several hills to cross, one of which was considered steep and would be "a severe test to teams drawing heavy loads in wet weather." The report continued,

> . . . that portion of the road which is now being built - between Sunshine Creek and the Oskondaga is easier travelled than parts of the broader and more finished way. The ground is covered with moss; it is in fact in a state of nature — the trees only having been removed. The men on this section are principally engaged in corduroying the marshy spots and also levelling stumps, for the object now sought is to provide a good road for the troops; the final construction of a permanent way being delayed for the present. . . . [28]

Both Russell and the reporter were optimistic, the latter even going so far as to write, "it is more probable that the road will be ready for the troops, than that the troops will be waiting to use it."[29] Then, in closing his report, he sounded a note of warning, "it may be well to remember, however, that up to the present time the weather has been exceptionally fine, and that long or heavy rain would make the red marl hills anything but easy to travel. Rain would also tell considerably in the soft, springy places, which are now the most pleasant parts to traverse."[30]

It was not rain, however, that imposed the first delays upon the hard-working crews. It was fire. How the fire started is not known. Usually such disasters are the result of human carelessness. Whether the fire at Thunder Bay was the result of some thoughtless act by one of the squatters along the line of the road, or by one of the workmen, or by some other agency is not clear. Apparently, it began not far from the roadway. Owing to the long spell of dry weather, the fire spread rapidly along both sides of the road, consuming some of the government shanties as well as stocks of squared timber carefully stacked for bridge construction and for culverts. It spread rapidly towards the bay, and special precautions had to be taken to protect the stabling and the various government structures near the edge of the clearing. Huyshe says that those buildings were saved only by the greatest exertions.[31]

Dramatic as a forest fire may appear, with the bright flames and spiralling columns of smoke, and the crash of dying trees that accompany such a disaster, the aftermath is an all-prevading sense of death and futility. That was how Dawson's work-force felt when they saw the extent of the damage the fire had inflicted; the destroyed bridges, the charred culverts, the smouldering cribwork, the still blackened trunks of trees lying across the roadway. And everywhere, the pervasive smell of burnt wood and peaty soil. Desolation and dreariness greeted Wolseley upon his arrival. That probably explains why he wrote with such lack of enthusiasm of the place he named Prince Arthur's Landing. "It had a depressing effect on our spirits," he said, "for go where we might, the scene was one of funereal mourning...."[32] Huyshe also deplored the devastation resulting from the fire but, looking to find the bright side, he remarked in his account of the Red River Expedition that the fire had, at least, destroyed the myriads of mosquitoes and black flies, and, for a few days, spared the soldiers some of the torment these insects would later inflict upon them.[33]

IV

There was, however, as Wolseley himself put it, no time "for either mournful or poetical reflections upon the manner in which such a fair spot had been converted into a dismal wilderness."[34] Troops moved steadily from the Sault to Thunder Bay until almost the end of June.[35] It was a matter of work, work, work, from daylight until dark, and often until late at night, fetching the horses, the waggons, the stores and the supplies ashore and conveying them from the beach to the depots that were set up to receive them. As Huyshe put it, "No drones allowed in the hive."[36]

The vessels were normally anchored about 275 metres offshore, moving out to about 800 metres whenever a breeze developed. In the first few weeks after Wolseley's arrival the weather was "delightful,"

Discharging suppies at Prince Arthur's Landing. Water Lily *is on the right.*

the heat of the day being tempered by a breeze from the lake in the evenings making it possible for the troops to sleep. The ships offshore were serviced by a large wooden scow that rejoiced in the name of *Water Lily.* She drew no more than a metre of water and with the aid of a cable, moved backward and forward between the anchored ships and the shore. Mr. Mellish of the Control Department, her master, was nicknamed "the Admiral." He was in charge of the unloading and became highly indignant when any person interfered with him on board his own "ship". [37] The unloaded cargoes were then moved up the beach by horse and waggon and placed in long rows under cover of hospital marquees.

For some of the soldiers, the journey over Lake Superior was a pleasant outing, particularly on vessels such as *Chicora* and *Algoma*, both of which were luxury vessels in their day and fitted out accordingly. Others were smaller with few conveniences. Neither Harman nor Tennant, writing years later, hints at any of the discomforts that apparently afflicted some of the lower ranks. One private soldier who preferred to remain anonymous, perhaps because his account was published during the actual period of the expedition, describes conditions that were distinctly unpleasant. Sleeping space on the vessels en route to Thunder Bay was "somewhat limited," particularly on board the schooners where the soldiers found their sleeping quarters "carpeted with dirty bilge water." On occasions the men slept

> ... on grain sacks, our heads pillowed on a comrade's legs and our own legs couched upon the body of another — on hay, where the horses were located, the warm breath of whose nostrils or the stamping of whose heavy hoofs were our reveille in the morning — in all crooks and corners of the lower deck in which it was possible to stow ourselves.[38]

There were other hazards, particularly for the men of the 60th on board *Frances Smith*. The captain of the vessel was drunk most of the journey, lost his way in a fog and nearly ran his vessel aground.[39]

When the infantry companies arrived, they immediately set up their own camps, establishing a small military hospital and erecting a redoubt as a defence work against a possible Fenian attack from Duluth. It was manned by a company of the 2nd (Quebec) Rifles under Captain L. C. A. L. de Bellefeuille. The Ontario Rifles pitched their bell tents along the lake shore, about 400 metres from the landing; the Quebec Rifles were located just beyond them, a small stream separating the two encampments. The 60th Rifles were located on the flank. Each unit was responsible for its own messing, and if we may believe

Prince Arthur's Landing, a contemporary sketch, 1870.

Lieutenant H. S. H. Riddell of the 60th, the British officers, regarding the whole expedition as something of an outing, disdained the services of a "professional cook." As far as the troops were concerned, a few good cooks could always be found among them; but the officers were expected to "rough it." That is why poor Lieutenant Riddell found himself appointed cook for the force commander. He wrote:

> I never saw a piece of pork cooked in my life, but determined to do the best I could. I seized some sticks, lighted them, threw a huge chunk of pork into a pot of water, put it on the sticks, and sat down to watch the effect. The fire was soon exhausted, and so was my patience; and, like a bad workman blaming his tools, I was just beginning to abuse the pork for not boiling, and the fire for not burning, when the arrival of the colonel put an end to my difficulties. He showed me, in the scientific manner of an old campaigner, how to dig a trench in the ground, and with stones and sticks to construct a fender over it, on which to place my cooking utensils; and the result was, that when dinner-time approached, a hard, tough mass of over-boiled meat was fished out of the pot, with the assistance of a forked stick, and served up, with tea and biscuits, as the mid-day repast of the officers.[40]

The redoubt at Prince Arthur's Landing, 1870, manned by soldiers from the 2nd (Quebec) Rifles.

Men and horses! The efficiency and response of both would depend in large measure upon their housing and feeding arrangements. And these, according to Huyshe, were "most satisfactory."[41]

In a reasonably short time the mixture of canvas tents and wooden sheds was transformed into what the *Globe* described as "an orderly and systematized station," the effect of which was "rather pleasing than otherwise."[42] The decorative abilities of the troops quickly became apparent and the lines were adorned with green curtains and rustic tables "which serve to give privacy to toilette and messing arrangements."[43] Streets were marked by signposts. Wolseley was pleased with the initiative displayed by the soldiers. If nothing else, it was an indication of good morale. Live cattle had been brought from Collingwood to be slaughtered as required, in order that the soldiers might be spared a salt pork diet as long as possible, with the result that fresh meat and potatoes were issued daily, accompanied by fresh bread. With Lake Superior only a few steps away, the normal daily ration could be supplemented with fresh fish caught by trolling. According to Huyshe "with hard, open air work and famous appetites, sickness was unknown."[44] The 60th Rifles opened a canteen which sold "good wholesome beer and little luxuries of diet ... but no spirits."[45] The need for relaxation was understood and there were field days and aquatic sports to keep the troops interested. One of the militia officers wrote:

> A most commendable measure adopted by Colonel Wolseley was that of practising the men in rowing. This was adopted on two grounds. First to accustom the men in handling the oar, which was to be their daily mode of propulsion, and second, to afford them some recreation. The men entered into it with the greatest spirit, and the result was several races took place which proved most interesting, and showed what stuff they were made of.[46]

The horses were less well cared for. Normal cavalry rations proved to be inadequate for the heavy draft animals and the hard work they were expected to do. Their ill-fitting harness became a constant source of collar sores. The commander seems actually to have derived a certain satisfaction from the fact that the harness, like the militiamen's boots, had been acquired through a Canadian government contract, rather than from the British Army stores, and that

Colonel Wolseley's tent at Thunder Bay, watercolour by William Armstrong, 1870.

both harness and boots proved to be unsuitable for the kind of usage they were obliged to endure.[47] The mosquitoes and flies, too, were problems that had not, apparently, been contemplated in Ottawa when plans were being made for the expedition. The veils were inadequate. Smudges were the only way to control the pests.

Wolseley's first task, after seeing his men and horses properly housed and fed, and defence works erected, was to assess the extent of the damage inflicted by the forest fire. He was impatient to move along, pressured as he was by the demand of the War Office to be sure to bring his regular troops back to central Canada in time to embark for Great Britain before winter set in. In company with Irvine, he made a preliminary tour of the Dawson Road, following the same route that Molyneux St. John had taken a fortnight earlier. It was obvious that there would have to be considerable rebuilding, particularly of the wooden bridges and culverts. When the troops asked Wolseley when they could expect to move on towards their final objective, his stock answer was "as soon as sufficient boats and sixty days' provisions are up at the place of embarkation."[48]

Wolseley's instructions were, therefore, that steps be taken immediately to repair the damage caused by the fire. To expedite the work, existing civilian work crews were to be supplemented by military work parties drawn for the most part, from the regular infantry battalion; and an advanced depot was established at a point where the road crossed the Matawin River about 50 kilometres along the road to Shebandowan Lake. Here at Matawin, it would be possible to house some 50 horses and waggons. The troops went to work willingly and with the characteristic adaptability of the private soldier. It was not long before the troops, Canadians included, while wielding their shovels, were bellowing the several verses of:

> 'Twas only as a volunteer that I left my abode;
> I never thought of coming here to work upon
> the road.[49]

When General Lindsay came to Prince Arthur's Landing towards the end of June, the soldiers were already coming to appreciate the full significance of his remark that the spade was just as important a weapon for the infantryman as his rifle. It was unfortunate, however, that the rains came before the road was finished. There were deluges in June and July that reduced the road to quagmire. Bridges, culverts, even parts of the road surface were washed away before it was possible to get the boats as far as Matawin Bridge, much less Shebandowan Lake. Days and hours had, therefore, to be spent effecting further repairs, just when time was of the essence. What else could be done but to keep up the road work and perhaps to sing?

> But never mind, we'll struggle on, not
>   heeding wind or weather,
> For we're sure to get along, if only we
>   pull together.
> If the girls of Manitoba are as kind as
>   they are charming
> The half of us will stop behind and
>   settle down to farming.[50]

If the Canadians were learning anything, it was the truth that adaptability is the mark of a good soldier, along with discipline and effort. At Prince Arthur's Landing, everyone had to labour, men and officers alike; and when work parties marched off each day, the officer in charge was to be seen carrying his own pick or spade, just the same as every private soldier who followed him. Usually the road work began not long after daybreak. Each man brought his own rations with him, ready for the task of the day, whatever it might be, preparing the corduroy by laying logs on the road-bed, or clearing ditches, and, between spades-full of earth or mud, swatting mosquitoes. At night, sleep was often hard to come by; whining insects, thick smoke smudges, scratching bodies and muttered oaths were not exactly designed to produce or encourage rest or relaxation.

Occasionally some of the soldiers over-indulged in alcohol. Military regulations have never deterred the bootleggers. When D. D. Van Norman, the Stipendiary Magistrate at Prince Arthur's Landing, complained to Wolseley that two canteens were in full operation, one for the 60th Rifles and the other for the Canadian Volunteers, Wolseley simply replied, "The issue of a pint of beer per man daily, within the precincts of the Military Camp, is a purely military affair, and I trust you will not consider it necessary to interfere with the arrangement." He admitted, however, that "Canteen men, in general, are a bad lot, and frequently endeavour to take advantage of their position, by selling liquor without the commanding officer's knowledge."[51]

"Singing and Preying",
a cartoonist's impression of the mosquitoes and flies during the Red River Expedition, 1870.

"Writing Home", contemporary cartoon, 1870.

The day to day experiences of the soldiers may have been uncomfortable in many ways, yet this was the kind of soldiering that many of the Canadians expected, even wanted. An anonymous volunteer who sent his contributions to the *Canadian Illustrated News*, remarked that at Prince Arthur's Landing, he and his companions learned "for the first time" to sleep in tents, rise early, struggle with a pick and a spade and still carry out military drill "which some of us, armed civilians, still had only thought of as the legitimate duty of a soldier."[52]

They had never thought in terms of hard, physical labour. The fortunate ones among them were those "to whom Nature and good living had not been too lavish in the bestowal of obesity," for men who were overweight suffered most from the heat. The writer was, obviously, one of the latter; if only because he retained a good sense of humour, asking the reader, "Have you ever seen a horse shake himself when just loosened from a heavy cart?" If the answer was in the affirmative, then perhaps they would have "a faint notion of the ecstasy of the moment when, on reaching the end of the day's march, the knapsack was taken from our backs." He continued,

> . . . taken altogether, it was not so unpleasant an excursion after all, — for the men had courage and endurance and goodwill, and strength, and brotherly feeling to one another; and the strongest helped the weak, — and when the day's work was over and all partook of that rest they had earned so well, and which was so welcome after the long hours of toil, many slept more peacefully and better upon the hard rock or the white sand, which fringed the edge of some beautiful lake, or failing these, upon the softer mud of some arduous "portage," than they were wont to do in the downy luxury of their distant homes.[53]

Making a corduroy road, a contemporary drawing.

Fort William from across the Kaministikwia River, 1873.

V

In the weeks immediately following the fire, Wolseley's principal preoccupations were those of morale, how to counteract "the heat-beat", as it was sometimes called, and how to counter the insects. At least, those were the more obvious problems as far as the troops were concerned. Even more demanding of the Commander's attention, was how to get his supplies to the point of embarkation on Sheban-dowan Lake. The road to Matawin Bridge, about half way to Sheban-dowan Lake, was in reasonably good condition, although it would not take much rain to reduce it to a morass and make movement, not impossible, but difficult and time consuming, especially for waggons bearing heavy loads.

Working, as he was, to a rigid time-table, scarcely had Wolseley completed his inspection of Dawson's road than he began wondering about establishing a depot at the point where the road intersected the Kaministikwia River on its way from Dog Lake to Fort William. That is why he undertook the construction of a redoubt at this point, some 23 metres long and a metre wide, together with a magazine and storehouse which, with two cannon, would be strong enough to "laugh at any Fenian attempts" to take possession of it. At the same time, however, he gave thought to the possibility of sending boats up the Kaministikwia to the point where it intersected the Dawson Road. Perhaps by using this water route he might accelerate the movement of supplies or, at least, speed the movement of his heavy water craft to Shebandowan Lake. After all, his horse-drawn waggons could only carry a single boat at a time and Wolseley had 150 boats to move.

The Kaministikwia had never been a popular route in the early days of the fur trade, owing to its shallowness in summer and its many rocks and boulders, to say nothing of the enormous barrier presented by the Kakabeka Falls. Graffenried had used it in the winter of 1816-1817 and voyageurs of the North West Company used it in summer. The Swiss had travelled over the ice and the Nor'Westers over water. But the latter had used only canoes, and with good reason. Wolseley sought the opinion of the Hudson's Bay Company factor, John McIntyre, who admitted that the British officer's scheme of using the water route might be feasible, but would be difficult with the weather changing for the worse. Dawson, however, came out strongly against Wolseley's proposal. He had discarded any idea of using the Kaministikwia as early as 1857, arguing that its shallowness and roughness in summer made it unsuitable for water transport. He had tried it and found it unsatisfactory. In his report he had written:

> It will at once occur that the rough and rocky Kaministiquia would be best avoided by making a road direct from Thunder Bay to Dog Lake, which would then be within half-a-day's drive of Lake Superior, instead of its taking nearly five days to reach it, as it did us by the Kaministiquia, although we were tolerably well manned and lightly loaded.[54]

In the years following 1857, Dawson never departed from this view that the Kaministikwia was not a river suitable for boat traffic.

Wolseley was, however, a stubborn man. As he saw the problem, every boat that he could get up the river to its junction with the road, would mean one less waggon trip between Matawin Bridge and the beach-head, and one more waggon ready to move supplies along to Shebandowan Lake. It was this kind of reasoning that led him to give instructions to Captain John Young of the 60th Rifles to undertake the experiment of moving boats up the Kaministikwia.[55]

On 4 June, at 0630 hours, a small force led by Captain Young and Lieutenant Edward Fraser of the 60th undertook to move four flat bottomed boats and two heavy Quebec-built boats up the river. They had, to assist them, a force of some thirty soldiers and a dozen voyageurs, the task of the latter being to guide and steer the boats once over the great barrier presented by the Kakabeka Falls. The distance to be travelled was about 72 kilometres, 19 of which were relatively quiet, and the remaining 53 filled with rocks and rapids.

The portage at Kakabeka Falls, 1870, from a contemporary painting.

The most difficult obstacle facing Young's party was the Kakabeka Falls. First seen by Jacques de Noyon in 1688, and sketched by Paul Kane in 1846, the falls were both magnificent and intimidating, symbolic of great strength and power. Paul Kane considered them superior even to "those of Niagara in picturesque beauty; for, although far inferior in volume of water, their height is nearly equal and the scenery surrounding them infinitely more wild and romantic."[56] Impressive as their wild beauty may have been to the artist, to Captain Young they presented the problem of dragging heavy boats up a portage nearly one and a half kilometres in length, with a slope at times approaching 45 degrees: and of men carrying loads on their backs up these same slopes with black flies feasting on their blood during the day time and mosquitoes doing the same thing at night.

The method of manhandling the heavy boats over portages was to use skids or rollers, short logs laid across the path at close intervals. A long towline was attached to the stem of each boat and passed through a ring bolt on the keelson and then run back again to the stem and secured there. One of the Canadian militiamen, Sam Steele, explained the procedure in these words:

> Then a man would take the end of the towline over his shoulder to lead in the right direction; two of the most powerful of the crew, generally voyageurs, placed

themselves at the bow with their backs against the side
of the boat, and braced themselves, while two or more
of the strongest men were at the stern. The rest strung
themselves along the towline or supported the sides of
the boat by holding the gunwales. Those on the towline placed themselves in pairs or half sections, divid-
ing the distance to the end of the line, fastening their
tumplines (portage straps) to the rope, passing the flat
part over the outward shoulder, and hauled on the
rope, bearing outwards a little. As the boat went along
the men at the bows lifted the stem over obstacles, such
as stumps, stones or high skids, and in this manner
they crossed the portage.[57]

This was muscle-tearing work. But even more physically exhausting
was the constant labour of carrying stores and tracking against the
current. Even in navigable sections of the river, the current was too
fast to permit rowing or poling. Hence the necessity of tracking. In this
procedure the voyageurs in the bow and stern remained aboard, each
with a pole to steer clear of the boulders on the shore. Again Steele
explains:

The remainder of the men took hold of the line, one of
them leading it the best way over land or along the
shore, while the rest passed the line over their shoulders. Often when the water was too deep near the
shore they ascended the bank, the leader passing the
rope in front of the trees while the others hauled on the
line as was most convenient, running along and passing one another when necessary. As a rule wading was
preferred to taking to the high banks. Frequently,
owing to the swiftness and depth of the water, one
would miss his footing and would have to hang on to
the towline whilst the other men steadied themselves
until he had regained his feet.[58]

It was, therefore, by sheer physical strength and unceasing toil
over seven days, combined with a positive knowledge of what to do,
that Captain Young, his voyageurs and soldiers slowly made their
struggling way up the Kaministikwia River as far as Matawin Bridge.
They were probably grateful when the Indians declared that it would

Tracking and poling up the Kaministikwia River, from a contemporary drawing.

be impossible to drag the boats beyond this point. To have done as much was an achievement. Because Wolseley was little disposed to accept any advice that went counter to his own opinions, Captain Young and those with him had their brief role to play in the history of the Red River Expedition. As stubborn as Wolseley, Dawson considered that the latter's insistence upon using the Kaministikwia was not only a misuse of men's muscles and skills, it was also a waste of the expedition's times and resources. According to his report, the boats "strong as they were, were found to have been sadly torn and scraped in the rapids, and had to be immediately placed in the hands of the builders for repairs."[59] That is why Dawson strongly urged, "the expediency of sending to Collingwood for more waggons." When he found his horses suffering from lack of adequate rations, he agreed to work with his military colleagues, and to send voyageurs to improve the portages and to organize some system "by which the boats might be, in as far as possible saved from damage."[60] That involved a close degree of co-operation between the civilian and military work crews. It was clear, both to the civilian and military officers in charge of the expedition that the voyageurs, men "rough, ready and inured to hardships, but holding all fixed rules and restraint in abhorrence," could never function effectively if brought under a system that demanded implicit obedience to a superior officer. The voyageurs themselves, generous and obliging though they might be, were in the habit of thinking and acting for themselves. Dawson, therefore, retained full responsibility for the voyageurs, organizing them and discharging such as proved inefficient. By the time the brigades of boats were ready to leave Shebandowan Lake in July, Dawson was able to man the various boats with carefully picked crews of "the most skilful voyageurs to be found in the country."[61]

Reluctant as he was to do so, Dawson submitted to Wolseley's determination to continue to use the Kaministikwia route. He therefore sent a number of his work crews to the Kaministikwia to prepare skids and lay them over the portage. Special teams of voyageurs were also selected to assist each boat and military detachment making use of the route. According to Dawson's statistics in his official report, between 6 June and 6 July no fewer than 101 boats were sent over the Kaministikwia to Matawin Bridge, served by 556 voyageurs and 471 soldiers.[62]

On 5 July Wolseley moved his headquarters to Matawin Bridge. Every effort was still being made to complete the road, but with work crews reduced in numbers. Even so, there were signs of progress. Captain Huyshe records that on 15 June waggons, drawn by bullocks, passed over it towards Shebandowan Lake; but it was disappointing that teams of horses still could not negotiate the road except with great difficulty.[63] Beyond Oskondagee to the Dam-Site "large gangs of men were at work . . . assisted by two companies of the 60th."[64] However, the region was still plagued with intermittent fires, alternating with rainstorms, both of which played havoc with new construction, the one destroying the crib work and the culverts, and the other creating fresh quagmires. In the hope of speeding the movement of the boats to Shebandowan Lake, Wolseley took another look at the river route. Once again, Captain Young was given the task, this time with one boat, of navigating the Matawin to Oskondagee Creek. The problem, or, as Wolseley put it, "the great nut to crack,"[65] was how to get the stores, supplies and equipment from Matawin Bridge to Shebandowan Lake.

The distance between Matawin Bridge and Oskondagee Creek was about 19 kilometres. For the first part of the route, to a point bearing the name of Young's Landing, the river was navigable. But beyond that the river became a succession of rapids, "the most difficult on the route,"[66] emerging from "a deep canyon with perpendicular walls, through which the current dashed at a great speed."[67]

It was here, at the canyon, that Young gave up. He had set out, deliberately, with an all-soldier crew, believing that a good soldier was as capable as a good voyageur. Now he realized that each was a specialist and that, with soldiers alone, further progress was impossible. At this point, Dawson stepped in with an offer of assistance. In his official report he wrote:

> Some interest had been excited by this experiment, which it was said was designed to show how much could be effected in the rapids independently of the voyageurs. Before the discouraging effects of this failure could spread far I had sent forward a band of voyageurs who took up the boats and, from that time forward, the boats, in this difficult section, were manned wholly by voyageurs. To get them all past the section just referred to, occupied a force of 120 men for upwards of a month and it had become necessary to spread so many people along the River, in this toilsome work of dragging boats up rocky channels that, much to my regret, I was compelled to reduce the force on the road.[68]

Camp of the 60th Rifles on the Upper Kaministikwia, from a sketch by Capt. C.M. Calderon.

Equally disturbing was the fact that the severe physical tasks being given to the Indians convinced a number of them to withdraw from the expedition. Fond as they were of voyaging, the labour they were expected to perform on this section of the waterway was so demanding of time and effort, and so distasteful, that they could not be persuaded to continue, in spite of being coaxed by the agent of the Hudson's Bay Company and the local missionary at Fort William. "Why," the Indians asked, "do you keep us dragging boats over rocks where there is no water to float them ...?"[69] They were aware of the fact that additional waggons could have been obtained from Ontario, and, as Dawson remarked, "their patience and endurance, under toil which they believed to be unnecessary and arising from a mistake, cannot be too highly commended."[70] When Dawson was moved to send his voyageurs to do the job that the soldiers could not do, he did so, not so much to save Wolseley's face, as to prove that his Indians were better men than the conceited English commander was disposed to admit.

What Dawson did was to seek out one of the local people to obtain advice and assistance. According to Sam Steele, Dawson asked Donald McKellar of Fort William "to go up to the Matawin station and get the boats up the Matawin and Shebandowan rivers to the Oskondagee," taking with him a crew of local Indians from the mission at Fort William. He gave him a letter to the foremen along the line authorizing them to give McKellar such men, boats and supplies as he might require, adding "see that you get the best, so that you will be sure to open up this route." McKellar selected ten Iroquois from Kahnawake, ten Sault Ste Marie Indians and ten Ojibways from Fort William. When they arrived at Matawin, they chose three boats. While these vessels were being prepared for the journey, Captain Young approached McKellar and said, "You can save yourself all this trouble, for there are not men enough in the expedition to take the boats up this river."[71] Remarks such as these from the soldier, Young, constituted a challenge to McKellar, the civilian, and a local man to boot. Early next morning, McKellar, with the Fort William Indians, followed by two other boats manned by Indians, set out on their journey. By nine o'clock the same evening they arrived at their destination, Ward's Landing on the Oskondagee. Here they were greeted by a much surprised and delighted Captain Ellis H. Ward of the 60th. The news of McKellar's success spread up and down the line from Prince Arthur's Landing to Matawin Bridge. Almost everybody was pleased. Almost, but not all. For some reason — could it have been jealousy or annoyance? — Wolseley made no mention of the voyageurs' accomplishment in the account of the expedition he published a year later in *Blackwood's Edinburgh Magazine.* However, to the rank and file and officers alike, the achievement seemed to indicate that, after all, they might be able to embark on the final stage of their journey to Red River, according to the commander's schedule.[72]

Simon Dawson proved his point with respect to the reliability and skill of his Indian voyageurs by this action; but he still felt compelled to report that the continued use of the water route resulted in unnecessary wear and tear on the boats; and that his carpenters had to be diverted from their other duties to make new oars and effect repairs on the damaged hulls, while his blacksmiths had to waste their time producing new oarlocks "as fast as they could." The fact was, according to Dawson, that waggons, in short supply at the outset, were now arriving in greater numbers and stores were accumulating both at Matawin and Oskondagee. From Oskondagee to Shebandowan Lake, the road, he admitted, was in "a bad state," but "never so utterly bad but that a yoke of oxen, with a waggon, could not take from eight to twelve hundred pounds [363 kg to 544 kg] weight over it, and horses with waggons, as well as oxen, passed frequently to that point."[73] That progress was being made on the road seems evident enough. The weather in July was considerably improved, and bad as the roads

The Dawson Road, 1870 from a sketch by Capt. C.M. Calderon.

might be, waggons and artillery were able to make their way over them; stores were also beginning to accumulate at Ward's Landing, about five kilometres from Shebandowan Lake. Work parties were already in the process of constructing a small wharf at McNeil's Bay close to the river exit from the lake, and here the repairs were made to the boats that had been employed on the water route.[74]

Early in July, members of the Red River Expeditionary Force were scattered all along the line from Prince Arthur's Landing to Sheban-dowan Lake. Some were working on the road; some were employed taking boats up to Matawin Bridge; some were freighting stores from Matawin to Young's Landing; others were doing the same from Calderon's Landing to Ward's Landing; and some were employed at Shebandowan Lake. It was not an easy task to keep all of these separate groups supplied with rations, but the cooks worked hard, and fresh bread was available throughout the weeks the troops were at Prince Arthur's Landing and along the road to the point of embar-kation.

That the great moment was in the offing was apparent to all when on 14 July, Wolseley moved his headquarters form Matawin Bridge to Ward's Landing.[75] He had selected 16 July at the date for the departure of the first boat bound for Fort Garry; and although for some time it appeared as if he might have to abandon his proposed schedule— man and nature seemed to conspire to thwart his intention— the or-ganization he had set up functioned reasonably effectively. Each day as the boats arrived at Shebandowan Lake, they were examined, repaired, fitted with rowlocks, rudders, masts and sails. The night of 15 July it seemed as if nature might have the last word when a terrific thunderstorm developed. It was St. Swithin's Day! Would the rains continue for forty days according to the superstition? "Sheets of water tumbling upon us in rapid succession" was how Wolseley described it. Private John Kerr of the Ontario Rifles considered it "the star storm of the season."[76] But it ended abruptly and on the morning of the 16th the troops were greeted with a bright sun, a clear sky and a good drying wind.[77] The wind brought surf to the sandy beach at McNeil's Bay; but it lessened as the sun rose. Officers and men rushed to complete their final tasks before the command to embark was given.

That Wolseley was able to keep to his time-table was, in large measure, the achievement of both the Control Department and the civilian engineering department under Simon Dawson. Wolseley was never prepared to admit that fact. However, Captain Huyshe, a relatively junior officer with no need to prove the quality of his leadership or to claim credit for all that was successful, felt free to pay tribute to the civilian element in Wolseley's force and in particular to Dawson who, he wrote, "worked untiringly and did all that one man could do to carry out Colonel Wolseley's wishes."[78] He also singled out one of Dawson's assistants, a Mr. Graham, who was responsible for ensuring that the boats, as they arrived at McNeil's Bay, were thoroughly overhauled and fitted out for the next stage of the long journey to Red River. Their destination was Fort Garry, 785 kilometres distant.[79]

Officers of No. 6 Coy., 1st (Ontario) Rifles-Capt. A. McDonald, Lieut. William McMurtry, and Ensign Hugh Macdonald.

On the evening of 15 July, a young militia officer at Oskondagee Creek, Hugh John Macdonald, was writing to his friend, James Coyne:

> I really believe that the devil got up this expedition for the purpose of getting hold of my immortal soul, as I am beginning to swear a little. The example set me by my Captain is not good, as I am sorry to say he does not bear the bites of mosquitoes, doubtless made by the Lord, with the patience of a Christian, and whenever evening approaches my ears are shocked by oaths. Since our arrival here we have been busy road making, not a very intellectual work, but I hope it won't last long as the first detachment of the 60th Rifles leaves tomorrow morning and we are to be the first Battalion to leave.[80]

CHAPTER SEVEN

Shebandowan to Rat Portage July-August 1870

I

16 July 1870! The day the first troops of Colonel Garnet Wolseley's Red River Expeditionary Force set out from Shebandowan Lake. The troops were elated, but then discouraged, as the day began with a rainstorm. When the clouds passed, everybody burst into action. All was bustle and excitement. The boats were checked and last minute repairs effected. Then the men moved to the embarkation wharf at McNeil's Bay where the final fittings were put into place — tillers, rowlocks, oars and sails — and where sixty days' provisions and camp equipment, munitions and personal belongings were loaded. There was the inevitable confusion, with staff officers and orderlies running about in all directions endeavouring to rectify mistakes and smooth out difficulties;[1] while regimental officers and non-commissioned officers were doing much the same thing, checking the men and the stores in their charge. Everywhere there was confusion.

That everything went as smoothly as it did may be attributed, in large measure, to S. J. Dawson, who had sent a force of voyageurs ahead to lay skids on the first portage to facilitate the passage of the boats. Moreover, Dawson had himself proceeded to the Height of Land to oversee the necessary arrangements to get the boats up a small stream connecting Kashaboiwe Lake with the summit pond. As he was returning, he encountered a messenger bearing a peevish note from Wolseley. It had been written the previous day. It read:

> Dear Mr. Dawson, — I have been obliged to start off Capt. Buller's brigade without either voyageurs or guides, the former were ready, with the exception of their cooking utensils, which had not turned up. . . . I have ordered Capt. Buller to halt on the first portage,

The starting point on Shebandowan Lake, 1870.

until I can send him both voyageurs and guides. Please send me word what I am to do. The carts are here also, waiting for your men to take them to the portages.

Dawson, of course, obliged. But he noted in his report:

I had been barely two days absent, and here matters were already in a mess. . . . At this time the voyageurs were by hundreds within easy reach of Shebandowan Lake, engaged in dragging boats to the Oskondagee or in scows conveying stores from Ward's to McNeil's Landing, and had only to be given warning to get ready at a moment's notice.[2]

Whether Wolseley would admit it or not, Dawson's role and that of the civilian voyageurs under his control were crucial to the success of the Red River Expedition.

Wolseley watched the whole proceedings, wondering if everybody and everything would or could be sorted out, and shouting that the expedition would start, even if the men had to go on working until midnight![3] By 2100 hours, three hours short of midnight, the first boats were ready, 17 in all, carrying two companies of the 60th Rifles, under Captains Young and Ward, and detachments of the Royal Artillery and Royal Engineers under Lieutenants James Alleyne and Frederick William Heneage.[4] According to Captain Huyshe, it was an evening of "surpassing loveliness."[5] The wind, that had been blowing hard most of the day, died down. So moved was Huyshe that, departing from his customary, straightforward prose, he indulged in a little hyperbole when he described the scene in his book:

> The lake lay calm and smooth as a mirror, reflecting in its placid bosom the varied tints of a mellow sunset, which tinged the fleecy clouds with wondrous hues. The measured dip of the oars, and the last faint hurrahs of the boats' crews, alone broke the calm glory of the summer evening, as we stood on the little wharf and strained our eyes to catch the last glimpse of the fast disappearing boats. . . . [6]

Wolseley, when he wrote his account, some six months later, used somewhat different metaphors:

> Except at this little spot, where we were all bustle and excitement, the scene had the stillness of death about it, which in the distance seemed all the more deathlike from the contrast between it and the noise immediately around us. This absence of animal or even insect life in the North American woods is one of their most striking characteristics.[7]

Obviously, mosquitoes were not about at the moment. Either that or Wolseley had forgotten their usually noisy attentions. Then he saw himself in history:

> The sail and the oar were to be our means of propulsion, as they had been those of the Greeks and Romans in classic times; and when arrived at the end of our 600 miles' [965 km] journey, we should have as much

difficulty and as far to send in order to communicate with even the nearest telegraph office, as Caesar had when he sent a messenger to Rome, announcing his successful descent upon our shores more than 1900 years ago.[8]

This was all very fanciful. But very nineteenth century. My own imagination suggests to me that Wolseley, instead of thinking about Julius Caesar, would have been saying to himself, "Thank God! They're off at last." A thought like that would have been much more in keeping with the occasion.

II

For the move to Fort Garry the Expeditionary Force was divided into several "brigades,"[9] each of which consisted of approximately 50 men. There were 21 brigades in all. Each boat carried ten or twelve soldiers, with two or three voyageurs, including a bowman and a steersman, upon whose skill the success of the expedition largely depended. "Fortunate was the officer," remarked Lieutenant Riddell of the 60th, "who secured for his boat the skilful Iroquois, the finest boatman in Canada."[10] Certainly, not all the voyageurs were of equal skill; but there were comparatively few who were not familiar with their responsibilities; although almost invariably the British officers who took part in the Expedition gave first place to the Indians from Kahnawake.

In addition to the soldiers and their own personal baggage, each boat carried 60 days' provisions of salt pork, beans and dried potatoes, flour, biscuit, pepper, salt, tea and sugar; and, in addition to these foodstuffs, an arms chest containing rifles, cooking utensils and grey army blankets and waterproof sheets. Lieutenant Riddell specifically refers to bottles of mosquito oil that were included in the supplies in each boat, adding however, that the oil was "not of the slightest use." He continued, "it smelt so horribly, that the men would seldom use it on their hands and faces, and much preferred being bitten by the insects it was supposed to protect them from." Riddell did admit, however, that "when the supply of coal-oil failed," the mosquito oil "came in handy."[11] The same young officer estimated the total weight carried in each boat, not including the camp equipment, at about 1500 kilos.[12] With each brigade, in one or other of the boats, went a carpenter's tool-box and other requisites for effecting repairs en route.

Of the boats, 31 were carvel-built; 16 were equipped with sprits, and the rest carried lug sails. The remaining boats, 119 in number, were clinker-built. Not all were equal in size; but the average length was 9.7 metres and the beam, 1.8 metres. In addition to these lumbering craft, the army staff had a light gig for their use and three *canots de maître* manned by Indians.[13] The gig was normally used by Wolseley's staff; he himself frequently used a canoe. Lieutenant-Colonel J. C. McNeill, V.C., the Governor General's secretary, stayed on at Shebandowan Lake to superintend the departure of the remaining brigades; this completed he and Mr. G. A. Jolly of the Control Department followed in a light bark canoe.

17 July was a Sunday, and Wolseley had "great difficulty" in pursuading his Iroquois to work. They said that they were "not engaged to work on Sundays, which was their only day for washing." Their desire for cleanliness was, however, amply compensated for by the promise of "an extra day's pay for the extra day's work."[14] The Indians had the upper hand and Wolseley knew it. He wrote in his *Journal of Operations*, "situated as the force now is, it is completely at the mercy of these Indians, nothing can be taken up the rapids" to the point of embarkation on Shebandowan Lake, "without their assistance, and when they have made three trips they consider that they have done a day's work, no matter what the time of day may be." He added, "They are however capital men, and very civil."[15] Their leader, Ignace Montour, had long known how to deal with white men. He had served for fifteen years under Sir George Simpson, "the little Emperor," and Dr. John Rae, the Arctic explorer.

When all the brigades of regulars had embarked in their water craft, the various militia companies began to assemble and to take their places in their boats. Wolseley waited around long enough to see the first two brigades of militia embark and then headed off in a fast canoe[16] to overtake the orderlies who had left earlier in the colonel's gig. By travelling light and with an Indian crew, he felt certain that he would overtake the brigades that had already embarked.

Meanwhile the militia soldiers continued to assemble at Shebandowan Lake and to embark in their boats. At each loading, apparently, there was the same confusion, the same meaningless haste that Wolseley had complained about as far as the regulars were concerned. The volunteers were no better. At the last moment, men shouting "where's my knapsack" or complaining loudly,"I have not got my blankets." "Such a scene!" remarked Captain S. B. Harman of the 1st (Ontario) Rifles, "But at last everything was ready, and away we went,

others taking our places and going through the same kind of thing."[17]
Each day the various brigades went through the process of loading
their boats and rowing towards the western extremity of Shebandowan Lake. The first of the British boats had left on 16 July; the last
of the Canadian boats departed from McNeil's Bay on 2 August. By
that time the whole expedition extended for a distance of approximately 240 kilometres from the bow of the first boat to the stern of the
last. Except in case of an accident, the troop-carrying boats were
expected to keep their own place in the line. After all, it was a military
expedition and not a boat race. Yet each boat seemed to develop its
own identity and its crew, a special *esprit de corps*. There was a
competitive feeling among the militia brigades.

Some of the boat crews, the Canadians in particular, were disposed to give names to their boats. No. 7 Company of the Ontario
Rifles christened their six boats, *The Leaky Sallie* (13 men), *Shoo Fly* (11
men), *Dreadnought* (11 men), *Fanny Latimer* (11 men), *Fairy Belle* (10
men) and *D.A.K.* (after one of the officers, Lieutenant D. A. K.
Macdonald). Sam Steele relates that the boat in which he travelled,
rejoiced in the name of *The Flying Dutchman*. She was, Steele writes,
"the worst boat in the lot, two feet shorter than any, and at least a foot
wider in the beam." Her name, when suggested, was received with
scorn "as it required nearly twice as much effort to move her through
the water as any other boat in our brigade." There was one boat worse,
Major James Macleod's *La Belle Manitoba*, "an immense boat . . . which
gave . . . much trouble on all the portages, and in rapids was very
clumsy and difficult to steer."[18] It is an odd feature of human beings
that they develop a tender feeling for, or dislike of, inanimate objects
and attribute to them pleasant or unpleasant human qualities. The
bestowing of such names seems to provide a focus for affection or, at
times, abuse. In any event, it was not long before *La Belle Manitoba*
became *La Belle Bummer*.[19]

Anxious not to press his men too hard, owing to the late hour of
the start of the first brigade, Lieutenant-Colonel R. F. Fielden of the
60th, who was in charge of the first wave departing from McNeil's
Harbour, decided upon a short cruise only. His boats, therefore,
pulled into a sandy beach along the lakeshore and were safely moored
for the night. The troops, wearied by the preparation for the departure, and elated at having got away according to schedule, chose to
sleep in the open. In this way they would be ready to depart bright and
early the next morning, set the pace for the boats that would follow,[20]
and keep well ahead of them. They did not, however, have much rest.

"One of the most violent thunder-storms I ever witnessed," wrote Lieutenant Riddell, who was with them, "passed over us that night: the rain for hours poured down incessantly, and the flashes of lightning were frequent, and of extreme brilliancy."[21] The soldiers huddled together under the tarpaulins and rubber sheets. But there was nothing to do but sit it out, and to move the boats, in early morning, to a safer anchorage, lest the wind blow them ashore. The wind did not abate until the evening; as a result they were a day late when they arrived at the Kashaboiwe Portage. Here they learned, for the first time, the practical lessons of how to negotiate a portage.

III

The drill at all the portages was similar. The stores and equipment would be carried over the portage first, and piled by the water's edge ready for reshipment. Then the crews would drag the boats ashore, and fasten the tow lines to the bows. The men, harnessed with portage straps and slings to the tow lines, would then drag the boats over the physical obstacle to be surmounted, the keels of the boats resting upon rollers or skids that had been previously cut and prepared by Dawson's workmen. Other soldiers would be required to stand on each side of the boat to steady her as she moved slowly along. The barrels and the boxes — the former much easier to handle because of the absence of square corners and sharp angles — were carried over the portages by the men using tump lines and portage poles, after the fashion developed over the years by the Canadian fur traders. Harman describes the tump line:

> . . . [it] consisted of a broad piece of leather, about the width of one's hand, and some 12 inches [30 cm] in length; to this was attached, on each end, two long pieces of leather tapering off, say to six feet [1.8 m] each. These were securely tied round the load, the broad piece being left clear, so as to be placed across the forehead, the load being carried on the shoulders.[22]

The portage poles were simply poles about five centimetres in circumference that were passed through loops of a rope sling. These were used to carry barrels and boxes, and could be handled by two men with comparative ease. These were popular at first, among men unaccustomed to the tump line, although, it may be noted, as the

Expedition progressed, there was a tendency to discard the poles and slings, and to use the tump line for everything, uncomfortable as the square boxes were to carry on the back. The worst problem for the soldiers with the tump lines was negotiating the rollers or skids used to move the boats. These skids had to be left in place for the boats and crews behind (and, of course, they had to be in position for the return journey). At the outset, some soldiers insisted that the rollers be removed while the barrels and boxes were being carried, and then relaid; but this practice proved too time-consuming and was soon abandoned. The demands made by portage duty upon the soldiers will be understood when it is realized that portages were often between one and five kilometres in length. Each man was, therefore, obliged to make, on an average, ten trips per day,

Portaging, "Fourteen Manpower" from a contemporary drawing, 1870.

Portaging, from a contemporary drawing, 1870.

before all the stores were moved. How little reality resembled the imaginative picture of soldiering that had encouraged the men to enlist!

It was fortunate for all concerned, that the first portage to Kashaboiwe Lake was a comparatively easy one, a little over a kilometre long, and over fairly easy ground.[23] Once they were safely on the lake, brigades were able to move along rapidly towards the height of land separating the waters flowing into Lake Superior from those flowing into Hudson Bay. Like so many of the lakes in this region of Canada, Kashaboiwe was studded with small islands. There was little noise or chatter, the principal sound in the ears of the soldiers was the steady click of the oars in the rowlocks and the splash of the oar blades as they dipped into the lake. Most of the oarsmen bent their backs to their task

Portaging, "An Evasive Pork Barrel"— from a contemporary drawing.

Portaging, "Back For a Load" from a contemporary drawing.

and were oblivious to their surroundings; others were struck by the beauty of their physical surroundings, the clarity of the night and the brightness of the stars. Everything seemed to be going smoothly.

The first break, in what some may have regarded as monotony, came with the appearance of a canoe from the Red River Settlement, which reached Kashaboiwe Portage from the west end at the same time Colonel Wolseley arrived from the east. In the canoe were four men, two Indians and a Métis. The fourth was a white man with letters from Donald A. Smith, the Canadian commissioner to Red River, and from other residents of the Settlement. The gist of the letters was that everything was quiet in Red River. Wolseley was highly suspicious of these letters and of the men who brought them. Was it possible that they might be spies sent by Louis Riel "to see what we were about and how we were getting on?"[24]

To the Canadian militiamen, the Red River men were curiosities. Men from the enemy camp, but, generally speaking, not to be taken seriously as spies. The Canadians therefore "joked with them on the size of Riel's army, and the time it had taken them to cover the distance from Fort Garry."[25] Wolseley made no effort to interfere with the

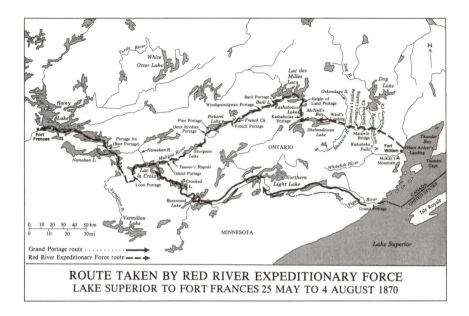

ROUTE TAKEN BY RED RIVER EXPEDITIONARY FORCE
LAKE SUPERIOR TO FORT FRANCES 25 MAY TO 4 AUGUST 1870

strangers — the more they saw the better was his general attitude — although he did make sure that they were kept well in the rear of the Expedition until he had a chance to receive a report from his intelligence agent, Captain William Francis Butler, whom he had sent through the United States to Red River and whom he expected to meet at Fort Frances.

On 24 July Wolseley reached the Height of Land Portage. This portage, approximately 365 metres long, marked the high point between Fort William and Fort Garry. Up to now the British and Canadian troops had been working against the current. Once over this portage they would be moving with the flow of water, at least until they entered the mouth of the Red River.

The Height of Land Portage was long and exhausting, but it did not present Wolseley's troops with any serious problems. However, the lake to which it afforded access did. Lac des Mille Lacs was a body of water of considerable size and filled with numerous islands. Lieutenant Riddell remarked that, owing to these islands the lake "well deserves its name."[26] Wolseley, in his journal, was rather more accurate, when he said it should have been called Lac des Mille Iles, for the islands seemed to be without number. What made its waters so confusing to navigate was the fact that the islands tended to obscure the route traditionally followed by travellers. "The only safe way" to navigate the lake, in his opinion, was "to steer a course by compass, for even the guides frequently lose themselves for a time."[27] Peter O'Leary, who made the same journey over the Dawson route several years after Wolseley and wrote a travelogue about his journey, described the lake as "one of the prettiest sheets of water I ever saw, not even excepting Killarney."[28] High praise from an Irishman! That other Irishman, Wolseley, saw it differently. He called it "a curiously shaped and straggling expanse of water, in which there are islands without number, many being of sufficient size to have great bays stretching for miles into them." In view of the lack of maps to help the troops find their way through this watery maze, perhaps Wolseley was justified in writing:

> One island so closely resembles another that it is wonderful how any of us found our way over the 20 miles [32 km] to be travelled before we reached the next portage . . . steering solely by the compass took one repeatedly into these large bays; and nothing is more disheartening than finding one's self in a *cul de sac* after a pull for many miles up one of these bays, and having to row back again to search for another passage.[29]

The scenery around Lac des Mille Lacs proved to be much pleasanter to the eyes of the soldiers. The fires that had devastated the vicinity of Prince Arthur's Landing, had not reached the interior of the terrain that appealed to sportsmen; country in which to hunt and fish, but not country in which to settle in the hope of making a living, was the general impression made upon the minds and memories of the soldiers. This is clear from various references to the rocky outcroppings, the thinness of the soil, and the absence of large timber to be found in contemporary accounts left by the troops. Harman, for instance, refers to the exposures of white quartz which were "repeatedly seen on the islands, and not unfrequently . . . taken for the sails of distant boats."[30]

From the portage of Lac des Mille Lacs to the next obstacle, Baril Portage, was about 32 kilometres. The problem here was a steep hill that stood out like a hog's back or barrel. It is apparently from this physical feature that the region and the portage received their names, although Sam Steele has a much more interesting explanation. In his account, he says that one of the early fur traders was carrying a barrel of rum in his boat. Fearing that a rival group might catch up with him and demand a share of the liquor, he ordered his crew to dig a hole and bury the barrel, and then to erect a headboard on which he inscribed the words, "A la Mémoire de Monsieur Baril." When the rival brigade passed the site, they concluded that some poor devil of a voyageur had been buried there. As good pious fellows they offered their prayers for the repose of the soul of M. Baril. On the return journey, the barrel was disinterred, the remains exhumed and, amidst much merriment, M. Baril's health was drunk with great enthusiasm.[31]

Whatever may be the truth of the naming of Baril Portage, there is no question that as an obstacle it was difficult and exhausting to negotiate. The Canadian militiaman, John Kerr, entered in his diary for 26 July, "Left at ten, and reached Baril portage, a distance of twenty miles [32 km], about 8 p.m., having had a head wind for sixteen [25] of them. A company of the 60th is here. The portage is an awful one, over rocks fifteen and twenty feet [4.5 & 6m] high, almost perpendicular. Distance, four hundred yards [365 m]."[32] A road, however, had been cut for the boats, skirting the hill and providing a relatively easy gradient. Nevertheless, when the volunteers arrived there, they found a British company still struggling over the portage. That meant, of course, that the Canadians had to wait, and Kerr gives hints of their dissatisfaction at having to sit and contemplate nature while the regular troops struggled to get clear of the portage. He noted in his

"In Camp", from a contemporary drawing, 1870.

diary, "The Canadian Volunteers were not permitted at any time to pass these seasoned troops from the Old Country."[33]

Occasionally, constant day to day contact led to problems of morale and to irritations of temperament. These are to be found in any organized group of people, obliged to work, sleep and play together over a prolonged period of time. Such negative items, however, are seldom found in the memoirs of participants, who prefer to remember the pleasant rather than the bitter aspects of group life. Which is just as well for all concerned. Bugler Joseph Francis Tennant, however, recounts one instance of a clash involving some members of the Quebec Rifles. One of them developed a boil, while on the expedition, which led him to avoid sitting. He was, as one might imagine, the victim of a certain amount of ribaldry, to which he submitted with a fair degree of dignity. However, when he was referred to by one of his comrades as a "dead-head passenger," he took offence and struck out, hitting his comrade in the face. Blood flowed. Quickly the aggrieved soldier returned the blow, straight from the shoulder, hitting his afflicted comrade on the chin and forcing him to sit down suddenly on the gunwale of the boat. There followed a look of surprise and then of pleasure! Instead of continuing the fight, the man who received the blow, thrust out his hand, exclaiming, "Now, you did it! Shake!" His troubles were over in an instant. The boil had burst! Tennant adds, "The crew grinned, even the stern Iroquois voyageur from Caughna-waga relaxed."[34]

Another illustration of life on the expedition comes from John Kerr who, writing about the expedition in retrospect, remarked:

> How we used to make the welkin ring with *My Old Grey Mare and I*, and kindred rollicking songs. . . . At night we'd sit around the camp fires, sing, and yarn about the day's doings. But no matter when we went to bed that blamed bugler would far far too soon blow reveille — or as the boys called it, revallee . . . though, for my part, I was usually up long before, getting the breakfast ready for our boat's crew. Many and many a night I hadn't more than an hour or two of sleep, for I had to stay up at night making bannocks, boiling beans and pork . . . so as to have as little to do as possible for breakfast. But, oh boy! How those boat-crews could stow away the grub! Ten or twelve hungry men can clean up a lot of stuff.

Then I had to have enough to serve for dinner and supper, because we stopped only about an hour at noon. So I usually had pork and beans and bannock enough to warm up at noon and night. Sometimes I let the bannock go, and then we had hard-tack, desiccated [sic] potatoes, dried apples and little else. The hard-tack I soaked in water for awhile, till it split, and I'd fry it in good pork lard. It made tasty eating, with a little sugar sprinkled on it.[35]

He added that the "desiccated" potatoes like beans and rice, swelled up a lot, making a rather "sticky mess." Philosophizing, he concluded, "still, we 'lived, moved and had our being' free from bodily ills."[36]

The passage of the next few miles involved several portages including the Brulé and French Portages leading into Pickerel (Koagas-sikok) Lake. These were not regarded as serious obstacles, perhaps because the troops, regulars and militia alike, were becoming more adept at controlling their boats and managing their cargoes. At French Portage, note was made of the first sighting of a humming-bird and "great quantities of Labrador tea"[37] (*Tedomo Polustre*) and "leeches" in the shallow, rushy portions of the lake.[38] A winding river, about 3.2 kilometres long, "thick with reeds and water lilies in flower" led into Pickerel Lake. Then followed, right after, two more portages, Pine Portage, so named because of the very fine pine trees in the vicinity, and Deux Rivières Portage. This latter was estimated to be 685 metres in length, "very steep and bad, requiring a great deal of work to fit it for the transportation of boats."[39] According to Wolseley's daily journal, ten Indians had been sent ahead to lay down skids before Lieutenant-Colonel Fielden arrived with the first troops of the 60th. While the soldiers were still struggling with the boats, Colonel Wolseley's party, in their canoe and gig, when ahead, blazing the way "at every point and turn of the route," so as to make the route easily visible for those behind. His purpose, well served by his action, was to save time for those coming behind, "for when," as he noted in his journal, "there is a doubt as to the true course, much valuable time is always lost, and no one likes to push on quickly when doing so may perhaps be leading them a long distance astray."[40]

Lieutenant Riddell considered the Deux Rivières Portage to be "one of the most difficult we had as yet encountered":

> ... in the centre of it was a high rock, up which a ladder of felled trees had been constructed; and at the side,

"Portage des Deux Rivières", from a contemporary engraving.

steps were cut for the men to carry their loads up. Had
one of the ropes snapped when hauling the boats up
this ladder, the men at work would, doubtless, have
received very severe injuries, and the boat been broken, to a certainty.[41]

Once embarked on Sturgeon Lake, the soldiers forgot the hardships of
Deux Rivières, absorbed, as they became, in the physical beauties of
the scene. Riddell quoted Longfellow when he caught sight of the
great fish from which the lake drew its name:

On the white sand of the bottom
Lay the monster Mishe Nahma—
Lay the Sturgeon, King of Fishes:
Through his gills he breathed the water;
With his fins he fanned and winnowed.[42]

But the King of Fishes did not long remain to survey his watery
kingdom. He was promptly speared by an Indian and cooked for the
officers' supper. And the roe, added Riddell, "was voted most delicious by all who tasted it."[43]

The officers of the 60th were not the only soldiers to take advantage of the fresh fish. John Kerr wrote that the Indian voyageur

attached to his boat, caught "several fine pike, pickerel and maskinonge" which he prepared as he said himself, to a "nicety."[44] He added to his account a story that the soldiers had barely seated themselves to enjoy their meal when one of their members suddenly jumped to his feet, let his plate of fish and pork roll into the fire, and shrieked that he had been bitten by a snake. As he rolled up his trouser leg, his comrades "stood ready with stones and sticks to kill the monster," only to discover that the creature inflicting the bite was, not a snake, but a small black ant.[45]

Harman, too, recalled the Deux Rivières Portage, noting in particular, a "tremendous storm of thunder and lightning, accompanied by heavy rain" that slowed down his brigade in negotiating the portage. When the troops endeavoured to erect their tents they found "no little difficulty in getting the tents to stand, as the locality being solid rock it was impossible, even in the crevices, to drive pegs so as to hold." The troops, therefore, tied the guy ropes around small boulders. Unfortunately, any severe gust of wind, would pull the rocks away and "threaten to demolish our canvas house." The night spent by the men of Harman's boat was, in his words, "cruel, sleepless, wet and cold."[46] With dawn came a burst of "golden sunlight," singing birds, and a morning "so glorious with its beauty and song, that we soon forgot our wetting and discomfort."[47] A good cup of strong tea and everybody was ready to resume the journey. The rain made the roads slippery and the footholds precarious, but all the discomforts were forgotten when they reached Sturgeon Lake, a "sheet of water" which "for picturesque scenery surpasses anything we had yet seen."[48]

Here, at Sturgeon Lake, Colonel Wolseley encountered a large *canot de maître* manned by Indians. It carried two men, one of them Wemyss M. Simpson, the member of Parliament from Algoma. These men had been engaged by the federal government to precede the expedition for the purpose of conferring with the Indians, arranging with them free passage for the troops through regions regarded by the Indians as their country. Both men had held interviews with the native peoples of the area, discouraging them from taking any actions hostile to the progress of Wolseley's soldiers. Wolseley had heard rumours that the Indians might well offer armed resistance to the troops. Although he had no doubt of his ability to brush the natives aside, he was apprehensive about the ability of his men, strung out in one long line like so many sitting ducks, to cope with sudden thrusts by Indians thoroughly familiar with the geography of the country and accustomed to move about rapidly in small canoes.

During the talks, the Indians demanded food and annuities and, above all, a formal treaty; but, in the end, they expressed their willingness to wait another year for formal treaty negotiations.[49] Wolseley was content. At least he could proceed without fear of armed interruption; the Canadian government could make whatever arrangements it wished after he had returned with his soldiers to Great Britain. Wolseley, therefore, expressed his satisfaction at the news that Simpson brought him. He was also interested in reports that men suspected of being spies for Louis Riel had been seen lurking in the vicinity of Rat Portage.

At the western extremity of Sturgeon Lake were four sets of rapids. Wolseley had heard gloomy accounts of these rapids, so he took them carefully. The soldiers disembarked and the boats were taken over by the Iroquois. The contents of each boat were then removed for the second rapid (this was the longest); but the third and fourth rapids were run with both the cargoes and the men aboard. Wolseley was delighted. He nailed a set of instructions to a tree at the first set of rapids, ordering the boats that followed, to halt, and wait until the Iroquois Ignace arrived and then to advance "precisely as he would tell them."[50]

The first of these cascades had a fall of one and a half metres; the second dropped another two metres. These were followed by a narrow reach of river for about five kilometres ending with a third descent of a metre, another stretch of water and two more rapids, at intervals of about three kilometres. The Indians assigned the task waited for the arrival of the various boats and then undertook to guide them. In the hands of experienced voyageurs, these rapids presented no particularly serious problems; but to men unaccustomed to running rapids the whole experience was unforgettable. Harman's account is dramatic; probably the best available of this experience, because it so firmly fixed itself in his memory. "We soon received our instructions," he wrote:

> . . . which were as follows: — All the men were to get out of the boats with the exception of four picked men, who were to take the oars, and the two guides, one at the bow, with his pole to direct the course, and the other at the stern, who was to steer by means of one of the sweeps shipped in a rowlock, . . .

The men not allotted to the boats walked over the portage.

> When all was in readiness the word was given, and they pushed off, every man with a firm hold of his oar, and his heart in his mouth, those on shore eagerly watching their comrades. As they near the broken water, the bowman, who has the post of honour, and who has been intently watching the current, hails his chum at the stern. Some words pass between them, at first quietly, and then excitedly; the helmsman takes it up, and calls upon the men to pull. "Pull hard, Nitchey," "Heligo permiscog Nitchey" (pull hard, boys), "Heligo permiscog shumogishie" (pull hard soldiers), and now they are in it; away they go tearing along, every man pulling for dear life, with his eyes starting out of his head. As they strike the roaring, seething waters the boat makes a bound, which fairly lifts them off their seats. Now they are in the middle of it, with the water dashing and foaming around them. Should they touch anything, a rock ahead, or a back eddy, God help them, is the thought which flashes through the minds of those on shore, but the guides know their work too well; they are now on the reach below, safely over, and with a shout, which is taken up by those on shore, land below the portage.[51]

Below the rapids, the men of Captain Harman's company found a barrel stave stuck into the trunk of a tree. It bore the printed words, "No. 6, Company Ontario Rifles, arrived here August 6, 1870, at 9.30 a.m., all well."[52] They too, had run the rapids safely.

After entering Lac La Croix, two exits were possible, both leading to Rainy Lake,[53] the one to the north, by way of the Maligne River and the other farther south via Namekan

"Running the Rapids", from a contemporary drawing.

Fort Frances, 1870, from a contemporary engraving.

Lake. From Wolseley's journal, it is clear that he followed the second route, owing to reports that there were two very dangerous rapids on the Maligne River, on which Donald A. Smith's canoe had been "twice broken during his recent voyage, although manned by the best Iroquois."[54] The route selected by Wolseley had several short portages; but they were not considered difficult. It was along this route that Fielden's 60th Rifles travelled. During this part of his journey Wolseley encountered several parties of Indians, noting only that all of them were "most importunate beggars," that the women were "much dirtier than the men," and that they were "most repulsive in appearance" and "covered with vermin, for which they are perpetually scratching."[55] He also drew attention in his journal to "the plant called poison ivy," indicating the unpleasant results that ensued when one picked it or touched his face or hands with it.[56]

Captain Huyshe likewise avoided the Maligne River, which he described as bare, swampy, filled with leeches and swarming with mosquitoes and black flies. He followed Wolseley's route, cutting a path over the Portage Nu (Bare Portage). When Fielden's men reached the same portage, Huyshe watched them with uncritical pride:

> It was quite a sight to see them arrive at a portage, to see the men spring out, unload the boats, and haul them over, the crews vying with each other as to who should

get everything over first. No delay or hesitation; as
soon as a barrel was handed from the boat, somebody
seized it, tied his portage strap around it, then off to the
other end of the portage running back to get another
load.[57]

As the commander's party continued towards Rainy Lake, they
encountered a strong northwesterly wind against which they were
able to make but little headway. However, they found compensation
in the presence of great quantities of blueberries. They were, he wrote,
"as large as cherries, as delicious as grapes, and with a bloom like a
peach, and no stones inside."[58] Small wonder that he and his party in
the gig ate them "until we could not stand, and then we lay down and
ate them again!"[59] The more prosaic Wolseley simply noted, "The
islands and rocky promontories have abounded with them [blueber-
ries] since we crossed the watershed. At this season they constitute the
staple article of food with the Indians."[60]

It was 0600 hours, 4 August, when Wolseley arrived at Fort
Frances. The post, one of those acquired by the Hudson's Bay Company from the Nor'Westers, was little more than a collection of one-
storied buildings standing on the west bank of the Rainy River, just
below a waterfall six and a half metres high. Wolseley took note of the
fact that there was a field of barley, wheat and potatoes close by and
a number of Indian lodges housing some Indians of the neighbourhood, who had assembled in order to hold a conference with him.
Huyshe considered Fort Frances a rather attractive location, describing it as "very charming, combining all the essentials of picturesque
beauty except that of mountain scenery."[61] The Hudson's Bay Company post manager gave up his room in his house to Wolseley, and
provided the commander and his staff with fresh vegetables. In
Huyshe's view, nothing could have been more acceptable than the
change to fresh vegetables. The officers "revelled" in the helping of
green peas, young potatoes and cabbages.[62] Wolseley appreciated, in
particular, the "luxury of a chair to sit on"[63] although he did not make
mention of it in his journal. A "luxury" was how Huyshe saw it. And
he added what Wolseley must have been thinking, a chair was really
a vast improvement over stumps and stones for any man's bottom.

The presence of the Indians meant the usual exchange of gifts and
importunities — gifts from Wolseley and importunities from the Indians. Wolseley had little to offer Old Crooked Neck and his companions. Nothing more than a few bags of flour, some pork and a little

tobacco. Nevertheless, he was able to reassure the Indians that the soldiers had no interest in acquiring their lands, and that they sought only a right of passage through the Indian country.[64] Wolseley was vastly relieved when the Indians accepted his presents and assurances and went away. He did not relish the idea of a hostile encounter with groups of hungry people for whom he could spare little in the way of provisions.

What he wanted to do at Fort Frances was simply to take a sharp look at his troops as they arrived from Shebandowan Lake, and to see them off again on the next leg of the journey to Fort Garry provided with fresh bread and, in some cases, with fresh vegetables. While Wolseley was at Fort Frances, Joseph Monkman, an English Métis from Red River, arrived at the fort, bearing letters from so-called "loyalists" in the Settlement, urging Wolseley to move with haste and suggesting that the best and shortest route would be by way of Lake of the Woods. This road, he was told, "with very little labour" could be made "passable for carts"; but Wolseley had had his fill of new roads, or roads under construction. He had no desire to risk the success of the Expedition on another such road.[65] In any event, he had made up his mind, even prior to setting out for the West, that he would travel the entire route by water. He later suggested that he was moved to this decision by the belief that Riel might prepare an ambush west of Lake of the Woods, and that it would be safer to continue along the Winnipeg River route; it probably would be the less obvious way of approaching the Settlement.

One other decision Wolseley had to make; that was to select the militia company to remain at Fort Frances as a garrison. That it would be an Ontario company was obvious enough; a Quebec company had already been ordered to remain at Prince Arthur's Landing. However, few companies wished to remain behind when their regiment moved along. When Major Macleod's company arrived at Fort Frances, the men hurriedly exchanged their clumsy *Flying Dutchman* for another lighter, even if slightly damaged craft, *The Girl of the Period*, and loaded her with supplies. The change was made with "frenzied eagerness," according to Sam Steele. "We received no orders," he wrote, "but there seemed to be something in the wind."[66] Whether their haste and obvious zeal made any impression on Wolseley is not clear; in any event it was not Macleod's company, but Captain MacMillan's that was slated for garrison duty. The MacMillan company had been one of the first to reach Fort Frances. Some of the other members of the Ontario Rifles felt sorry for MacMillan's men. They would miss all the excitement of taking part in the capture of Fort Garry; but if we may judge from John Kerr's account (he was one of those who was obliged to remain at Fort Frances), everybody seems to have had a jolly time at the Hudson's Bay Company post, with sports, swimming, rowing, and football. The soldiers even formed a Glee Club. Between various recreational activities, they kept a close watch on the Indians lest any agents be sent from Red River to tamper with their loyalty to the Crown,[67] and waited patiently for the orders to move on to Manitoba. On 23 August, Adams G. Archibald, the new Lieutenant-Governor of Manitoba, passed through Fort Frances on his way to Fort Garry. He was serenaded by the Glee Club. In return, he provided the garrison and the Indians with a magic lantern show. Then he continued his journey. Not until the beginning of September did No. 7 Company receive instructions to move. By that time, the British regulars were returning to central Canada.

IV

About three kilometres from Fort Frances, just as he was approaching from the east, Colonel Wolseley had spied a figure standing on a rock at a point where Rainy Lake flows into the river of the same name. The figure then stepped into a small canoe and paddled towards the commander's boat. As soon as they were within hailing distance of each other, Wolseley shouted, "Where on earth have you dropped from?" The reply came, "Fort Garry, twelve days out, sir."[68] The speaker was Captain W. F. Butler, whom Wolseley had engaged as an intelligence agent to go to Red River and then report to him on the situation there as well as on the attitudes of the people of the United States.

Butler had left Montreal on 8 June. He had travelled by the Grand Trunk Railway to Toronto (where he purchased the "full costume of a Western borderer"),[69] and then on to Detroit, Chicago, Milwaukee, St. Louis, Duluth and St. Paul. He became thoroughly aware of the American jubilation at Wolseley's check at Sault Ste Marie. He listened to many predictions that the British military expedition against Louis Riel would never reach the Red River Settlement — "swamps would entrap it, rapids would engulf it; and if, in spite of these obstacles, some few men did succeed in piercing the rugged wilderness, the trusty rifle of the Metis would soon annihilate the presumptive intruders."[70] He wrote later, "Such was the news and such were the comments," that "I ...read day after day, as I anxiously scanned the

W.F. Butler,
Wolseley's Intelligence Agent.

columns of the newspapers for intelligence."[71] Moreover, he kept hearing talk of Fenian aid to be sent to Riel; arms, men and ammunition "to aid the free sons of the North-west to follow out their manifest destiny, which, of course, was annexation to the United States."[72]

In St. Paul, Butler found all kinds of contradictory reports circulating about the Red River Expedition. Some were to the effect that Riel was tired and anxious to turn over the government of the settlement to the Canadians; others stated that Riel was actively preparing to oppose Wolseley by force and was on the watch for Canadian spies crossing the American frontier on their way to encourage unfriendly elements in the Settlement. Probably Butler was a little too intent on asking questions and on picking up bits of information. It was not long before he began to hear rumours that there was a British officer in St. Paul acting as a spy for Wolseley, a report which, he himself admitted, "did not intend in any manner to make the days pleasant in themselves nor hopeful in the anticipation of a successful prosecution of my journey in the time to come."[73] He, therefore, left St. Paul early in July, travelling by train to Sauk River and St. Cloud. St. Cloud was the terminus of the railway. Butler then had to continue his journey to Fort

Abercrombie by stage-coach. After three days of great discomfort — involving passing one night sleeping on the hay in a local barn in preference to the local hostlery at Pomme de Terre — he caught his first glimpse of the yellow, muddy waters of the Red River of the North. Here he was subjected to horrific rumours of "a large band of the Sioux Indians . . . ready to support the dictator [Riel] against all comers," and of a "vigilant watch" being kept at the frontier at Pembina "for the purpose of excluding strangers who might attempt to enter the Settlement from the United States." There were even more discouraging rumours about the fate of Wolseley's troops. They were doomed to disaster; why, already 40 Canadian soldiers had been lost in one of the boiling rapids of the route! "Not a man will get through!" was the general verdict — or wishful thinking — of the Americans with whom Butler chatted. All of this, as Butler noted, told in a loud voice to a roomful of Americans, "had no very exhilarating effect upon me as I sat, unknown and unnoticed, on my portmanteau, a stranger to every one."[74] Unknown and unnoticed? One must wonder.

Despite his apprehensions and the hordes of mosquitoes, Butler set out to hitch a ride to Georgetown, where he found the steamboat *International*. She was a flat-bottomed craft, "propelled by an enormous wheel placed over her stern," nothing much to admire in her lines, with a cracked roof and scarred bow and hull, her engines, "a perfect marvel of patchwork — pieces of rope . . . twisted around crank and shaft, mud . . . laid thickly on boiler and pipes, little jets and spirts of steam . . . coming from places not supposed to be capable of such outpouring."[75] What was even worse, the vessel seemed to have the capacity for catching fire every time a gust of wind sent the sparks from her boilers flying along the deck. For a man hoping to lose himself in the crowd, Butler had a certain capacity for drawing attention to himself, by shouting for help, only to find the local passengers staring at him with "surprise and pity."[76] Obviously his alarm was unwarranted. Perhaps it was his English speech that attracted attention. In any event, he arrived safely at Pembina on the morning of 20 July. The steamer made a short stop at the American frontier post, only long enough to impress Butler "with a sense of dirt and debauchery." Going ashore to see if there were any letters awaiting him there, he noted rather unkindly, "some of the leading citizens came forth with hands stuck so deep in breeches pockets, that the shoulders seemed to have formed an offensive and defensive alliance with the arms, never again to permit the hands to emerge into daylight unless it should be in the vicinity of the ankles."[77] After he had re-embarked, the stern wheel of *International* started, and within minutes, Butler noted, he was "within the limits of the Red River Settlement, in the land of M. Louis Riel."[78]

As the vessel approached Fort Garry, Butler began to wonder what he would do. He had seen Métis horsemen galloping along the road from Pembina towards Fort Garry, and suspected that they were bringing Riel news about the strange Englishman on board *International*.[79] Striking up an acquaintance with one of the passengers, Willie Drever, a resident of Red River and an acknowledged opponent of Riel, he and Drever planned to jump ashore as the vessel swung around, before she actually drew up to the dock. It meant abandoning some of his luggage, but, with his Colt six-shooter and his 14-shot repeating carbine, Butler joined Drever in leaping into the shallow water and climbing up the bank, while the local crowd gathered on the wharf to greet the ship.[80] Drever had promised to find a horse for him, but when the horse did not appear within a reasonable time, Butler set off on foot in the direction of Lower Fort Garry. Alexander Begg, who kept a diary of local events in Red River wrote, under the dateline 20 July:

> The Steamer International came in this evening. As it rounded coming into the Assiniboine from the Red River it touched the point nearest Fort Garry when Willie Drever and a stranger jumped off. The stranger disappeared mysteriously and Wm. Drever went home. Soon afterwards W. Drever was arrested on account of the suspicious actions of himself and the stranger in thus jumping off the boat. The stranger said to be one Butler or Baker left some baggage on the boat.[81]

With the assistance of local people, Butler made his way safely to the Lower Fort where he met Chief Henry Prince and a number of Indians. Amid several rounds of "Ho, Ho, Ho's," Butler told them that the "arm of the Great Mother was a long one, and stretched far over seas and forests" and gave them presents of tea, tobacco, flour and pemmican.[82] Then, when he turned his attention to making preparations for his departure to join Wolseley, a messenger arrived from Fort Garry. He carried a note from Louis Riel, inviting Butler to visit the Upper Fort!

The invitation came as a great surprise to the English officer. He wondered if it were genuine; or whether it might be a trick. Had Riel not imprisoned Butler's boat companion, Willie Drever? And was the Provisional Government flag not flying from Fort Garry? Despite advice from his new acquaintances, Butler decided to accept Riel's invitation; he would visit the Upper Fort and see for himself. In his account, written in 1871, he claimed that he laid down the condition that the Union Jack should replace the Provisional Government flag, and that Riel must show his good faith by releasing Drever who had been imprisoned in Fort Garry.[83] What he did not know, apparently, was that on 22 July, Riel had already received a copy of Colonel Wolseley's Proclamation, dated 30 June, addressed to "The Loyal Inhabitants of Manitoba"; and that the Proclamation had been published in *The New Nation* under Riel's personal supervision.[84] Butler was, therefore, in no danger when he set out for Fort Garry. In any event, he carried a letter from the Bishop of St. Boniface, which he felt confident Riel would honour.

On 23 July Butler recorded that Drever had been released and that his own luggage, left behind when he quit *International* several nights before, was waiting for him at Fort Garry. As he neared the fort, he saw *International* lying at her moorings, and encouraged by a wave from her captain, he approached the gate of the old Hudson's Bay Company fort. It was open, a sentry leaning lazily against the wall. The exterior "looked old and dirty," the muzzles of one or two guns protruding through the embrasures in the bastion "failed even to convey the idea of a fort or fortress to the mind of the beholder," and the only troops he saw were "lounging about" the square. On the two flag staffs flew two flags, the Union Jack and "the fleur de lys and a shamrock on a white field."[85] While Butler waited for a few moments playing billiards with one of Riel's staff, Riel entered the room. Butler looked up and saw:

> ... a short stout man with a large head, a sallow, puffy face, a sharp, restless, intelligent eye, a square-cut massive forehead overhung by a mass of long and thickly clustering hair, and marked with well-cut eyebrows — altogether, a remarkable-looking face, all the more so, perhaps, because it was to be seen in a land where such things are rare sights. .... He was dressed in a curious mixture of clothing— a black frock-coat, vest, and trousers; but the effect of this somewhat clerical costume was not a little marred by a pair of Indian moccasins, which nowhere look more out of place than on a carpeted floor.[86]

Moccasins may have appeared strange to an English officer, accustomed to more elaborate surroundings; but they were not out of place in Fort Garry in 1870, or even much later. Riel expressed his regret that Butler should have shown such distrust of the Métis that he had chosen to land in a surreptitious manner, to which Butler replied that he was alarmed by the reports circulating in the United States that the Provisional Government was preparing to offer armed resistance to Colonel Wolseley. Riel replied, "Nothing was more false. . . . I only wish to retain power until I can resign it to a proper Government." But he made it clear that he would not resign it to the local opposition. "I will keep what is mine until the proper Government arrives."[87] A few questions about Wolseley's force, which Butler answered with a minimum of detail, and the interview was over. Butler looked around what he described as "the dirty ill-kept fort,"[88] and then drove back to the Lower Fort. He had seen inside of Fort Garry and talked with the president of the Provisional Government. There was no further reason for him to remain in the Red River Settlement; and before sundown he embarked in a small canoe manned by Indians, and set off down the Red River, on his journey to report to Wolseley. Meanwhile, back at Fort Garry, men were being engaged "from all parts of the Settlement" (French, English and Canadian) to "go to work on the road to the Lake of the Woods" in an effort to finish the road for the use of Wolseley's soldiers.[89]

With a light craft and an experienced crew, Butler made fast time against the current of the Winnipeg River, and within twelve days he intercepted Wolseley on Rainy Lake. Now he was part of the expedition he had wanted to join nearly two months earlier and was returning to Fort Garry with the main body of Wolseley's troops. There was, however, no question of their using the road from Lake of the Woods. They would go all the way by water.

V

Colonel Wolseley was not in a good mood when he left Fort Frances in the early hours of 10 August. On the previous day he had learned to his disgust that some of the men of "K" brigade of Ontario militia had decided to ease their burdens by opening the barrels of pork they were carrying and draining out the brine. Twenty-four of thirty-one barrels had been tampered with, making the contents unfit to eat. No one admitted responsibility for this silly and dangerous act, although it was popularly believed that the militia men had been put up to it "by an old sergeant of the Royal Canadian Rifles serving with them." Wolseley admitted to being "very angry when he heard of this."[90] But his anger diminished as he set off in his canoe for Rat Portage, accompanied by the gig carrying Huyshe and Denison. They passed rapidly through the luxuriant country of the Rainy River, beyond the old and now abandoned post erected by the Nor'Westers. It was all easy going. The several rapids presented no problems; it was even possible to rest the canoemen and let the craft drift along with the current. The next morning the commander's party took breakfast at "Hungry Hall", a small trading post, so-called because a former occupant had almost starved to death there. Near the location of the post the troops encountered a messenger bearing letters from Red River appealing to Wolseley to make all possible speed and promising the active assistance of "loyal" elements in the colony when he should arrive with his troops. Progress was easy, the water was smooth and, with a rising wind on the lake, the men in the gig hoisted a sail. The Indians in the canoe, however, did not like the wind and refused to continue as the lake waters became rougher. Annoyed at their refusal to obey orders, Wolseley transferred to the gig, Lieutenant Denison being required to take his commander's place in the canoe.

It was not a wise move. Without the help of his Indian guides, Wolseley had no choice but to become his own navigator and astral navigation was not one of Wolseley's accomplishments. For the next

The Hudson's Bay Company post at Rat Portage, from a contemporary engraving.

two days, he sailed among and around the islands of Lake of the Woods, getting no place and blaming his predicament, not on himself, but on Simon Dawson's map — "a very inefficient and inaccurate chart," he called it.[91] Finally, on 14 August, he encountered some Indians who, in return for a present of biscuits and tea, expressed their willingness to direct him to Rat Portage. He arrived there safely that night about 2000 hours. Wolseley may have been a conceited man, but he was not a stupid one. He had learned a lesson. "To attempt to cross the Lake of the Woods without a guide is a feat which Colonel Wolseley will not attempt a second time," is what he noted in his journal.[92] Huyshe tactfully observed only that the party in the gig arrived at Rat Portage tired and hungry, "having fasted all day."[93] When Wolseley published his anonymous account in *Blackwood's*

The Falls at Rat Portage.

Edinburgh Magazine in 1871, he chose to see his experience in a somewhat romantic light:

> To lose one's way upon an expanse of water like the
> Lake of the Woods, and to wander about in a boat, as
> the writer did, through its maze of uninhabited is-
> lands, where no sound was to be heard but the dip of
> the oars at regular intervals, or the distant and weird-
> like whistle of the loon, is to experience the exquisite
> sensation of solitude in all its full intensity. . . . Oh! if it
> were not for the trouble of having to cook one's own
> dinner, how delicious would be existence passed in the
> society of nature![94]

Much more practical than his soliloquizing about the beauties of solitude (if only meals could be served in proper fashion), was Wolseley's prompt action at Rat Portage in making arrangements for guides to be sent back to Fort Frances to conduct the brigades across the Lake of the Woods, and also for guides for the Winnipeg River.[95] At Rat Portage he was joined by McNeill and Jolly, on 15 August, twelve days out of Shebandowan Lake. From them he learned of the locations of various brigades of Lieutenant-Colonel Casault's battalion of Quebec Rifles, strung out along the water route from the Height of Land Portage to Portage Nu, not far from Fort Frances.[96] Apprised of the exact location of each of the component parts of his force, Wolseley despatched a report to Lieutenant-General Lindsay for forwarding to the Horse Guards, London.[97] Then he was ready for the next stage of his journey, the dreaded descent of the Winnipeg River.

Meanwhile, the various brigades of soldiers were on their way to Rat Portage.[98] This was the jumping-off point for the journey down the Winnipeg River. Butler, travelling in his light canoe with his Indian paddlers, went along with them. He described the scene on Lake of the Woods in good nineteenth century literary form:

> Never before had these lonely islands witnessed such
> a sight as they now beheld. Seventeen large boats close
> hauled to a splendid breeze swept in a great scattered
> mass through the high-running seas, dashing the foam
> from their bows as they dipped and rose under their
> large lug-sails. . . . How the poor fellows enjoyed that
> day! no oar, no portage, no galling weight over rocky

ledges, nothing but a grand day's racing over into the heavy seas. I think they would have given even Mr. Riel that day a pipeful of tobacco; but Heaven help him if they had caught him two days later on the portages of the Winnipeg![99]

On arrival at Rat Portage the troops made ready for the last portion of their journey to Fort Garry. Butler remained here for a couple of days in order to receive instructions from Colonel Wolseley, when he should show up. Then, on 15 August, he, too, was ready to start down the river. His immediate task was to engage guides for the two regiments of Canadian Militia, to help them reach Fort Garry safely.

CHAPTER EIGHT

Rat Portage to Fort Garry August 1870

I

First travelled by Vérendrye and Jemerais in 1733, the Winnipeg River served for many years as the principal water highway for traders and explorers alike, travelling between Canada and the great prairies. During the mid-nineteenth century, the Canadian explorer and geologist, Henry Hind, made several journeys to the west on behalf of the Canadian government.[1] He chose to follow the Winnipeg River. As a consequence of Hind's writings and of those of others who preceded him, the Winnipeg River acquired a somewhat fearsome reputation.[2] Here is how Hind described the river:

> In its course of 163 miles [262 km], it descends 349 feet [106 m] by a succession of magnificent cataracts. Some of the falls present the wildest and most picturesque scenery, displaying every variety of tumultuous cascade, with foaming rapids, treacherous eddies, and huge swelling waves, rising massive and green over hidden rocks. The pencil of a skilful artist may succeed in conveying an impression of the beauty and grandeur which belong to the cascades and rapids of the Winnipeg; but neither sketch nor language can portray the astonishing variety they present under different aspects; in the grey dawn of morning, or rose-colored by the setting sun, or flashing in the brightness of noon day, or silvered by the soft light of the moon.[3]

Hind was not exaggerating. All the travellers who made the journey by way of the Winnipeg River, attested to its picturesque scenery, to the enormous vigour of the Slave Falls, and to the strength and variety of the thirty-odd water falls and rapids that marked its course. The travellers of 1870, such as Colonel Wolseley and Captain Butler, who travelled by canoe, were able to appreciate to the full the thrill and excitement and the tensions of running the rapids. They never forgot the experience. In his *Narrative*, Wolseley wrote:

> There is no more deliciously exciting pleasure in the world than that of running a really large and dangerous rapid in a canoe, or in a small boat. As your frail skiff bounds over the waves, ever and anon jumping as it were from a higher to a lower level, whilst the paddlers or oarsmen tug away with might and main, and the outcropping rocks are cleverly avoided by the skilful bowsman and steersman, every pleasurable sensation is experienced. As each boat turned into the slack water below the rapid, one took a long breath of relief, and the world and life itself seemed to be different in the calm stillness then from what it was when we were dashing through the roaring, rushing waters in mid-stream.[4]

II

What of the soldiers, who travelled the same route in their heavy boats over the same rapids? Here is militiaman Steele's account of his experience at the Grande Décharge:

> Big Mike, the powerful and skilful Iroquois, although of Major Macleod's boat, took the bow of ours also, and Captain McMillan, who had remained at the summit to see his boats safely through, came in our craft, which was the last, and sat in the stern sheets near Big Neil McArthur. I had the stroke oar (we took turns at it), and, as we approached the crest, set the pace, but just as we passed over it, rowing our best, Neil's oar snapped like a pipe stem and the boat swung into the tremendous waves on our right, rolling and pitching over them, and hurling several of the crew from their oars into the bottom of the boat. Captain McMillan tried to hold my oar down in the rowlock to enable me to row, but it was impossible; we were quite helpless, and death stared us in the face as we surged past the rocks and whirlpools at a great speed, while Big Mike stood

towering in the bow wielding a heavy oar as if it were a light paddle. His long hair streamed in the wind, his coal black eyes glared at the angry waters, and he handled his oar with such effect that the boat came safely through, landing us far below, and his compatriots on both sides of the Décharge, who, with our comrades of the brigade, were watching the outcome with great anxiety, joined him in wild whoops and the shrieks of triumphant laughter.[5]

The journey was not, however, all a matter of whoops and shrieks and chivalrous enthusiasm. There was a great deal of dry monotony, prosaic tediousness and sheer drudgery, shared by officers and men alike. Wolseley saw it: but he did not, as commander of the force, share in it. The hard labour of portaging, like the running of the rapids, tended to become a contest between individuals, a display of human strength and conceit. Steele tells about one of the guides, "a tall, dark, and powerful-looking voyageur, with a full black beard and moustache," who carried two barrels of pork and 1000 rounds of ammunition in a single load. It weighed 240 kilos, but "the burden was an awkward one and nothing to be gained by it except to show the man's great strength." There was no lack of men who could carry their barrel of pork, or an arms chest of 90 kilos "without any difficulty." Steele himself carried his share of pork together with his knapsack "or another pack." One of the officers of the 60th, Ensign Algernon St. Maur, later the Duke of Somerset, "frequently packed two barrels of pork on his back, 400 lbs., [181 kg]" and Captain Redvers Buller "always took at least 200 lbs. [90 kg] and sometimes 300 lbs. [136 kg] at a trip." Steele concluded, "everyone of us, on account of the training given by the heavy work, became much stronger than when he started, although he was then in good condition."[6]

Of all the physical obstacles Wolseley's men encountered on the Winnipeg River, the Grande Décharge, the Slave Falls and the Seven Portages were probably the most formidable. However, the soldiers were no longer novices in the voyageurs' skills. Their reaction to the physical problems of running rapids and portaging had been sharpened by experience and they had developed routines that made it possible for them to complete their journey with the minimum of physical losses. When they passed Islington Mission, at least the Londoners must have wondered how or why such a name should have become attached to so remote a region. Butler suggested that it might have been homesickness that "tempted" the local missionary, "in a moment of virtuous cockneyism . . . to commit this act of desecration."[7] It is not clear if Butler was thinking of Canada or London when he wrote the word "desecration." Beyond Islington, known locally as the Mission of the White Dog, was the Grande Décharge, "a narrow cleft between high granite rocks, which force it down a steep incline with tremendous fury."[8] As Captain Huyshe was descending this rapid, he lost a rowlock, his oar almost touched the towering cliff and only the skill of a voyageur saved the boat from overturning. In so doing, the voyageur broke his paddle, but immediately seized a scull and forced the boat's bow round with it. Huyshe admitted that it was a "close shave."[9]

Slave Falls, Wolseley believed, were the most beautiful rapids or falls he had yet seen.[10] The name was derived from an Indian legend, of which two versions appear to have been current; one was to the effect that two Sioux Indians, taken prisoners by the Ojibways and enslaved, were bound back to back and sent over the falls to be dashed to pieces on the rocks below. Lieutenant Riddell had a much more romantic version when he wrote about a female slave who, "maddened by long-continued cruelty" on the part of her Ojibway captors, stepped into a canoe above the falls and pushing off from the shore, wrapped her deerskin robe about her and glided into the cataract" to find rest in the surging waters below."[11] Whatever the truth of the story, there was no doubt in Captain Huyshe's mind that the falls were "one of the most beautiful bits of the river."[12]

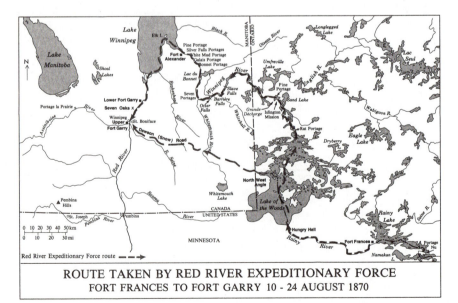

ROUTE TAKEN BY RED RIVER EXPEDITIONARY FORCE
FORT FRANCES TO FORT GARRY 10 - 24 AUGUST 1870

The portage around the Falls, located some 365 metres to the right of the Falls, was 685 metres long. The canoe portage was shorter. It was located just around a jutting ledge of rock, perilously close to the Falls. "Very dangerous," observed Wolseley, "except for skilled boatmen well acquainted with the place."[13] It was here, on 18 August, that Wolseley finally overtook the leading brigades of the Ontario Rifles, who were encamped for the night. It was the commander's strong desire to get ahead to Fort Alexander, in order to take personal charge of the regulars in the last approach to Fort Garry, and so he pushed ahead rapidly. Following the Slave Falls came the Barrière, then the Otter Rapids and the Sept Portages. These last were about five kilometres in length, a succession of water falls, rapids, whirlpools and eddies. None of these rapids was really difficult as far as skilled boatmen were concerned. Nevertheless, the picture they presented was one of a succession of dangerous back currents, rapid water, twisting whirlpools and hidden rocks, all of which required constant care and strict attention. A false stroke, a momentary hesitation, held the possibility of death, or at the very least, a cold dunking and a smashed boat. It was perhaps fortunate that there were few distractions along the banks, only the repetitive green and grey of woods and craggy rocks. Captain S. B. Harman, the Canadian militia officer, found this section of the journey "very arduous,"[14] if only because of the frequent occasions when it was found necessary to disembark, unload the boats, drag them a few yards and then reload to re-embark.

Finally, on 20 August, after negotiating the Galais and Bonnet Portages, the White Mud Portage, the two Silver Falls Portages and the final Fine Portage, it was an easy run to Fort Alexander, the Hudson's Bay Company post, located not far from the mouth of the Winnipeg River. Here Wolseley arrived, about an hour before sunset, to find the whole force of regulars, including the gunners and engineers, as well as the several companies of the 60th Rifles waiting for him. The next morning he despatched instructions to the commander of the Ontario Rifles at Fort Frances, to set out at once for Fort Garry, travelling by way of the North West Angle and the new road leading directly to Upper Fort Garry. All mails were directed to be sent by that route henceforth. Now that he was with his own kind, British regular soldiers, the commander became, once more, all that was implied in the description he was later to hear, "all Sir Garnet".[15]

It is not surprising that Wolseley and the men who accompanied him made much of the difficulties they encountered in descending the Winnipeg River. They were, after all, novices in the techniques of white water navigation. It should be remembered, however, that Hudson's Bay Company boats had long used the river as a highway, and the carrying places were obvious and in good condition. Moreover, in August the water level was low and the worst places had lost their terrors. The portages, while numerous, were short. It is clear from the accounts of the Expedition that the troops had no real problems on the Winnipeg, however exciting their experiences were to greenhorn boatmen. Good guides had been obtained at Fort Frances. The labour involved was trying to men unaccustomed to such work; but the actual dangers did not equal those that Canadians had faced

Officers 1st (Ontario) Rifles. From left to right: Staff Sergeant Douglas, Brigade Major James MacLeod, Major Griffiths Wainwright, Adjutant Captain S. Parsons.

for generations on the Ottawa, or its tributaries such as the Gatineau, or those of the St. Maurice, over which Canadian lumbermen had travelled for years. Nor were they any worse than those which Major Crofton had faced when he led 347 soldiers, 17 women and 19 children to Fort Garry in 1846.[16] Nevertheless one must confess to feeling a certain sympathy for Captain Huyshe when he wrote, on reaching Fort Alexander, "No more portages, thank God!"[17] He was exhausted. Like his comrades, who travelled in the heavy boats, he was weary of rivers, boats, rocks and portages.

Here, at Fort Alexander, larger and more imposing than Fort Frances, and located on high ground some 15 metres above the river level, the troops were greeted by Donald A. Smith of the Hudson's Bay Company. It was a happy occasion. Huyshe was ecstatic. Fresh bread and butter! He had seldom "enjoyed anything more thoroughly," and the "pipe of peace which followed it." Not the least of all was "the happy consciousness that the hateful portage-strap would cease to gall our foreheads for some time to come."[18]

III

Relying on local gossip as dependable military intelligence, Wolseley decided not to wait for the militia but to push on promptly, despite the fact that he had promised to assemble his force at Fort Alexander. The troops might discard tump lines and portage straps; but there was no rest or relaxation for them. The next day, after divine service — it was Sunday, 21 August— the officers and men of the British regulars again embarked in their river craft. For a few short hours there was no rowing or poling. With a favouring breeze behind them, the 50 boatloads of men and arms bore up for Elk Island and landed on a sandy beach about 32 kilometres from Fort Alexander. On the following day they rose at 0300 hours. They embarked once again and moved off in a southerly direction towards the mouth of the Red River. Here the shallow waters made it necessary for them to follow a narrow channel, already marked with a buoy and stake. Shortly after noon the leading boats landed, a meal was served, and once again the soldiers took to the oars, with Lieutenant Butler and Assistant Controller Irvine in the lead boat with orders to report anything unusual or suspicious.[19] Behind followed Wolseley and behind him, Lieutenant-Colonel R. F. Fielden of the 60th. The boats bearing the troops were drawn up in two lines. At long last, Wolseley's Red River Expeditionary Force was moving up the reed-fringed river that gave the force its name. Lieutenant Riddell of the 60th was struck by the contrast between the country in which he was now moving with his commander, to that through which he had travelled ever since his arrival at Prince Arthur's Landing three months earlier. From the dramatic to the dull, from the exciting to the commonplace. Here were no rocks, no forests, no running streams, no thundering waterfalls; only flat ground, a slow-moving river lined with rushes, swamps and vast numbers of ducks, geese and other waterfowl.[20]

While the troops were still some kilometres short of the Lower Fort, they encountered a band of Indians. They were Swampy Crees, led by Chief Henry Prince, whom Lieutenant-Colonel J. S. Dennis had endeavoured to enlist to help the beleaguered William McDougall back in December 1869. There was the customary exchange of presents and palaver, of pork and flour in return for expressions of welcome and loyalty, all enlivened by the clatter of a *feu de joie*. Wolseley did not mention it in his journal, but Huyshe was struck by the fact that nobody, not even the Indians, seemed to know what was happening in Fort Garry. Was Riel going to offer resistance or was he not?[21] Hoping to obtain information of some kind, Wolseley sent a messenger to the officer in charge of the Hudson Bay's Company post at the Lower Fort, William Flett. All that Flett could offer was the information that Riel was still in charge at Upper Fort Garry and that Bishop Taché was expected to arrive at any moment in St. Boniface with an amnesty for Riel in his pocket.[22] The only positive news was that of far-off events in Europe where the armies of Napoleon III were suffering humiliating defeats at the hands of the Germans.[23]

Again reveillé at 0330 hours. A cup of tea and the troops began to move. At 0800 hours they had breakfast, this time at the Lower Fort. Here began the preparations for the expected battle. The boats were lightened; and with four days' rations only, the soldiers re-embarked, to continue the advance towards the Upper Fort. Captain Butler, as intelligence officer, was sent on horseback to examine the country on the right bank of the river. The *Globe* reporter wrote of him, rather unkindly, but not untruthfully as

> ... being somewhere, doing something for our security
> — we do not know exactly what; but the idea of a man
> patrolling an unknown country with a seven-shot
> revolving-rifle, gives his services great value in our
> eyes.[24]

*Henry Prince, Chief of the Indians
in the lower Red River valley.*

Captain N. W. Wallace's company of the 60th formed the advanced guard. His task was to skirmish across country between the river and the road. His men were to keep about 400 metres ahead of the boats and to detain all persons proceeding up river. Wallace's force was, however, to keep in touch with the main body at all times by means of flag signals.

During the course of the afternoon, Captain Wallace's men brought in several detainees for questioning. They also acquired "a motley collection of horses, ponies, and mules."[25] Wolseley refers briefly to these in his journal, stating that Wallace's company was mounted "on ponies and in country carts."[26] In his entry for 24 August he refers to mounting "the Colonel and his Staff."[27] Both Riddell and Huyshe found the country horses more amusing than useful. Riddell says that these animals were brought in front of the astonished company, and the men told-off, as they stood in the ranks, to mount them. "Please, Sir, I can't ride," said one rather frightened soldier, imploringly. "I don't care a rap; get onto that mule," said the colonel aggressively, pointing, as he spoke, to a half-starved looking brute with a foal standing besides her. The unhappy soldier looked at the animal, approached cautiously and, watching his opportunity, clambered on its back and, "in company with the foal, took up his position in the ranks of the Light Cavalry."[28] Huyshe says that the men thought it "fine fun", except possibly those who did not know how to ride, to scour the country as "Mounted Rifles."[29] One man, a bugler, did not think it "fine fun" for when sounding his bugle, he was tossed "gracefully into a ditch close by," as soon as the first notes of his bugle sounded in the ears of the terrified animal.[30] Would not the Métis buffalo hunters have been convulsed by the comedy provided by Wolseley's impromptu cavalry?

While the horsemen slowly advanced, they were kept company by the infantry, and by the gunners with their cannons mounted in the bows of the boats — gunboats on the Red River! By evening the men were within nine and a half kilometres of their destination. Here Wolseley decided to halt. Outlying picquets were thrown out on all sides of the camp, and anyone coming within the cordon of sentries was detained. Meanwhile rain began to fall. All night it poured down. The picquets were drenched to the skin, as they huddled around their camp fires, with no cover from the storm. They did not know that, not far away, Riel was watching them from horseback. Neither did they know what the next day would bring. They knew only that the Canadian components of the Red River force were too far away to be of any help. Wolseley, however, was not interested in the two militia battalions; he was looking forward to an encounter between his regulars and the Métis. He wrote in his *Narrative*, "The 'shave' that night was, that we should have a fight; and it was well that we had something to cheer us, for a more dreary attempt at repose it is impossible to imagine."[31]

IV

24 August was something of a letdown. Both for Wolseley and for the troops of the Red River Expedition daylight came slowly and sullenly. The rain continued to descend in torrents. Everything was wet. It was difficult even to light the fires. The skirmishers steathily moved forward to a position about 365 metres in advance of the main column. Nearby a few inhabitants of Winnipeg turned out to see the fireworks. But there were no fireworks, no flag flying from the fort, no opposition. Only empty guns and an empty fort. No arrests were made; no attempt was made to pursue and capture the Métis president or his associates. Many of the soldiers had looked for glory at the

(Form No. 1)

Montreal Telegraph Company,

Connecting with all the Principal Cities and Towns in

CANADA AND THE UNITED STATES.

Office, opposite Merchants' Exchange, St. Sacrament St.

Terms and Conditions on which all Messages are received by this Company.

In order to guard against and correct as much as possible some of the errors arising from atmospheric and other causes appertaining to telegraphy, every important message should be REPEATED, by being sent back from the station at which it is to be received to the station from which it is originally sent. Half the usual price will be charged for repeating the message, and while this Company in good faith will endeavour to send messages correctly and promptly, it will not be responsible for errors or delays in the transmission or delivery, nor for the non-delivery of REPEATED messages, beyond two hundred times the sum paid for sending the message, unless a special agreement for insurance be made in writing, and the amount of risk specified on this agreement, and paid at the time of sending the message. Nor will the Company be responsible for any error or delay in the transmission or delivery, or for the non-delivery, of ANY UNREPEATED message, beyond the amount paid for sending the same, unless in like manner specially insured, and amount of risk stated herein, and paid for at the time. No liability is assumed for errors in cypher or obscure messages; nor for any error or neglect by any other Company over whose lines this message may be sent to reach its destination, and this Company is hereby made the agent of the sender of this message to forward it over the lines extending beyond those of this Company. No agent or employee is allowed to vary these terms, or make any other or verbal agreement, nor any promise as to the time of performance, and no one but a Superintendent is authorized to make a special agreement for insurance.

JAMES DAKERS, Secretary.   HUGH ALLAN, President.

No. of Words _____ 740   No. of Message _____

B   Montreal, 31. 8. 1870

By Telegraph from Fort Garry 24 via St Cloud 31st

To Mrs Wolseley
                Care Military Secy.
                        Montreal

I arrived here safely this
morning Riel and Company bolting
from Fort as we arrived
no fight in them hope
to be back by first
october

                G. J. Wolseley

        Collect 82
            & 439

Wolseley's telegram to his wife, 24 August 1870.

price of fatigue. All they found was fatigue at the price of glory. Most of the Red River men who had supported Riel either went home or into hiding, hoping to be forgotten. Those who called themselves "Loyalists" were loud in their expressions of disappointment, and belligerently urged the arrest of the principal leaders of the Provisional Government or offered themselves to act as the government's agents to effect these arrests. Wolseley, however, wisely prohibited his troops from acting as policemen on behalf of the "Loyalists". In any case, he lacked any authority to issue warrants of arrest. What he did do, was to free his troops from further military duties for the rest of the day and give them a chance, after a long period of drought, to drink Winnipeg dry. The civilian, Alexander Begg, one of the English-speaking Manitobans not unfavourably disposed towards Riel, wrote:

> Too much praise cannot be accorded to the 60th, for their honourable and just behaviour on their arrival at Fort Garry. Their conduct at that time is a page in the history of their regiment, which they may be proud of; and the people of Red River will never forget their short stay amongst them. No one was insulted; no one was interfered with; no one was harmed; everything went on pleasantly. Coming off a trip such as the men had gone through, it is not to be wondered at if they indulged rather freely in liquor, — what body of men would not do so. . . .[32]

Wolseley's intelligence officer, William Butler, who was not a Manitoban, wrote, "A wild scene of drunkenness and debauchery amongst the voyageurs followed the arrival of the troops in Winnipeg," encouraged, apparently, by the fact that the village "produced, as if by magic, more saloons than any city of twice its size in the States could boast of."[33]

It was not just the voyageurs and Indians who participated in this period of "unbridled celebration."[34] When James Macleod and Sam Steele arrived several days later with the militia, they found the muddy streets of Winnipeg "littered with bodies of drunken settlers, Indians, and one pet bear on the loose." According to some of their descendants, the Drevers were still ladling out rum to boozy celebrants in front of Rothney Cottage.[35]

Had Wolseley been named Lieutenant-Governor, as he had hoped, and possessed the civil authority to do so, he might have taken steps

The Hon. A.G. Archibald, first
Lieutenant-Governor of Manitoba,
1870-73.

to control the situation. Then again, he might only have attempted to pursue and arrest former members of the Provisional Government. Certainly that was on his mind. He made no effort to conceal the fact that he considered Riel and his councillors to be dangerous "rebels". The Canadian government, careless though it had been in preparing the Red River population for the transfer of their country to Canada in 1869, had wisely ignored Wolseley's not so subtle hints to give him political as well as military powers. Instead of naming Wolseley civil governor, Ottawa appointed a bilingual civilian, a Nova Scotian, Adams George Archibald, as the Queen's representative in the newly formed province. Archibald was neutral and not closely associated with the federal government in Ottawa; certainly not with the Ontario pressure groups that had so loudly demanded the despatch of a punitive, military force to Manitoba.

It was Archibald's neutrality that explains why his nomination was well received in the western province. In the interval between 15 July, the date fixed for the establishment of the new province, and 15 August, when it was expected Archibald would assume his new responsibilities, the Governor General, Sir John Young, undertook to act as temporary Lieutenant-Governor. It was the federal government's pronounced desire that the new Lieutenant-Governor should arrive at Fort Garry before, or at the latest, at the same time as Wolseley's men should reach Fort Garry. Unfortunate delays prevented him from doing so. On 23 August, the day Wolseley was approaching Fort Garry, Archibald had barely reached Fort Frances, where the militiaman, John Kerr, was a member of the choir that serenaded him.[36] He hurried on as quickly as possible, making use of Dawson's road from Lake of the Woods; but he lost the race to Wolseley.

About 1600 hours on Friday 2 September, word reached Wolseley that Lieutenant-Governor Archibald was on the last leg of his journey. A guard of honour of the 1st (Ontario) Rifles was ordered to parade and preparations were made for the militia gunners to fire a salute. Finally, about 2030 hours, Mr. Archibald arrived; the honours were given and acknowledged, and Archibald paid a suitable tribute to Colonel Wolseley:

> I take the earliest opportunity in my power to congratulate you on the magnificent success of the Expedition under your command. I can judge of the work you have had to do all the better from having seen for myself the physical obstacles that had to be met and overcome, obstacles which I assure you exceed anything I could have imagined.
>
> It is impossible not to feel that the men who have triumphed over such difficulties must not only have themselves worked well, but also must have been well led, and I should not be doing justice to my own feelings, if I were not on my arrival here to repeat the expression of admiration extorted from me, as I passed along, in view of the difficulties you had to meet, and which you have so triumphantly surmounted.[37]

Meanwhile the regulars were preparing for their return to central Canada. Wolseley had ordered a strong picquet to patrol the streets until all was quiet;[38] and only a few bewattled Ontario soldiers were caught drinking to any extent after their first night in Winnipeg. The voyageurs and the returning settlers were the people who provided the real problem. Neither were subject to military discipline. They could do as they pleased. Butler says that the Iroquois became "terribly" intoxicated and refused to go to the boats.[39] Eventually discipline took over, and on 29 August two companies of the 60th, in uniforms now ragged and patched, started down the Red River, bound for Fort Alexander. It was not exactly an orderly departure, not as Wolseley would have liked it. At first the Iroquois refused to get into the boats. Then there was the black bear — a trophy mascot recently acquired by the 60th. Here is Butler's picture of the departure:

> What a business it was! Drunken Iroquois tumbling about, and the bear, with 100 men after him, scuttling in every direction. Then when the bear would be captured and put safely back into his boat, half a dozen Iroquois would get out and run a-muck through every thing. . . . At length they all got away down the river. Thus, during the first week of September, the whole of the regulars departed once more to try the torrents of the Winnipeg. . . . [40]

On 10 September Wolseley took his leave of Lieutenant-Governor Archibald. In his canoe he soon overtook the more slow-moving soldiers. The return journey of the 60th Rifles was uneventful. The weather was good, the flies and mosquitoes had vanished and the route was familiar. When the troops arrived at Shebandowan Lake, they found waggons waiting to transport the baggage to the ships at Prince Arthur's Landing. For the soldiers themselves, it was an easy two days' march from the lake on which they had embarked a little over two months previously, to the beach where they had set up their encampment in May. On 18 October Lindsay reported the safe arrival of the British contingent in central Canada.[41] Several weeks later, both Lindsay and "the teapot general," as Wolseley was now called by the men of the 60th, were on the high seas, on their way back to England. One soldier had been left behind at Winnipeg. He was William Butler. The fact was, he did not choose to go. The Canadian West was getting into his blood and he wanted to see more of it.[42]

V

This was not the way that Sir John Macdonald or Bishop Alexandre Antonin Taché had hoped the troubles in Red River would end. Even as late as the day Wolseley departed from Fort Garry, Macdonald was still making a bid to keep a British garrison in Canada.[43] The *Globe*, the Prime Minister and the Bishop were all in agreement in querying the advisability of the British decision to shuck their colonial responsibilities. "Is it to be expected," asked the *Globe*, "that on this handful of people shall be thrown the defence, and development of this half-continent?"[44] Taché feared that "disorders" might rip the Settlement apart, were the British not to remain over the winter,[45] and Sir John Young, the Governor General, was inclined to agree with him. Why should the British troops not remain in Red River until the heat engendered by the events of 1869-1870 had cooled during the winter of 1870-1871? But the British government would countenance no such proposal. The Colonial Secretary simply replied:

> . . . when the authority of the Dominion has been duly established in Manitoba, the responsibility for all internal measures will rest with the Colonial Government, and it appears to Her Majesty's Government, that any attempt on their part indirectly to interfere with the local administration would be unjustifiable, and would by weakening the authority of the Dominion tend to produce those disorders which Bishop Taché apprehends.[46]

CHAPTER NINE

Manitoba's First Year 1870-1871

I

When Wolseley's troops arrived at Fort Garry on 24 August, they were expecting to do battle with the armed supporters of the Provisional Government. Whatever the politicians may have had in mind when they authorized the military expedition, Wolseley and his men believed that battle was the basic purpose for which they had been recruited. It is clear from Wolseley's own writings that he quite anticipated resistance from Riel and the need to use force against the Métis. In his *Narrative* he wrote:

> Sensible men who had but recently returned via the United States from Manitoba said that our force ought at least to be three times stronger than it was: that Riel was on the look-out for our advance, and intended to defend step by step and mile by mile the difficult country we should have to pass through, where a few good huntsmen, accustomed to the woods, could annihilate an army; in fact, that General Braddock's fate was in store for us. . . . Never did any expedition have more lugubrious prophecies made concerning it.[1]

Threats of annihilation, however, did not frighten the soldiers. If anything the troops were, according to their commander, "encouraged by intelligence received from Red River announcing Riel's determination to show fight."[2]

Was Riel really determined to pit his Métis against Wolseley's soldiers? The historical evidence suggests that he was not. He had failed to anticipate the strong reaction that the shooting of Thomas Scott aroused in Ontario; but at no time did he consider throwing his supporters into a stand-up battle with Wolseley's regulars. The simple fact is that he did not have the soldiers to do so. Riel's men, Métis tripmen and hunters, crewmen from the western fur brigades, men noted for their toughness and turbulence, men unemployed during the winter months, were, once the summer returned, off to the plains and the western rivers, to resume their normal activities. The buffalo hunters, too, superb horsemen every one of them, all potential dashing cavalrymen, were also absent from Fort Garry during the summer season, leaving Riel's French cavalry officer, Norbert Gay, with only a handful of "soldiers" to carry out manoeuvres. Hardly a sufficient force with which to take on Wolseley's troops. In any event, what good would prairie horsemen have been in the rocky declivities of the Dawson route?

The only force that might have interfered seriously with Wolseley's march would have been an Indian one. The local Indians, however, had never been part of Riel's entourage. Chief Henry Prince believed that he had more to gain from continued support of the Great White Mother, and Crooked Neck had early arrived at the same conclusion. The Saulteaux never showed any disposition to throw in their lot with Riel and the Provisional Government. In any event, they were not accustomed to fight in large numbers as were the Sioux.[3]

Moreover, what reason had Riel to disbelieve Wolseley's profession of peaceful intent as indicated in his Proclamation — a document that Riel had helped publish in the *New Nation*? Was it logical for him to conclude that the promises of an amnesty, given by Bishop Taché and Father Noel Ritchot, were, at best, misunderstandings on the part of the two clergymen, or, at worst, deliberate falsehoods on the part of the politicians?[4] Probably more than anything else, it was the hope for an amnesty, uncertain though it was, hard on the adoption of the Manitoba Act by the Canadian Parliament, that persuaded Riel and his councillors to accept Wolseley's assurances that his was an expedition of peaceful intent, assurances that reduced the military expedition of 1870 to little more than a demonstration of the Canadian soldier's ability to adapt to his surroundings and his capacity to overcome physical difficulties, when well equipped, well motivated and well led.

II

As early as 6 December 1869, Sir John Young, the Governor General of Canada, issued a Proclamation promising an amnesty to all

Monseigneur Alexandre Taché,
Bishop of St. Boniface, 1870.

those who had taken part in the initial Convention that met at Fort Garry to draft the "Bill of Rights". Donald A. Smith had a copy of Young's Proclamation in his pocket when he addressed the mass meetings of January 1870; but, for some unexplained reason, he did not produce it and make it public. When Bishop Taché, hurriedly returned from the meeting of the Ecumenical Council in Rome at the request of the Canadian government, to assist in the work of pacifying the Red River malcontents, he stopped over in Ottawa to discuss the Red River situation with the Canadian ministers, Sir John A. Macdonald, Sir George Cartier and Joseph Howe; and from them he received full authority to promise an amnesty to the man who had seized Fort Garry and set up his Provisional Government. Macdonald expressly stated that "not only will there be a general amnesty . . . but . . . the Canadian Government will stand between the insurgents and all harm."[5]

Early in March, Bishop Taché was back in Red River. When he arrived in St. Boniface, Métis soldiers asked Riel's permission to wait on the Bishop and receive his blessing. Riel would not have dared to refuse this request. He himself however, held aloof. "Ce n'est pas Mgr.

Taché qui passe, ce n'est pas l'Evêque de St. Boniface, c'est le Canada qui passe,"[6] he is alleged to have said. If true, it was a shrewd observation. Riel was more than a little suspicious of the Bishop, whom he regarded as another Canadian agent. He therefore placed a guard at the entrance to the Bishop's home, and while not interfering with His Grace's movements, kept himself informed of the identity of those persons with whom the Bishop was in contact. On 11 March, Taché interviewed Riel, Lépine and other Métis leaders, told them that the Canadian government was favourably disposed towards them and assured them that the Governor General's Proclamation of 6 December covered all offences up to the present date. He gave them his solemn word that all irregularities of the past would be overlooked and forgiven. Taché felt justified in what he did and what he said, convinced that the assurances he had received in Ottawa embraced everything up to the time of his return to Red River.[7]

The Canadian ministers, whatever their private opinions may have been, did not consider it politically desirable to expand upon the vague terms of Sir John Young's outdated Proclamation or to proclaim the amnesty which they had so freely promised. They were taken aback by the strength and malignancy of public opinion in Ontario. Howe, was, therefore, hedging the issue when he wrote Taché to the effect that the amnesty was a matter solely for Queen Victoria, not for the Canadian Cabinet. Howe's letter is enlightening. He wrote:

> I am confident that when you regard the obstructions which have been interposed to the adoption of a liberal and enlightened policy for Manitoba, you will not be disposed to relax your exertions until that policy is formally established.[8]

Here was no disavowal of Taché's conviction that an amnesty had been promised; no instruction to the Bishop to correct any statement that he had made to the Métis; only a request to continue in his role as an intermediary between Ottawa and Fort Garry.

When the delegates authorized to go to Ottawa by Riel's Provisional Government reached Ontario, two of them, Father Ritchot and Alfred H. Scott, were arrested on a charge of complicity in the "murder" of Thomas Scott. However, following the intervention of the federal government, the charges laid against the two men were dropped. Ritchot and Black — Scott was more or less a cypher and played little part in the discussions — began the negotiations that led, in a few short weeks, to the adoption of the Manitoba Act by the Federal Parliament. Ritchot insisted upon an amnesty for the leaders of the Provisional Government, making it quite clear that, in his opinion, Sir John Young's Proclamation of 6 December did not cover the situation as it existed.[9] The priest from St. Norbert was a tough negotiator, quite impervious to fine words and flattery. Assurances, however nicely worded, were simply not enough. He wanted nothing less than a positive statement about the amnesty. All he ever received was Sir George Cartier's advice to forward a petition to the Queen, and the Minister's personal assurances that the Governor General would support it. In his journal Ritchot wrote:

> I refused to do so at first and I ended by consenting because it is only a matter of form, I was told, that it was necessary to forward a document to Her Majesty and that the Governor was a little embarrassed at the thought of presenting it himself lest he should compromise himself.[10]

Although Ritchot yielded to the blandishments of Cartier, he remained uneasy. The whole affair seemed to be developing into a kind of run-around between Cartier and the Governor General; and so he returned to Red River. He took with him no written document, only great unease of mind. How much trust could really be placed upon oral assurances? Particularly those of politicians? The questions bothered him. And they bothered Taché. If only because the sole positive action so far taken by the federal government had been in the direction of organizing a military expedition to be sent to Red River. Accordingly, Taché once more packed his bag and returned to Canada early in July, determined to obtain something definite out of Sir George Cartier. Discussing the whole question once again with Sir George in Montreal, Taché agreed to go with him to see the Governor General, who was at that time observing the magnificent scenery of Niagara Falls.

The movements of the Bishop and the Cabinet Minister were not unknown in Toronto. Word had been leaked to the Ontario "Loyalists" that Taché and Cartier were discussing Manitoba and Riel, and G. T. Denison, the mainspring of the anti-Riel agitation in Ontario, resolved to make the province too hot a place for both the Bishop and the Minister. Aware that the presence of the Minister of Militia in

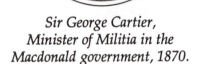

*Révérend Noel-Joseph
Ritchot of the parish of
Saint-Norbert.*

*Sir George Cartier,
Minister of Militia in the
Macdonald government, 1870.*

Toronto, in all probability, would be recognized by a guard of honour, Denison hastened to get in touch with Lieutenant-Colonel W. S. Durie, the Deputy Adjutant-General of Military District No. 2. He threatened that should any attempt be made to mount a guard of honour for Cartier, he, Denison and his friends, "would take possession of the armoury that night;" they "would have ten men to his one, and if anyone in Toronto wanted to resist," they were "ready to fight it out on the streets." Durie replied that Denison "was threatening revolution," to which the belligerent "loyalist" replied, "Yes, I know I am, and we can make it one. A half continent is at stake, and it is a stake worth fighting for."[11]

Of course there was no revolution. All that happened was that Cartier and Taché detrained at Kingston. While Cartier took a steamer to Niagara, Taché travelled through the United States, reaching Niagara Falls by way of Buffalo. The interview with the Governor General was held at a local hotel, the Clifton House. Sir John Young had been a strong proponent of military action against the Métis during the early months of 1870, considerably more so than the Prime

Minister. To the Governor General, Riel had been and still was, a rebel. As Governor General, it was difficult for Young to come out openly and parade his Orange sympathies, but they were always there. They were part of his Ulster heritage. Yet his role as Governor General imposed upon him at least the appearance of neutrality. At the meeting at the Clifton House he was, therefore, cool in his manner, although not very collected. Taché, too, was cool, and very correct. All that Young did was point to the Proclamation of 6 December, accompanying his gesture with the words, "Here is my proclamation, it covers the whole case." Then he added, "See Sir George Cartier; he knows my views upon the subject, and he will tell you all."[12] It was no more and no less than he said on several previous occasions. Young made no new promises, leaving the Bishop with the feeling that everything was as it had been before. Nothing had been added; nothing had been retracted. Taché departed in a state that was collected but not very cool. As he left, Adams Archibald entered. The Nova Scotian had come to be sworn in as the new Lieutenant-Governor of Manitoba.

Taché returned, disappointed, to St. Boniface. All he carried with him was the already familiar oral promise from Sir George Cartier that an amnesty would be forthcoming from the Crown, and that this amnesty would cover everything, including Scott's execution. On 8 August the Bishop set out for the west, arriving in St. Boniface on 23 August, the morning Wolseley's troops set off in their boats, rowing upriver from the Lower Fort, flanked by an improvised cavalry and taking every precaution against any possible surprise, except the one that greeted them — silence. No booming cannon fire; no rattle of musketry; no opposition. Several members of the Provisional Government came to the Bishop's house to be assured that there was nothing to fear. There would be an amnesty. It was only then that the Bishop learned, to his consternation, that Wolseley's soldiers were slowly making their way to Fort Garry from the Lower Fort. They looked as if they meant business — military business.

Taché could hardly believe the news. Then, next morning, when he opened the door of his house, he could see them, green-coated soldiers, engaged in what, to Taché's eyes, appeared to be a warlike manoeuvre. A month earlier Riel had written to Taché about a welcome for the troops and the Lieutenant-Governor "with enthusiasm"[13] and an official reception. These were now out of the question. On the morning of 24 August, the so-called "missionaries of peace" looked much more like the apostles of war. Riel's world and his hopes evaporated. The Bishop wondered if he had been misled by the politicians, including the Governor General.

III

Following the flight of Riel and his principal councillors on the morning of 24 August, the Red River Settlement, temporarily at least, was without a civil government of any kind. Colonel Wolseley's authority did not extend beyond control of the soldiers serving under his command. He was, therefore, unable to issue warrants for the arrest of any civilian, whether bartender, voyageur, Indian or Métis buffalo hunter. From a purely legal standpoint, Riel's Provisional Government probably had the best claim to represent civilian authority. It had, at least, received a certain cachet from the fact that the federal cabinet, including the Prime Minister and his principal colleagues, Sir George Cartier and Joseph Howe, had received its delegates and negotiated with them the terms of the agreement by which Red River would enter the Canadian Confederation as the Province of Manitoba, and from the embodiment of those terms in a formal Act of the Canadian Parliament. As the Red River delegates were departing from Ottawa, Ritchot, had asked who would govern Manitoba, pending the arrival of the Lieutenant-Governor. Cartier replied, "let Mr. Riel continue to maintain order and govern the country as he has done up to the present moment." He added, "Let Riel maintain peace and not make *des sottises* . . . because he has to-day to fear enemies who will make him believe that we are hostile to them. The Fenians also will make efforts to deceive him." Then, having been assured by Ritchot that Riel was quite capable of carrying on the local administration on an interim basis, Cartier added, "Let him continue till the Governor arrives."[14]

Riel's flight on 24 August posed an entirely new problem. Without Riel and his councillors, the Provisional Government, for all practical purposes ceased to exist. What was the alternative source of authority? Wolseley took the view that the Hudson's Bay Company, as the last government immediately prior to Riel's assumption of power, possessed what might be considered a residual power. Although he knew as did everybody else, that the Company was highly unpopular,[15] not unreasonably, he turned to Donald A. Smith, as the senior representative of the Hudson's Bay Company, asking him to assume the responsibility of Governor *pro tem*. Smith was not unaware of the weakness of his position, but he agreed to do so. As a

Donald A. Smith

result, the Hudson's Bay Company, although for only a brief period between 24 August and 2 September, became the *de facto*, if not the *de jure* civil authority in the new province. Smith issued an appeal to the people of Red River and authorized the establishment of special constables to maintain some kind of law and order in the Settlement. It could only be a temporary arrangement, and no man could have been happier than Donald A. Smith when Archibald finally arrived to assume the lawful responsibilities of the civil power in Manitoba on 2 September.

Three days after Wolseley's occupation of Fort Garry on 27 August, during the brief Smith period, the first Canadian soldiers began to arrive in the Red River Settlement. At about 1800 hours, Major Griffiths Wainwright, with two companies of the Ontario Rifles, reached Fort Garry. He had been delayed at Lake Winnipeg by the same wind and rain storm that had given so damp a greeting to the 60th when they took possession of Fort Garry on 24 August. On the following day Wolseley and Donald A. Smith inspected the buildings at both the Upper and Lower Forts. Their purpose was to determine the suitability of these buildings, formerly used for commercial purposes, as military barracks during the months to come. By 31 August all the Ontarians had arrived. The Quebec regiment was still *en route*, as was also the Ontario company travelling overland from Lake of the Woods. It was Wolseley's choice that the 1st (Ontario) Rifles should be stationed at Upper Fort Garry with one company, under Captain Henry Cook, sent to occupy the Hudson's Bay Company post at Pembina on the Canadian-United States frontier. The 2nd (Quebec) Rifles were to be housed at Lower Fort Garry. The decision to billet the Quebec corps at the Lower Fort, may well have been determined by the fact that the Ontarians had preceded them in the march from Prince Arthur's Landing to Fort Garry. If we may believe John Kerr, the Upper Fort was not a very comfortable billet. In a letter to his father, dated 23 October 1870, he wrote, "Fort Garry is a pretty place at a *distance*, but go near and you are disgusted with the filth and dirt which is seen on all sides. Everything is awfully dear here . . . wood is a very scarce article, hardly any timber around the place. And cold!"[16]

Some members, at least, of the Ontario Battalion had joined the Expeditionary Force under the stimulus of the anti-French and anti-Catholic agitation of *Canada First* and the Orange Order. It might, therefore, have been more diplomatic to domicile the Ontarians at the Lower Fort. Here they would have been among the downriver Scottish and English-speaking population that had largely held aloof from events of the autumn and winter months. The Ontarians would there have been well away from St. Boniface and the French-speaking parishes on the Red and Assiniboine Rivers. By the same token, to have billeted the Quebec Battalion at the Upper Fort would have had the effect of easing tensions in the upriver parishes. To place the Ontario militiamen so close to the main French settlements indicated considerable lack of political judgment on Wolseley's part. When the new commander, Lieutenant-Colonel S. P. Jarvis, succeeded to the command on Wolseley's departure, he found himself pretty well committed to this rather insensitive arrangement of the battalions.

IV

The most pressing problem facing Lieutenant-Governor Archibald, on his arrival in Red River on 2 September was that imposed upon him by those members of the local population who had responded with such alacrity to Lieutenant-Colonel Dennis's appeal to arms in December, 1869; the men who assumed the title of the "Friends of Canada". Men such as John Shultz, Joseph Lynch, George MacVicar, Thomas Lusted, James Ashdown, Peter McArthur, John

O'Donnell and others who, for what they had considered their bounden duty, had been forced to spend days and nights in the cold and cheerless cells of Fort Garry. Some of them had escaped and returned to Canada; others had found refuge in the Scottish parishes or at Portage la Prairie; still others had made their adjustment to the changing political situation within the Settlement. But most of them were still harbouring resentments that were, in some instances, to be carried unto the second and third generations. Certainly the first generation continued to nourish resentments against Riel and the various members of his Provisional Government, and looked forward to redress or revenge. Their logical allies were any Ontarians whose motive in volunteering their services in the 1st (Ontario) Rifles was to

revenge the shooting of Thomas Scott, and who, according to Archibald, had "taken a vow before leaving home to pay off all scores by shooting down any Frenchman that was in any way connected with that event."[17] In his evidence before the Select Committee appointed by the federal government to ascertain the causes of the "troubles" in the North West in 1869-70, Archibald stated that, on his arrival in the Red River Settlement, he found feelings between the English Canadians and the French Métis in Manitoba, "one of intense dislike"[18] for each other. He pointed out that when the volunteers took discharge from the Ontario Rifles, some of them joined forces with the "Friends of Canada". R. G. MacBeth refers to the early weeks of the Archibald administration as a period of "great unsettlement." He wrote:

Lieutenant-Colonel S.P. Jarvis, Commanding Officer 1st (Ontario) Rifles, who succeeded Colonel Wolseley as senior officer in Manitoba, 1870.

188

The soldiers, released from the struggle of the half-military, half-voyageur life they had led for the past few months, were more or less disposed to take advantage of any opportunities that offered themselves for the somewhat fast and furious pace allowed by the codeless life of a frontier; and as they looked with some bitterness upon the half-breed population, as on those whose compatriots had imprisoned many and murdered one of their countrymen, conflicts more or less sharp were not infrequent on the streets of the straggling village.[19]

On the other hand, Alexander Begg, a Quebec-born anglophone, who had come from Canada to enter a business partnership in Winnipeg with A. G. B. Bannatyne, and who lived through the exciting days of the Red River Rising which he described in his books and diary, was inclined to blame, not the militia soldiers, but the old "Friends of Canada," for the nasty violence that marked the early months of the Archibald administration. The volunteers, he wrote, on the whole "behaved well, and soon won their way into the favourable opinion of the residents, although there were a few turbulent characters among the soldiers, who gave their officers a good deal of trouble."[20]

The first step taken by Archibald in the direction of easing the tensions so obvious within the Settlement, was to insert in the *New Nation* newspaper, a notice that he would hold a levée on 6 September at which his commission as Lieutenant-Governor of Manitoba would be read. Former members of the Council of Assiniboia, members of the clergy of all denominations and "a good representation of the men of business and the farmers of the Settlement" were invited to attend. Neither Louis Riel nor Ambroise Lépine was present; but one guest who accepted Archibald's invitation was Thomas Bunn, the English-speaking half-breed from St. Clements, who had been a member of the first Convention and who had, on a motion by Louis Riel, chaired the mass meeting of 19 and 20 January 1870 when Donald A. Smith presented Canada's case to the shivering multitude standing on the square of Fort Garry. Bunn had also served as secretary of Riel's Provisional Government. The attendance at the levée was good and Archibald was pleased. The one sour note was an effort on the part of the "loyal" element to distribute inflammatory leaflets urging the people of Winnipeg to "Tar and feather Tom Bunn"; "Who consorted with murderers?— Tom Bunn"."[21] Despite these disturbing activities on the part of hostile demonstrators, Archibald was generally satisfied with the public response. It was, indeed, with some satisfaction that he wrote to Ottawa on 10 September:

> My efforts have not been without some success, as I learn from all quarters. I am glad to find that my views of the course which ought to be pursued, meet with a general measure of acceptance, even from those who might, under the circumstances, have been supposed to be the least likely to acquiesce in those views.[22]

However, a few warming words accompanied by a few warming drinks did not remove the bitter taste of past memories. For several years, violence remained a familiar aspect of political life in Manitoba,[23] owing in large measure to the absence of any effective police force and to the presence in the Settlement of a number of men intent upon perpetuating the memory or avenging the death of Thomas Scott. On 13 September, Elzéar Goulet, who had acted as second-in-command of the Métis soldiery under Ambroise Lépine, while fleeing from a hostile mob, suffered death by drowning. Perhaps some of the volunteers were responsible; perhaps civilians were to blame for the actions that led to Goulet's death. It was easy enough to escape the law by accusing the soldiers. Certainly the historical evidence is not conclusive. Sam Steele, who was on duty with his men the night of Goulet's death, taking boats out of the Assiniboine River where they had been moored and placing them on skids near Fort Garry, relates that "two travel-stained horsemen . . . rode up to us and asked if we had seen a man named Elzéar Goulet, who, one of them stated, had commanded the firing party which shot Thomas Scott." When they found that the soldiers could provide no information "they wheeled quickly and rode off at full speed towards Winnipeg."[24]

The same night it was reported in camp that the two strangers had found Goulet seated in a local pub. When they accosted him in a menacing manner, the poor frightened man took to his heels. He ran towards the Red River, closely pursued by his accusers. Steele's account is, of course, based on hearsay; but it has a certain ring of truth about it. He stated that when Goulet "arrived at the bank he turned and threatened to shoot, but they called to him 'Fire away!' Seeing that

S.B. Steele, 1st (Ontario) Rifles,
in the early 1900s.

they would not be denied, he jumped into the river, and when he attempted to swim across, shots were fired and he sank."[25] Steele added:

> The horsemen had been followed by a crowd of people, amongst whom were two of our buglers, mere lads. No other soldiers were present, and neither of these took part in the chase, nor is it likely that any of our men would have taken part in the pursuit of the unfortunate man, even had they known that he was one of the murderers of Scott.

Steele did admit that there were in the battalion

> ... about a dozen very wild spirits, but they were kept in control by the strict discipline maintained in the regiment, and, what is sometimes better, the fear of the displeasure of their comrades, who in ways which soldiers have, could make their lives intolerable.[26]

In any event, at the time Goulet drowned, "a strong party of military police was in the town night and day, and as they were remarkable for their attention to duty, it is a certainty that they would be aware of any part taken by soldiers and would have arrested the delinquents on the spot."[27] The next day, Major Wainwright, acting on rumours he had heard from "interested parties who wished to put the blame on the military to save others," paraded the troops in the camp and accused them of being "a lot of hot-headed fanatics who had aided and abetted the death of Goulet." Steele believed that the reports of the involvement of the soldiers were circulated by "persons who would not hesitate to make political capital out of the circumstances" and who were anxious "to have the blame shifted from their shoulders to ours."[28] In this way, the military became victims of a hostile press in various parts of Canada.

One of the buglers to whom Steele referred in his statement was Joseph Tennant. He too wrote about the death of Goulet. His account differs somewhat from that of Steele. Tennant says categorically that "some" soldiers were in the pub on 13 September when Goulet was identified, and that they rushed to seize him. Whereupon Goulet dashed away, plunging into the river in an effort to swim to the St. Boniface side. Tennant described it:

> Fearing they would be balked of their prey, the frenzied mob in pursuit hurled missiles of all kinds at the hunted man and stoned him to death in the water. Goulet was a man of quiet disposition, who fell a victim to circumstances.[29]

Like Steele, Tennant resented the highly coloured accounts that appeared in the press, and the attacks that were made by sensation-mongering journalists who wrote about the "lynching" of Goulet. He added, "The whole Battalion should not have been blamed for the mad act of a few. Volunteers who came to this country to uphold law and order deeply resented the attacks . . . made upon them as a regiment. . . ."[30]

Another unfortunate violent death was that of James Tanner, an English Métis who was killed by being thrown from his buggy when his horse was frightened by unknown persons. Once again the soldiers were blamed. And once again bugler Tennant felt aggrieved. "There are bullies in every school," he wrote, "and the Ontario

Volunteers had their share of them, with all the blame attached to the battalion for the bad conduct of a few."[31]

Returning from a visit to the lower end of the Settlement, Lieutenant-Governor Archibald found the people in Winnipeg and St. Boniface greatly excited as a result of Goulet's death. He therefore gave instructions that steps should be taken immediately to investigate the circumstances surrounding the killing. Since he had not yet got around to establishing a police force, he issued instructions to Mr. H. J. G. McConville, a bilingual lawyer recently arrived from Montreal, to conduct an investigation on behalf of the Crown, sparing "no pains to find out the facts and to do all that was necessary to vindicate public justice."[32] This action he followed by appointing a number of Justices of the Peace, including representatives of all groups within the province, French and English, whites and Métis.[33]

McConville began his investigation of the death of Goulet by issuing twenty subpoenas. Dispositions were taken in writing and other witnesses were examined orally, but little real information was obtained. It did not help McConville that, of the two commissioners appointed to look into the Goulet case, one, Solomon Hamelin, understood little English, and the other, Robert McBeath (the father of the author, R. G. MacBeth) understood only a minimum of French. McConville was, therefore, required to act as interpreter as well as to conduct the investigation. He had problems. Some of the witnesses, "under the belief that this was an inquiry held secretly for the purpose of finding guilty parties, without any consideration of impartiality or justice," were unwilling to say anything.

When such evidence as could be extracted from these reluctant witnesses had been assembled, the two Justices of the Peace could not agree as to what action should be taken. One was prepared to grant warrants against three men, the first against the man who had "incited" the mob, the second against a soldier "who had pursued the deceased," and the third, against a man who had been "foremost in the pursuit" of Goulet;[34] the other commissioner stated that he "could not grant warrants against the soldier, or against the person looked upon as having incited," but that "he was ready to grant one against the party who had been foremost in the pursuit and chase of the deceased." There is no identification in the official reports of any people involved; only McConville's statement that "the most guilty, I have no doubt, according to the testimony, it would appear, is a civilian who came from Upper Canada some time ago."[35] McConville prepared a draft warrant of arrest, but it was never served.

Tanner's death was the subject of a Coroner's inquest on 2 December. Again no action could be taken. The verdict in this case was simply that Tanner

> ... died from a fracture of the skull, caused by his being thrown out of a waggon, while the horse in the said waggon was running away, and that the said horse was caused so to run away, wilfully and maliciously, by two persons unknown to this Jury, thereby causing the death of this said James Tanner.[36]

It is easy, a century or more later, to be critical of Archibald and the provincial authorities in Manitoba in those early weeks of provincial status. Perhaps a better appreciation of the problems faced by Archibald can be gained from a glimpse of the situation as seen through contemporary eyes. A historical review published by the *Manitoban* at the end of 1871, read as follows:

> The antagonism between the English and French races divided the country into two hostile camps. . . . It required great tact, great courtesy, and great firmness to dispel the elements of danger and bring about a better state of affairs. To this task the Lieutenant Governor devoted himself. . . . Gradually, the seething excitement began to subside, and in the course of a few months, a feeling of safety and security dawned upon all classes, and our people, in the usual employment of peace, began to forget the troubles and turmoils through which they had passed.[37]

An immediate result of the Goulet affair was the formation of a Manitoba Police Force, the command of which was given to Captain F. Villiers of the 2nd (Quebec) Rifles. Villiers was an accomplished horseman and, according to MacBeth, a "handsome but somewhat dissipated officer, who did good service for the time."[38] His second-in-command was the Vicomte Louis de Plainval, who subsequently succeeded Villiers in the command. A Frenchman by birth, he, too, was a member of the Quebec Rifles. Tall, handsome and distinguished looking, he had "a ringing baritone voice." An odd qualification for a policeman, perhaps, but one which earned him the regard of John Kerr,[39] and, doubtless, the music-loving citizens of Winnipeg and St. Boniface.

Louis de Plainval,
2nd (Quebec) Rifles, chief officer of
the Manitoba constabulary.

Archibald had expected to recruit his police force from the civilian population, but the response was less enthusiastic than he had hoped. It was, therefore, with a certain irritation that his Provincial Secretary, Alfred Boyd, wrote to "the Gentlemen resident in the parishes of St. Andrew, St. Peter, St. James, Kildonan, and Headingly, and in the Town of Winnipeg" who had petitioned the Lieutenant-Governor for the establishment of a police force, telling them that, although the government was offering "a rate of wages higher than is given in any of the older Provinces," nobody had come forward in any of the parishes indicated to offer their services "in the indispensable work of protecting the public peace."[40] He stated that the soldiers, stationed in Manitoba were "never intended to act as policemen" and were not to be employed in that capacity. In fact, wrote Boyd, "no free country asks or suffers soldiers to perform police duties," except when called in to aid the civil power in the event of an emergency. Without police "it is absolutely impossible to carry on civil Government in the country, or provide for the emergencies of the present, much less enter into and carry on with vigour and impartiality the enquiries to which you refer in reference to the past."[41] Since there was too little time to bring in policemen from the other provinces, the provincial authorities had no choice but to ask the military authorities to detach a number of men from military duties to enable the province to field a suitable police force. That is how and why soldiers from the two rifle battalions stationed in Manitoba, became members of the Manitoba Constabulary. In the spring when the soldiers had completed their tour of duty, several of them merely exchanged one uniform for another. John Kerr was one of them. According to Kerr, "a few" members of the Manitoba Constabulary were drawn from the civilian population, but the majority had entered Manitoba with the two volunteer battalions of the Wolseley expedition.[42]

In his summary of past events, the editor of the *Manitoban* wrote:

> We may say of the police, which has now been organized for a year, that first year though it be, and with all its shortcomings, it may fairly challenge comparison with that of older countries. For the last nine months, life and property in this Province have been as secure as in any Province in the dominion. [43]

Along with the organization of a police force came the construction of a jail. The only one existing in the country at the time of Archibald's arrival had served as a military hospital for the troops. It was not an adequate lock-up; "its doors had so often yielded to pressure from within, that it could hardly be looked upon as a place of safe custody." A police station was therefore built in Winnipeg and a suitable building in the Lower Fort rented from the Hudson's Bay Company, was repaired and remodeled for the purposes of a provincial jail and penitentiary.[44]

V

Rather than pursue former members of the Provisional Government with warrants and threats, Archibald devoted much of his time and most of his efforts to organizing the civil administration. His declared object was to conciliate all groups, French, English and Métis, and to avoid identifying himself with one faction or the other. In this he succeeded, although at the sacrifice of personal popularity; impartiality is rarely the way to win friends or gain adherents. He made no effort to seize Riel or any of his supporters. No amnesty had yet been proclaimed and warrants for the arrest of Riel, Lépine and O'Donoghue had been applied for. Writing to Sir George Cartier, the Lieutenant-Governor expressed his view that the flight of the leaders of the Provisional Government was "the best solution . . . while feeling runs so high as it does at present, an attempt at arrest . . . would have been met by resistance, and in the end we would, perhaps, have had to call out the military. . . ."[45] He therefore took steps to name Alfred Boyd, a local merchant as provincial secretary, and Marc Girard, a French Canadian and former mayor of Varennes, Quebec, as the first members of his Executive. He then issued commissions to a number of local men to act as magistrates and ordered a census to be taken. This last revealed that Manitoba had a population of almost 12,000 people, including 5,757 French-speaking Métis, 4,083 English-speaking Métis, 1,565 whites and 558 Indians.[46] Then the Lieutenant-Governor called for a provincial election. The results seemed to justify the policy of striking a balance among the diverse racial elements of the province. Among those elected were French-speaking Métis and English-speaking settlers, men who had supported Riel and some who had opposed him. That explains why in the early years of Manitoba's history, proceedings both in the legislature and in the courts, were conducted in French as well as English, and speeches from the throne were read in both languages. The fact was that Archibald, who was bilingual, was, to all intents and purposes, Premier as well as Lieutenant-Governor.

Perhaps it was just as well, as Archibald had told Cartier, that the principal leaders of the Provisional Government did absent themselves for a while from the vicinity of Winnipeg and Fort Garry. Bitter memories are seldom conducive to peaceful and orderly conduct. A discreet presence, or better still, a temporary absence from the political scene usually goes far towards cooling tempers, farther even than an official amnesty. The state of public opinion, not just in pockets of settlement in Manitoba but also in parts of central Canada, made it politically difficult for the Canadian Cabinet to confirm publicly the oral assurances of an amnesty given to Bishop Taché and the Rev. Noel Ritchot by Sir George Cartier. Alexander Begg, a sympathetic first-hand observer of events in Red River during 1869-1870, later expressed his doubts that an official amnesty would, in fact, have served "to protect Riel and the other leaders from the fury of men who were on the look-out to take revenge upon them for the killing of Scott." He added, "had they been arrested they would probably not

Alexander Begg,
Winnipeg merchant and journalist
(1839-1897).

have received an impartial verdict at the hands of any jury empan-
elled to try them." Begg believed that "The course afterwards adopted,
of inducing Riel and Lépine to leave the country, for a time was
therefore, the best in the interests of the whole country, as thereby
peace was assured."[47]

That the federal government was anxious to placate the Métis
population seems obvious enough. Cartier, for instance, encouraged
a number of Quebeckers, including Joseph Royal, Joseph Dubuc and
Marc Girard, to go to Manitoba to provide political leadership for the
French community, and nominated Francis Johnson as a special
commissioner for establishing courts in Manitoba. Girard, Royal and
Dubuc were strangers in the west; Johnson, at least, was a familiar
figure to Manitobans and the Métis recalled him with mild affection
as a friendly former Governor of Assiniboia. They were to remember
Archibald in the same way.

Not long after Goulet's death, Lieutenant-Colonel Jarvis went on
leave, and until his return to Fort Garry in the winter, the garrison
command was taken over by Lieutenant-Colonel Louis-Adolphe

Casault, the officer commanding the 2nd (Quebec) Rifles. He was an experienced soldier who kept his troops in Red River busy with parades two or three times a day, including parades in full marching order at 1430 hours with 32-kilogram packs and ammunition. According to one of his non-commissioned officers, "the drills were those of a rifle regiment of that time, every movement had to be done very smartly, double time was the rule, and from extended order we occasionally made rushes of one thousand yards [914 m] or more."[48] After about two and a half hours of this exhausting exercise, the proceedings wound up with a march-past "at all the paces." Not for nothing had Casault spent his early years in the ranks of the French Foreign Legion and as a commissioned officer in the British 100th Regiment of Foot. According to Sam Steele:

> These manoeuvres did us a great deal of good, brushed us up until we were wellnigh perfect, and taught us how little food a healthy Anglo-Saxon really requires. The afternoon drills in marching order were in fun styled "Ladies' Parades," on account of the interest that the fair sex took in our movements, particularly the pretty wheels on and off the passing line. One of the young ladies remarked to an officer, "It is charming to see the regiment out in the afternoons; the men look so nice with the little boxes on their backs!"[49]

Early in December the elections for the Legislative Assembly were held. Party feelings ran high and, because voting was done openly and not by ballot,[50] there was a great deal of noise, shouting, threatening and rioting. All of which kept the local constabulary busy, as well as the military picquet. Steele was on duty on that occasion. He wrote "our officer ordered us to load with ball, and it seemed at one time that we might have to fire; but, fortunately, the disturbance was quelled without it, though there were many broken heads."[51] The election was a victory for the moderates. In particular, it was also a defeat for John Schultz and those Ontarians like him, who tended to see the North West simply as a western extension of the province of Ontario.[52]

VI

Meanwhile the soldiers of No. 1 Company of the Ontario Rifles were employed on outpost duty on the Canada-United States frontier.

They located their camp in a meadow on the bank of the Red River, just north of the American post of Pembina. There were a few poplar trees in the vicinity and some bush. Neither was much use for shelter and merely posed an added hazard in the event of a prairie fire.[53] Outpost duty was much more relaxed than duty at Fort Garry. Instead of garrison parades, Tennant wrote about evening singsongs , including Handel's *Hallelujah Chorus* which sounded in the writer's ears as "Sally, I hardly knew yer." An oratorio with a vengeance! Then came the winter, and that too with a vengeance. The company moved from canvas tents to the more substantial protection afforded by the Hudson's Bay Company post. Even so, the soldiers suffered considerably from frost-bite. But there were some advantages. In their permanent quarters the soldiers had a chance to clean up and to sleep in beds. The officers took over the residence of the Hudson's Bay Company Trader in charge and the troops occupied the bastion at the northwest corner of the fort. The relaxations were simple — cards, checkers, writing letters and dances, with music provided by a mouth organ. Weekdays were spent on route marches and drill. There was also the Sunday church parade with the service conducted according to the Anglican prayer book. Tennant writes about the officer who conducted the religious services:

> The stern old veteran of many campaigns shouted as if he was giving orders on parade. After the doxology, and without change of voice, would be a warning to some poor innocent, that the next time he kicked over the traces his daily grog ration would be stopped. If it was near the end of the month, notice was given to get ready to settle accounts in ten minutes; all being made in the same tone and it left one in doubt if it formed part of the litany "Good Lord deliver us and incline our hearts to keep Thy laws."[54]

During the winter, some of the soldiers made an effort to learn French. Others engaged in winter sports, or put in time sawing firewood. Occasionally they were permitted to exchange visits with the American troops stationed just south of the international boundary line. Almost inevitably there were fistic encounters that prompted the old American annexationist, Enos Stutsman, to send reports to the St. Paul paper, about the "Ontario banditti" who crossed the frontier "with heavy military belts and sword bayonets" to attack the poor,

Enos Stutsman, one of the principal
American annexationists at Pembina

peaceful citizens of the United States, in their own country, "thus creating a reign of terror on the border." "Bosh!" wrote Tennant.[55] It was a fair comment. At least on New Year's Day, there were friendly exchanges of visits (and kisses when women were present) that did not arouse the national sensitivities of the miserable Stutsman.

With the arrival of spring came thoughts of returning to civilian life. The Canadian government had anticipated that a number of the men who had enrolled in May 1870 would take discharge on the expiration of their one year's service, either to accept the promised grant of 64 hectares (160 acres) and to settle down as landed immigrants, or to return to Ontario. Six of the men at North Pembina opted for discharge and took the steamer *Selkirk* down the Red River to Winnipeg. At Fort Garry steps were taken to organize provisional companies of those men who preferred to remain another year in the armed forces in Manitoba. These provisional companies were placed under the command of Major Irvine of the Quebec Rifles. Among the officers who elected to remain in the west were Captain William Herchmer and Lieutenant John Allan. The soldiers who took discharge were entitled to free grants of 64 hectares of prairie land and a pre-emption of the same size. However, like many Métis who were entitled to special land grants under a provision of the Manitoba Act, some soldiers were either swindled out of their land or persuaded to sell it for miserably small sums.[56] Others settled down to farming. Still others sought employment on the Dawson Road, and a few trekked to the west, as far as Fort Edmonton. Those who preferred to return to central Canada embarked at the North West Angle of Lake of the Woods and retraced the route they followed the previous year, as far as Prince Arthur's Landing. All told, the official records show that 17 officers and 83 non-commissioned officers and men of the 1st (Ontario) Rifles took advantage of the opportunity to return home. Twelve men who had already been discharged, did the same.[57] This time they all travelled with considerably less effort than previously. There were steam tugs to tow them on the lakes![58] There was no official welcome when the first returning volunteers reached Toronto. But one veteran soldier who saw them as they detrained on 14 July, was heard to remark, "Well, those are something like soldiers!"[59]

CHAPTER TEN

The Fenian Raid in Manitoba 1871

I

William Bernard O'Donoghue had never been a wholly trusted or trustworthy adviser to Louis Riel. He was a Fenian and, as such, saw political events in Red River, not through the eyes of a native Métis, but through those of an Irish nationalist who hated Great Britain and British institutions. He could empathize with the nationalism implicit in the Métis movement in Red River in 1869-1870, but he could never become wholeheartedly identified with it. He could work for Riel, but not with him, because he never really shared Riel's native background or his sentiments.

To O'Donoghue, the principal object of the Red River rising had been to strike a blow at Great Britain and her empire, not to secure British acceptance of Riel's political ideas. The best way to injure Great Britain would be to mobilize the Métis horsemen into an instrument to annex the North West to the United States. It was O'Donoghue who encouraged the activities of the acknowledged annexationists in Red River, men such as the two American agents, Oscar Malmros and H. M. Robinson, or the bartender O'Lone, or those pernicious meddlers from Pembina, Stutsman and Rolette. It was O'Donoghue who insisted upon including the shamrock on the Provisional Government flag. That is why, even though at one time he had worn the soutane,[1] he was able to stand by calmly and witness the shooting of the Ontario-born Orangeman Thomas Scott, and refuse to intercede on behalf of the condemned man. And why, during the passing of the summer months of 1870, he had become more and more dissatisfied with what he regarded as Riel's drift towards compromise with the government of Canada. Even so, he remained at Riel's side until the arrival of Wolseley's troops, hoping that the Métis leader might, at the last moment, be convinced that his future lay in seeking an alliance with the United States.

W. B. O'Donoghue,
the Fenian who was a member of
Riel's government and who led the
raid of 1871.

Not long after Wolseley's departure, the leaders of the former Provisional Government held a secret meeting at St. Norbert, the village south of Winnipeg, where the Métis movement had taken off eleven months earlier. The 1870 meeting was held on 17 September. The purpose of the gathering was to draft a memorial to be sent to Ulysses S. Grant, President of the United States. During the discussion there were several sharp exchanges between Riel and O'Donoghue, the latter insisting that the Métis seek incorporation into the American republic. Riel, however, was opposed to the idea of Red River becoming a northern extension of Minnesota; and the final document prepared by the Métis, simply asked the American President "to intervene with the Queen," to ensure an investigation of Métis grievances and reparations for "violated pledges". In order to mollify O'Donoghue, the Métis gave the sulky Irishman responsibility for seeing that the document reached Washington, a tactical error for which Riel was not responsible.

With the Métis letter in his hands, O'Donoghue was able, with the aid of annexationist sympathizers in Pembina, including among others, Joseph Lemay, the United States customs agent, to "amend" the letter to Grant, omitting all reference to the Queen and inserting a paragraph asking the President of the United States to "take all such steps as Your Excellency may deem appropriate and proper, to enable us to enjoy the blessings of life, liberty, property, and the pursuit of happiness, under a Government of our own choice, or in union with a people, with whom we may think we can enjoy these blessings."[2] To O'Donoghue's great disappointment, his trickery served no good purpose. He received no encouragement from Grant, probably because the United States President had already been briefed by a more reliable secret agent, J. W. Taylor. Grant greeted O'Donoghue with an amiable countenance, but returned a chilly response to the Irishman's request for military and political assistance.

II

Disappointed, although not subdued, O'Donoghue turned to the Fenian organization for help. He told the Irish Brotherhood, not altogether truthfully, that President Grant's reply had been encouraging, and even less truthfully, that even though Riel had not openly endorsed annexation, the Métis people generally, would throw in their lot with the Fenians once they saw Fenian soldiers and heard the sound of Fenian bugles. The members of the Brotherhood were wary. They were woefully short of funds and lacked stomach for another fruitless foray into Canada. They had already tried several times to make headway in that direction, but on no occasion had they won Canadian support. Their last effort, at Eccles Hill in May 1870, had been a disastrous fiasco. Facing only militia troops, the soldiers of the Brotherhood had suffered a serious reverse, and their leader, John O'Neill, had landed in a Yankee jail. Oddly enough, the irrepressibly optimistic O'Neill was prepared to support the equally hopeful O'Donoghue. Other Fenian leaders, however, more realistic, were less enthusiastic. Angrily, O'Neill resigned his presidency of the Brotherhood, declaring that he would act on his own. He was going to support O'Donoghue and would invite other Fenian officers to join him. Colonel Curley alone responded to O'Neill's histrionics.

Together with O'Donoghue, O'Neill and Curley began raising money and enlisting recruits for still another attack upon Canada. This time discouragingly little of the first and few of the second were forthcoming. What the Fenians did not know was that their every step and action was being reported to London and Ottawa, by a British

John O'Neill,
one of the few Fenians who
supported O'Donoghue in 1871.

secret agent, Henri Le Caron.[3] The cards were stacked against O'Donoghue and his handful of miserable Fenian supporters. Their only hope of success lay in an enthusiastic response from the Métis of Red River.

Aside from Le Caron's reports, the Canadian government was not unaware of what O'Donoghue was doing. It was no secret in Ottawa, during the next twelve months, that Fenian officers were trying hard to recruit unemployed workmen and Civil War veterans living in Minnesota and the Dakotas, and that an attack on Manitoba was in their minds. Most people in Manitoba were likewise aware of what was going on and they were alarmed. What was there to stop a strong military force moving north down the line of the Red River? The British troops were gone. They had returned home with Wolseley. The Canadian garrison was diminishing in numbers; even the little garrison at north Pembina had been withdrawn. The unknown, and perhaps decisive, factor would be the attitude of the native peoples. Would they or would they not join O'Donoghue and his Fenian friends?

The Fenians themselves were counting heavily upon Métis support. To enlist Métis backing, O'Donoghue's tactic was to portray his movement as no more than the continuation of the struggle to which so many of them had committed themselves in 1869 under Louis Riel's leadership. O'Donoghue's error was that he never realized that, during the past year, while he had been out of the sight and mind of the Métis, he had lost credibility, while Louis Riel had strengthened his hold over the mixed blood population. There was no way the Irishman could challenge Riel, despite the spreading reports that the Fenian army numbered, not just hundreds, but thousands! In the final analysis, it was Louis Riel, not O'Donoghue, who would determine the Métis attitude. Fortunately for the Métis and for the people of Manitoba, Riel was disposed to listen to Bishop Taché rather than to O'Donoghue. The Irishman did not strengthen his position by lying to Taché, telling him that he was in no way tied up with the Fenians, and that he was simply interested in attracting immigrants to Manitoba. Taché was not deceived. When he met O'Donoghue in the United States, mounted on a "magnificent charger" and wearing "golden spurs," accompanied by several men all bearing military titles, he knew that the Irishman was not telling the truth.[4] Taché neither believed him nor wanted the Métis to throw in their lot with him. The Bishop had already pressed the question upon Riel, when he first learned of O'Donoghue's activities, and Riel's reply had been unconditional. "I am in no way tied to the Fenians", he said. "You may be certain that neither I nor any of my friends will join the Fenians; we detest them because they are condemned by the Church."[5] When Taché repeated these remarks to Noel Ritchot, the priest from St. Norbert said simply, "I have known for some time that there was no doubt" what stand the Métis would take so far as the Fenians were concerned.[6]

Meanwhile, on 2 October 1870, Lieutenant-Governor Archibald learned from Gilbert McMicken who, as Commissioner of Police for the Dominion of Canada, was a federal intelligence agent, that the Fenians at Pembina were now ready to move into Manitoba. Archibald, therefore, issued a Proclamation on 3 October warning the public that "a band of lawless men, calling themselves Fenians, have assembled on the Frontier Line of the United States, at or near Pembina" with the intention of carrying out "a raid into this Province from a country with which we are at peace, and to commit acts of depredation, pillage and robbery and other outrages upon the persons and property of Our loving subjects, the inhabitants of this

Province." He enjoined all Manitobans to assemble in their parishes and to enroll themselves in their local defence corps and select their officers. He assured Manitobans that there were experienced troops in the province and that the public was quite capable of repelling "these outlaws." He concluded with the words, "Rally, then, at once! We rely upon the prompt response of all Our people of every origin, to this, Our call."[7]

Following the publication of Archibald's Proclamation, meetings were held throughout Manitoba, and on the next day, 4 October, volunteers began to come forward in considerable numbers to enrol in *ad hoc* units. By Friday, 6 October, Archibald was able to muster no fewer than 1000 men, including two strong companies of what might be termed Canadian "regular" infantry and several volunteer companies of riflemen, commanded by experienced officers such as Major Irvine, Major Peebles and Captain David Gagnier. In addition, a small number of Métis, French and English, volunteered as mounted scouts. These latter were promptly stationed at various positions throughout the southern part of the province, with instructions to keep close watch on all roads leading north from the United States. The employees of the Hudson's Bay Company organized a special company under Donald A. Smith; and additional companies were formed under W. N. Kennedy and Stewart Mulvey, both of whom had served with the 1st (Ontario) Rifles. Since these volunteer soldiers lacked uniforms, Major Irvine issued them with capotes from the Hudson's Bay Company stores.[8]

It was late on 5 October when positive word reached Archibald that the Fenians had actually crossed the frontier into Canada. These reports, however, were vague as far as numbers were concerned. All that Archibald could ascertain was that the invaders totalled 50 to 100 men "with a large body in the rear." This was confirmed by further accounts received on the morning of the 6th. On that day Archibald gave the order to "advance a body of troops to meet the enemy."[9] Two companies of 200 men, including 80 from the full-time service companies at Fort Garry, with arms, ammunition, equipage, provisions, medical stores and a mountain howitzer, set out to find and to do battle with O'Donoghue's and O'Neill's Fenians. According to the Lieutenant-Governor, the afternoon was "wet and cold, and the mud made travelling difficult and disagreeable, but the spirits of the men were excellent. The alacrity and cheerfulness they displayed was most creditable."[10] Less creditable was the fact that "a number of Irishmen living in the villages around, suspected of Fenianism were arrested by self-constituted policemen without complaint or warrants."[11]

Ambroise Lépine,
a Métis leader who supported Riel
against O'Donoghue in 1871.

In the French parishes a considerable number of Métis, formerly associated with the Provisional Government, were examining their consciences. On 28 September, a committee, including Louis Riel, Ambroise Lépine, Pierre Parenteau, André Nault and others assembled at the Riel house at St. Vital, south of St. Boniface. Their object was to talk about O'Donoghue and what the Métis response should be to the impending threat of invasion led by their former colleague. They were agreed that the federal government had not carried out the pledges it had given, both to Bishop Taché and to Father Ritchot; nevertheless, as a group, they were disinclined to support the Fenians. Rather they preferred to "pronounce themselves in favour of the advantages already possessed by virtue of the Manitoba Bill, and not to allow themselves to be carried away by the contingencies, farther than to ask, loyally and with moderation, the fulfilment of the clauses and of the things guaranteed by our arrangement with Canada."[12]

The Métis committee met again on 5 October. This time a vote was taken on whether the Métis would support Archibald's call to arms or maintain complete neutrality. There was no question of joining

O'Donoghue, however the Irishman might choose to explain his actions. The vote was 12 to 1 in favour of the Canadian government. Word about this vote was obviously passed to Archibald who, in a public statement, addressed "the People of the Province of Manitoba" as follows:

> On Wednesday, I issued a proclamation, calling upon you to assemble and enroll in your various parishes. Copies were distributed all over the Province, and by the evening of Thursday, the people of every English parish had met, had made up, and sent to me lists, shewing 1000 men, ready at a moment's warning to shoulder their muskets and march to the front. In the French parishes, meetings were also held, and by the same evening, I was assured, upon unquestionable authority, that my proclamation would meet with loyal response. I suggested that it should be such as to admit of no misinterpretation, and received the assurance that it would assume a shape entirely satisfactory.[13]

During 6 and 7 October, the Métis continued to enrol in the various parishes. On 7 October, Louis Riel wrote to Archibald from St. Vital:

> [Our conduct] as several trustworthy persons have been prayed to inform you, has been worthy of faithful subjects. Several companies are already organized and others are being formed. Your Excellency has been able to convince yourself that we, without having been enthusiastic, have been devoted. As long as our service shall continue to be required, you can count on us.[14]

As early as 4 October, Father Ritchot had written to Archibald, explaining that Riel was reluctant to place himself at the head of a Métis force without "some guarantee that the proceeding would be looked upon with favor" by the Crown. He therefore asked for "some assurance that will shelter him from any legal proceeding, at least for the present."[15] Not only did Archibald provide Riel (through Ritchot) with the assurance requested,[16] he crossed the Red River to St. Boniface on 8 October, in company with Joseph Royal, the Speaker of the Assembly, Marc Girard, the Provincial Treasurer, and Captain

MacDonald, who was commanding the troops at Fort Garry in the absence of Major Irvine, to meet the assembled Métis. In order to avoid embarrassment, Riel was not presented by name to the Lieutenant-Governor, although it is impossible to believe that Archibald did not recognize the Métis leader. The Métis levies received Archibald with a *feu de joie* and loud cheers, and Girard, in the name of all ranks, assured the Lieutenant-Governor of "the loyalty and devotion" of all Métis people. Archibald replied, tactfully, thanking everybody "very cordially" for "the assurance given in their name", and promising to make known to the Governor General "this demonstration of their feelings."[17] The Reverend J-B Proulx in St. Boniface confided to his diary:

> Generally I hear it said that the English are really frightened, . . . that's a good thing; that they have received a slap is not so bad. If the Fenians really number 1500, only the Métis horsemen can stop them. The English have said that the Métis count for nothing; they are now going to find out.[18]

III

Meanwhile, O'Donoghue's raid, like a damp squib, sputtered momentarily and then came to an inglorious end. On the morning of 5 October, between 40 and 50 buckeens,[19] led by O'Neill and Curley, crossed the frontier and occupied the Hudson's Bay Company post at North Pembina. It was the same post in which a company of the Ontario Rifles had spent the previous winter. The operation was carried out early in the morning. Guards were posted and prisoners were made of all Canadians present, including W.H. Watt, the Hudson's Bay Company officer in charge and his two clerks. The Fenians then began loading their waggons with goods of every kind from the Company shelves. An action, incidentally, which does not suggest that they were looking forward to a lengthy stay!

At this point, a small detachment of American troops in Pembina intervened. The U.S. Consul in Winnipeg, J. W. Taylor, had informed the State Department on 11 September that large quantities of arms were stored at, or near, Pembina, and that he feared the construction of the Northern Pacific Railway in Minnesota and the Dakotas had attracted "several hundred desperate characters" to the region. He suspected that if a Fenian raid was in the offing, robbery would, most

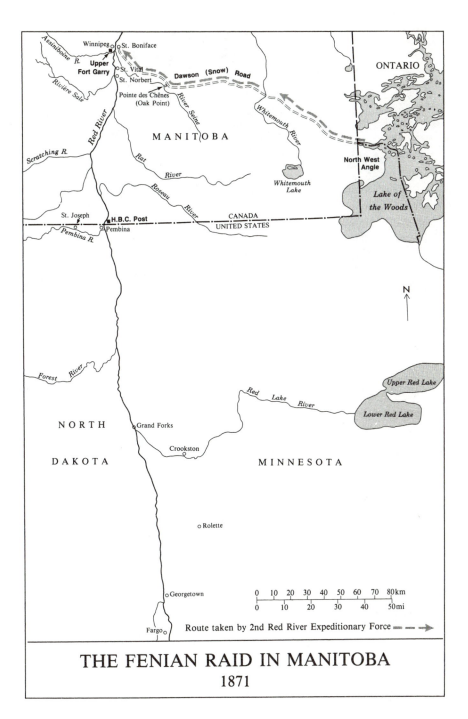

THE FENIAN RAID IN MANITOBA
1871

Route taken by 2nd Red River Expeditionary Force ▬ ▬ ▶

Archibald acknowledging Riel's and Royal's offer of Métis assistance against the Fenians, 8 October 1871.

likely, be the principal motive.[20] Early in October, Taylor reported O'Neill's presence at Pembina. He expressed his opinion that discontent among the Métis was sufficient to encourage a raid or attack on southern Manitoba, but not sufficient to provide for its success.[21] The American officer in charge at Pembina, Captain Lloyd Wheaton, discussed all possible developments with Taylor, who asked the Lieutenant-Governor if he had any official objections to American troops entering the province to round up the Fenian raiders should they attempt any military operations on Canadian territory. Archibald welcomed the suggestion. Wheaton, therefore, acted promptly. Giving the Fenians enough time to commit themselves, he hurried over the frontier, with two under-strength companies of the 20th Infantry. They travelled in waggons which they concealed in a ravine near the trading post. Here Wheaton formed his men into a skirmish line and approached the fort. Inside the Hudson's Bay Company post he captured the Fenian leaders and ten men *in flagrante delicto* (redhanded), with 94 muskets, 11 sabres and 12000 rounds of ammunition. Some 40 or more additional Fenians were collected and marched back to the United States. Most of the so-called Fenian "soldiers" were released on legal technicalities; apparently with the connivance of the United States commissioner.

O'Donoghue was not among them. He was picked up some miles away, ironically enough, by several French-speaking Métis, who

The Canadian fort at Pembina in 1871, as drawn by Joseph Tennant, one of the soldiers stationed there.

J. W. Taylor,
U.S. consul and secret agent who
offered assistance to Archibald
during the Fenian Raid in 1871.

214

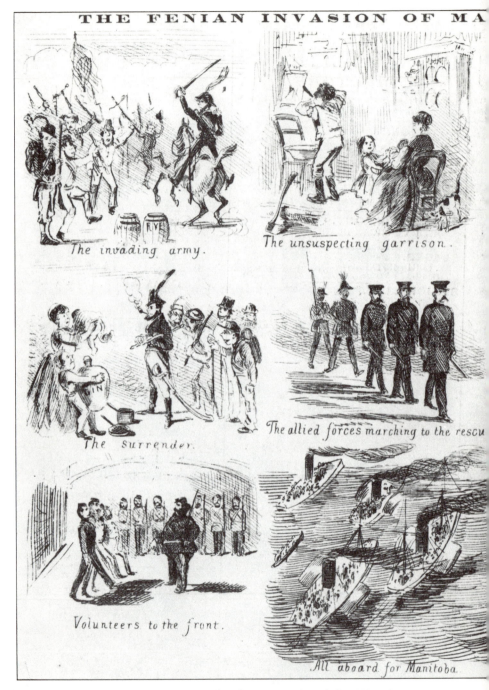

The Fenian Raid, 1871, as portrayed by the cartoonist of the Canadian Illustrated News, *1871.*

ITOBA, IN TWELVE TABLEAUX.

e advance guard.

The attack.

anic; skedaddle of the invaders.

The country is in danger! Planning its defence

Arrival at Fort-Garry. — where's the Enemy?

Return of the gallant army covered with mud and glory.

turned him over to the Canadian customs officer. He, in turn, handed the Irishman to Wheaton. But when Major Irvine requested Wheaton to give the prisoner to him, Wheaton replied that O'Donoghue was no longer in military custody. He had been delivered to the civil authorities on a charge of violating the neutrality laws of the United States.[22] In the end, of course, O'Donoghue was released, even though the Canadians wanted to charge him with robbery. This, however, would have meant a long wait while extradition proceedings could be instituted. It was hardly worth the time and cost.

The Fenian Raid on Manitoba was over.[23] It had degenerated into a simple case of thievery, but the people of Manitoba did not know that on 5 October. It took another twenty-four hours before any positive news reached Winnipeg. Even then, there was the possibility that North Pembina was only a distraction and that Winnipeg and Fort Garry, the main objectives, might be approached by another route. There were still Fenians hanging around Pembina according to the Canadian customs agent, P. B. Douglas, who wrote to Archibald on 7 October: "Bands of men and numbers of strangers from St. Paul and elsewhere are passing and repassing this place and all over; very suspicious looking characters; they are very inquisitive as to essentials."[24] Reporting local gossip Douglas added, "A strong raid is *imminent* very very soon.... Hurry! Hurry! An attempt will be made on Fort Garry, and especially if successful here." He added reassuringly, "The half-breeds and Indians here appear to be loyal, and only want strong support to make them active and efficient soldiers."[25] On the same day Riel, Lépine and Pierre Parenteau wrote to Lieutenant-Governor Archibald telling him that several Métis companies had been organized and others were in the process of formation. They closed their letter with assurances that "so long as our services continue to be required, you may rely on us."[26] Meanwhile Irvine's troops and the volunteers were not recalled to Fort Garry on the capture of the Fenians at North Pembina. Supplemented by Métis scouts, they continued their march, veering towards the southwest, in the direction of the Métis settlement of St. Joseph.[27] Not until 13 October did the Lieutenant-Governor write *finis* to the O'Donoghue affair. In a Proclamation issued on that date and published in the *Manitoba Gazette*, Archibald informed the public that the Fenians, "the bands of miscreants — the scum of the cities of the United States," who had collected south of the border "for purposes of plunder, robbery and murder" had been attacked and dispersed by American troops "as they were crossing the frontier." With regard to O'Donoghue, he regretted that the Americans had released him, "for reasons which I am unable to comprehend." He concluded:

> Nevertheless, the raid for the moment is over. If re-newed, it will not be immediately. If the Fenians were men actuated by ordinary reason, it would never be renewed. But they are not. They will trade, while they can, upon the simplicity of their dupes, and hope by excitement to replenish their exhausted exchequer. There is nothing in the wickedness or folly of any scheme to prevent their attempting it.[28]

Two months later, the Colonial Office expressed satisfaction that "the appeal to defend the frontier" had been "so promptly and loyally responded to."[29] On 2 January 1872, Joseph Howe, as Secretary of State for the Provinces, passed on Lord Kimberley's congratulations to Archibald.[30] By this time O'Donoghue and his Fenian adventurers seemed very much a thing of the past; gone and soon to be forgotten by Manitobans as well as by Canadians.

The French language newspaper of St. Boniface, *Le Métis*, also expressed its satisfaction at the conclusion of the Fenian Raid. On 19 October the editor wrote:

> At last, thanks be to God, our country is safe. O'Donoghue can no longer seriously threaten us; our brave volunteers have showed up well; the American Government has fulfilled its obligations and has under-stood in which direction its interests lay. French and English, marched together, facing the same dangers to defend their common interests and today everybody has returned to his own fireside.[31]

There is nothing equal to an external threat to encourage internal political unity. At least, for the moment, the turbulent rhetoric of local politics, the hootings, the threats and the assaults were set aside in Manitoba.

IV

Meanwhile, in Ottawa, all was excitement. The exaggerated accounts of what was happening in western Canada, appearing in the daily press, had the immediate effect of stimulating the federal authorities into activity. On 3 October, Archibald had acquainted the Secretary of State for the Provinces with the information that he had obtained from Gilbert McMicken about probable Fenian intentions to attack Manitoba,[32] forwarding a copy of his Proclamation. Ten days later Archibald wrote again, pointing out that O'Donoghue was believed to be still in the area, and urging the despatch of "additional" troops. These, he suggested, might be sent overland, by way of the American railway system, under the guise of "private citizens." Above all, it was essential that the soldiers be in Red River "before the winter sets in, if you wish to consider the country safe."[33]

Ottawa had, however, already taken steps to send reinforcements of Canadian soldiers to Manitoba. Learning of the Fenian threat from the newspapers, the Canadian authorities had, without delay, instructed the Adjutant-General, Colonel Patrick Robertson Ross, to send 200 troops to reinforce the Provisional Battalion at Fort Garry. Lieutenant-Colonel W. Osborne Smith, the Deputy Adjutant-General

Major Irvine addressing the anti-Fenian volunteers at Fort Garry, October 1871.

of Military District 5, was ordered to proceed at once to Manitoba, by way of the United States, to assume command of Her Majesty's forces in the western province. On arrival he was to make all arrangements necessary for the transportation of troops over the Dawson Road from the North West Angle of Lake of the Woods to Fort Garry.[34] The actual command of the troops, *en route*, would rest with Captain (Brevet Lieutenant-Colonel) Thomas Scott of the 42nd Brockville Battalion of Militia, a veteran of Wolseley's expedition of the summer of 1870.

Because the Department of Militia had already experienced the difficulties of mobilizing militia soldiers and sending them to Red River, the Second Red River Expedition moved with a minimum of delay and an absence of most of the problems that had proved so irritating to Colonel Garnet Wolseley. On 21 October, only nine days after the decision had been taken to send additional troops to Red River, the recruits had been documented, examined and equipped, and arrangements completed for the purchase and distribution of supplies and the chartering of trains and vessels. Following the precedents established in the First Expeditionary Force, troops were selected both from Ontario and Quebec.

Among those who volunteered at this time was George Adshead of London, Ontario. A militiaman, a private soldier belonging to the 7th Light Infantry, he volunteered on 17 October 1871, "for six or twelve months service ," on the sudden call of the Canadian Government for "200 men to proceed to Fort Garry to reinforce the two service companies now there; the cause being anticipated invasion of Manitoba by Fenians from Minnesota."[35] On 19 October Adshead left London for Toronto, along with 25 other recruits from western Ontario. In Toronto they joined men from other Military Districts. Among them was Justin Griffin, who wrote a complete account of his experiences and later published it, under the designation of "A Private Soldier." Meanwhile, the Adjutant-General's staff in Ottawa not only arranged for the necessary supplies, but also, following the procedure of 1870, engaged a number of voyageurs to navigate the tricky waters to be travelled between Prince Arthur's Landing and the Lake of the Woods.

The first group, including that to which Adshead belonged, arrived in Collingwood, the port of embarkation, on the evening of 19 October. On the day following, all of the new recruits were re-examined by a medical officer. "A few men were sent back home, much to their apparent disgust," according to Adshead, who had just received his sergeant's stripes.[36] The next day, on the 21st, the troops were inspected by Colonel Robertson Ross, now the senior military officer in Canada, after which they were marched to the wharf where they were given arms and accoutrements and then they embarked on board *Chicora*. Griffin, whose diary reveals his aspirations to become a "literary" writer, describes the departure of the troop ship on 21 October in this fashion:

> The day was pleasant and the water calm, so that all were in good spirits as we rapidly glided away amid the cheers of the assembled crowd. Before the shades of night had fully settled down upon us we were nearly out of sight of land, but though we could not now gaze upon the beauties of *terra firma*, many of us found pleasure in standing upon the deck and viewing the moonlit waters of Georgian Bay.[37]

Both Griffin and Adshead commented upon what they saw, although the first was inclined to refer to "a cloudless sky and the moon in all her splendor," while the more practical sergeant noted, "one man arrested during the evening for drunkenness." The next day, Adshead entered in his diary:

> Oct. 23. Pretty good sea on & a good many men sick. Abt 10 P.M. I lay down on deck under the lee of the house, after all the men had turned in, as there was not enough accommodation in the berths, the Captain roused me out between eleven & twelve & kindly offered me the use of his own cabin, saying at the same time he should have to come rather often during the night to look at the chart.[38]

The troops passed through the Sault Canal during the night. Some of them, however, like Griffin, perched themselves on a table in their stateroom in order to catch a glimpse of the river and the canal and "the back-ground formed by a range of high hills, clothed with the rich verdure of an evergreen forest."[39] All that Adshead had to say was, "Passed the Sault St. Mary Canal during the night."[40] Later the same day, the remainder of the soldier's kit was handed out to each man. It consisted of two heavy blankets, two oil sheets, a fur cap, a pair of leather mitts, a pair of moccasins, a pair of ammunition shoes, a red woollen nightcap, or "chute" as many of the troops called it, a muffler, and two strong and warm over-shirts, such as were worn by the soldiers of the British regular army. These last were, apparently, extra large. According to one soldier, a man 1.8 metres (six feet) in height, his issue overshirt fitted him "like a sentry box."[41] Other items included two knitted undershirts, two pairs of knitted drawers, four pairs of socks, a pair of suspenders, two linen towels, a hold-all with needles and thread, blacking brushes, clothes brush, a large clasp knife, fork, spoon, tin-plate, tin-cup, and about a pound of soap. All of this, when added to the greatcoat, rifle, accoutrements and 60 rounds of ball ammunition and a pair of snowshoes, made a sizeable load for any man to carry.

On the 24th *Chicora* rounded the Isle Royale and made her way into Thunder Bay. About 1 p.m. the vessel cast anchor opposite Prince Arthur's Landing. She was unable to draw up to the small pier, and all the men and supplies on board were landed by means of a scow operated between the vessel and the shore. *Chicora's* companion ship, *Frances Smith*, had already arrived at Prince Arthur's Landing with horses, teamsters and voyageurs.[42]

There were no delays. About 0300 hrs the first group of Quebec soldiers set off up the road to Shebandowan Lake, followed at intervals by other troops. Adshead found the road "very rough & muddy."[43] The soldiers made good time, nevertheless. It was late in the season and the ground froze on the night of 26 October, while a light snow covered the trees and the country-side. The practical-minded Adshead thought the land "poor," but admitted that it was "picturesque and in summer time would no doubt, look very nice, provided there were no flies to make a man d—n the country." The simple fact that he had found his quarters comfortable, "with a good supply of fresh beef," (twelve head having been killed the day before and cut up in joints for the troops), beans and tea "with hard tack accompanyment," may account for his comment in his journal, "slept like a top."[44] Griffin also slept well, "covered with ice and snow" and with his greatcoat "stiff enough to stand alone," draped over his body.[45] The next day being "fine and frosty with clear air," the first troops made ready to set off on the journey to Fort Garry. Sergeant Adshead was in charge of No. 2 boat. The voyage began at 1400 hrs with a small tugboat towing six troop boats. It made for the head of the lake, a distance of 40 kilometres and arrived there by 2100 hrs.

Meanwhile Griffin's party was still at Kaministikwia Bridge. He therefore had ample opportunity to wonder at and to write about the "surpassingly beautiful scenery to be found in this region of rocks, lakes and rivers."[46] Not until Sunday, the 29th, did he embark in his water craft. He reached Kashaboiwe portage by noon, and after crossing the portage, hoisted sail. Towards seven o'clock "in the midst of a blinding snow storm" — a hazard never experienced by Wolseley's men — the troops, of whom Griffin was one, reached the Height of Land portage. They crossed without difficulty, taking shelter in the shanties erected by the federal government for the use of immigrants and travellers making their way to Manitoba. After a restless night in their cramped quarters, the troops prepared to continue their journey. The snow was now 30 centimetres deep over the portage "which, with the ice on the lakes, makes everything have a wintry appearance."[47] That probably explains why Griffin did not embark on Lac des Mille Lacs until 1100 hrs.

Adshead's men, too, were having their problems. He reached the same portage on 28 October, and the troops had "a big war dance round a large camp fire," probably to keep the blood circulating and the men "in good spirits". But the unfortunate sergeant did not get much rest. He "tried to sleep across two flour barrels but failed," was the laconic entry in his daily journal on 28 October. He added on the 29th, "everyone looking seedy — with seedy looking weather."[48] There was some talk about halting for a while and building more shanties, but, when the weather began to show signs of improvement, the troops pushed on. That, after all, was their first priority. However, they did have the good fortune to come across a group of Indians who willingly parted with some "splendid pike," in return for a few biscuits and plugs of tobacco. In any event, they arrived safely at the extremity of Lac des Mille Lacs without losing their way, although they had to break a centimetre and a quarter of ice for a distance of 450 metres as they pulled in to the shore. "Bitterly cold night but calm" was Adshead's entry in his daily journal.[49]

Behind Adshead, just entering Lac des Mille Lacs, Griffin was noting in his diary on 30 October, "spent a very uncomfortable night, during which very few of us got any sleep, and those few not being much refreshed by it."[50] Griffin's companions were full of complaints about the depth of the snow, and the difficulty of having constantly to row against the wind. They encountered the same Indians that Adshead had met, gave them a little hardtack, but did not get any fresh fish in return. About dusk, after rowing about 50 kilometres they came in sight of Baril Portage. As if it were not enough of a test of their fortitude to overcome the several portages barring progress into Sturgeon Lake, there was another problem, every day growing more formidable: the formation of ice along the river banks.

Meanwhile, Adshead's troops crossed Baril Portage and the others, including French Portage (Portage des Français), an obstacle that Adshead considered "a beastly one." And with reason. It had taken his men until 2200 hrs to get everything over and the boats reloaded. Not until 0300 hours were they free to eat supper, pitch their tents and turn in. Then, it was up again after only a few hours. Even so, everybody seems to have worked willingly, and the voyageurs proved to be competent men. According to Adshead, they navigated his boat down French Creek, a narrow stream "in some places little wider than the boat and full of snags, shoals and small rapids" without any mishaps. Indeed, they worked so well, that they caught up to one of the Quebec boats that had left Thunder Bay a day ahead. Both boats set out the following morning to race to Lac Lacroix. But there were still more portages to cross. Describing one of them, Adshead wrote

> ... two men and an Indian (Iroquois) took the boat thro' the Chute, called Cedar Rapids ... boat went thro' like a shot — We stuck on the rocks shortly afterwards (twice), this river is full of them — passed the wreck of a boat which was smashed in the rapids two years ago — Pulled five miles [eight km] to Tanner's Rapids where we portaged boat etc. abt 50 yards [45 m] then down stream to Island Portage four miles [six and a half km], portaged boat about 100 yards [91 m] where we arrived at 4:30 P.M., portaged boat etc., had a snack & started downstream two miles [three km]— At 5:30 P.M. were taken in tow by a small tug to cross Lake Lac la Croix, 30 miles [48 km], arrived at Loon Portage, 200 yds. long [180 m], at 11:30 p.m.[51]

Griffin's experiences were not much different. His boat survived the Baril, Windisgostigwan, French, Pine and Deux Rivières Portages — the last having been made easier by the building of bridges over two ravines through which everything had previously had to be manhandled. Although, as Griffin noted, "there was some excitement and danger for us in drawing the boats up and down the short hills still remaining, and in crossing bridges, which have no railings."[52] Griffin knew what he was writing about. He himself "had a narrow escape from a broken leg, and perhaps from death itself," when his leg was caught between two long skids, with the boat on top of them. Thanks to the quick action of several soldiers who "exerted their entire strength to restrain the boat in its motion down the hill," it was possible for Griffin to pull his leg clear.[53] It was a close call for the amateur soldier-boatman! But dangers were usually forgotten in competitions between the boat crews. One detects a note of satisfaction in Griffin's statement that, on 1 November, his boat "overtook the Quebec company,"[54] and the two crews camped beside each other. That there should be instances of rivalry between boat crews was only natural. There was always the stimulus of trying to reach the portage first, if only to find the best campsite and to escape working into the late hours of the evening; and the excitement of pitting one's skill or strength against that of a rival crew, or the amusement of watching men, some of whom were totally unfamiliar with the art of rowing, demonstrating their skill or incompetence against others equally well or poorly endowed. According to Griffin:

> Those who happen to be looking on at the time take great delight, in using such expressions as, "That's it, all together, one after the other," and similar taunting words, which are usually taken in good part, though sometimes an angry retort is given by some of the quick-tempered ones.[55]

On 6 November, Adshead's boat arrived at Kettle Falls. The next day it reached the landing place at Fort Frances. The boat in which Private Griffin was labouring had arrived at the same place about half an hour before, at 2000 hrs. Griffin was quick to look around. He noted the stout oaken fence enclosing several blockhouses, at Fort Frances, and the men at work building steamers for Rainy Lake and the Lake of the Woods. "These steamers," he wrote, "together with the tugs on the smaller lakes and the improvements to be made on the portages, will make this route much pleasanter as well as more useful next year." He obviously liked the place, its falls, its fertility, and its Indian burial ground; although he was inclined to query the use of the term "burial ground" for a place where "the coffin is suspended in the air, six feet [1.8 m] above the ground, each being sustained by four stout stakes."[56] He predicted a great future for Fort Frances, located as it was "in a fertile tract of country, at the head of a magnificent and beautiful river which is swift enough to furnish an almost unlimited water power, and in the vicinity of one of the richest mineral regions in the world."[57]

The soldiers, however, had no time to linger and rhapsodize. The journey westwards continued the next day. This time the various boats set off down the lovely, winding river, dashing over the Manitou Rapids, fortunately without mishap. At the Long Rapids the men followed a footpath three kilometres long beside the river, leaving the navigation of the boats to the voyageurs. This was Indian country and Griffin was inclined to let his imagination run a little as he wrote about his "bright visions of the future." He could see "comfortable farm houses in place of the wretched wigwams now scattered along the banks," and "broad fields of waving, yellow grain and herds of sleek cattle" instead of the reality of "prairie grass and the wild beasts of the forest."[58] After supper, the troops spent a few hours at rest, and then resumed their journey shortly after midnight. Further progress proved difficult, owing to the wind. Another 24 hours were spent simply waiting for more favourable conditions. Even then, the troops found it possible to move ahead only a few kilometres. The heavy water was too much for the steam tugs, which were in constant danger of being swamped. Some of the men were "terror struck" by the menacing waters — at least, those who were not miserably seasick.[59] In Adshead's boat, the practical, methodical sergeant seemed to be most concerned by the fact that there were only a few days' rations left.[60]

The continuous winds were accompanied by a declining temperature and the formation of ice, which made the journey more and more difficult for the tug boats. However, by 12 November, Colonel Osborne Smith's armada was estimated to be only 19 kilometres from the North West Angle of the Lake of the Woods. As the boats tried to work their way closer to the shore, the ice became heavier, and the tug boat crews attached an "armour plating of sheet iron" around the bows to help them break the ice.[61] Finally, the decision was taken to continue the rest of the way, over the ice, on foot. For the moment, however, the troops had no choice but to take refuge on a small island. Adshead explained the circumstances in few words: "the wind changed to the NNE and blew half a gale accompanied by some snow and freezing hard. Spent a miserable night, first part of night blankets wet through & afterwards frozen stiff, tent all ragged and torn."[62]

On the 13th, about noon, orders were given to begin the march. After a "very scanty meal of slap-jacks and fat pork in a half-cooked state," the soldiers set out for the North West Angle at one o'clock. Here is how Griffin described it:

> Our march led us through half-frozen marshes, in
> which we were continually sinking over the ankles
> and over smooth, slippery ice, against a strong and

piercing cold wind, the ice being so thin that we were obliged to march in single file at intervals of from 5 to 10 paces, which gave the force the appearance of a skirmish line taking ground to its right or left. Even with this precaution several men broke through, but were soon assisted out by their comrades; the smoothness of the ice and the strength of the wind frequently caused some of us to lose our footing, and the fall being accelerated by the burden of nearly one hundred pounds [45 kilos] which each man carried, many a bruise and sprain was the result.[63]

However, by 1700 hrs they sighted shanties on the shore of the North West Angle, and the heart-warming fires that were a great encouragement to those still farther away. Both promised warmth and comfort to men who had completed what was estimated to have been a 19 kilometre march, but seemed so much longer to the troops. The practical Adshead noted in his journal

Arrived at the Angle a little after 5 P.M., very thankful that our boat pulling and portaging is over, and so successfully. Slept in the open and on a splendid bed of hay & had the best sleep since Thunder Bay. Lots of fresh beef & other provisions ready for us here, having been waiting for us some days, there are also about twenty waggons & carts.[64]

The worst was, indeed, over. The next few days' marching was easier. Carts were available to carry the heavy baggage, and although the weather was cold and the footing slippery, there was a happy change of diet from pork to beef, and lots of straw and bedding to improve the hastily erected shanties. In the early hours of 16 November — reveillé was at 0330 hrs — the troops set out and marched for 40 kilometres without a halt, reaching the Métis settlement of Pointe de Chêne or Oak Point. It snowed most of the day and was still snowing the next morning. Hardly surprising, perhaps, that a few historically-minded among the troops, should have recalled to mind the great Napoleon Bonaparte's struggling withdrawal from Moscow in the winter of 1812-13, just two generations earlier.[65] Sergeant Adshead, however, was not thinking of Napoleon when he noted briefly in his journal of 17 November:

Turned out at 3.30 A.M. Marched at seven o'clock. Couldn't get away sooner in consequence of a heavy fall of snow, therefore were unable to find the road across the prairie; had a heavy march of 17 miles [27 km] to Little Point du Chêne, a place, as far as I can [see], of one house, here we camped for the night. Hard frost with fresh breeze & snow, very cold, got served out with some potatoes which were very acceptable. A man of the Quebec [battalion] had a narrow squeak from freezing to death.[66]

On Saturday, 18 November, the troops were up again at 0330 hrs and on the march an hour and a half later. As they neared the Red River, a couple of men in a cutter provided a bottle of whisky to each squad — "a God-send" Adshead called it — and by one o'clock the troops shuffled into St. Boniface. Here they halted, to smarten up a bit before crossing the Red and the Assiniboine Rivers on the ice, and marching into Fort Garry to the tune of "The British Grenadiers" played by the military band. A good crowd of people witnessed their arrival. That was all. The circumstances did not seem to call for

Upper Fort Garry as Sergeant George Adshead would have seen it late in 1871, watercolour by E.J. Hutchins.

anything more. That night a drowsy Adshead wrote in his journal, "The two Service Companies who occupied the Fort till our arrival, showed us every kindness and we found a good substantial meal ready for us."[67] It was the least the garrison troops could do. After all, their reinforcement had spent 28 days on the march, days of extreme physical discomforts and dangers exceeding those experienced by Wolseley's troops the year before. The success of the Second Expedition was important, if only because it proved to all concerned, Manitobans of French, English or Indian origin, Canadians and Americans, Canada's interest in and determination to hold and defend the territories it had acquired from the Hudson's Bay Company. Moreover, it stimulated in the participants themselves a new and greater sense of their own identity as Canadians.

Winnipeg, 1872, the capital of Manitoba, from a contemporary print.

CHAPTER ELEVEN

The Provisional Battalion and the Establishment of M.D. 10 1872-1874

I

The despatch of two militia rifle battalions to Red River in 1870 and the hasty improvisation of local militia companies to meet the threat imposed by O'Donoghue's and O'Neill's raiders in 1871, brought home to the federal Department of Militia the need to organize effective military units within the boundaries of the new province of Manitoba. As an integral part of Canada, Manitoba was, of course, subject to the requirements of the federal Militia Act; but no steps were taken until 1872 to establish properly maintained militia units inside the provincial boundaries. That is why the military command at Fort Garry had been obliged to put together *ad hoc* home guard units, bearing the names of their commanders, rather than territorial designations, on the occasion of the Fenian Raid. The reinforcements intended to fill the vacancies left by the departure of time-expired soldiers from the battalions which had accompanied Wolseley, arrived a month and a half *after* the Fenians had crossed the frontier. Had it not been that O'Donoghue was unable to muster the support he expected from local sympathizers, "the men of the movement" as they were known in Manitoba at that time, the situation might have become truly embarrassing for Canada.

It was to meet just such a situation that Lieutenant-Colonel Osborne Smith, when he led his men over the Dawson route in October-November 1871 carried with him formal instructions from the Department of Militia to establish a new Military District in Manitoba to be designated M.D. 10, over which he was to assume command. This meant that, henceforth, there would be a permanent and official military presence within the new province. Smith was a good choice for the appointment. He had served in Crimea with the British 39th

Lieutenant-Colonel Osborne Smith,
D.A.G., engraving from a
photograph by Notman.

Foot, the Dorsetshire Regiment, and subsequently come to Canada with his regiment. After retiring from the British Army he settled in Montreal and accepted a commission in the Victoria Rifles. Responding to the call of duty when the government of Canada sent militiamen to the frontier during the tense period of the American Civil War, he took charge of the First or Western Provisional Battalion at Sandwich, to which several Montreal regiments contributed troops. In 1865 Smith was named Assistant Adjutant-General in command of the troops in the Eastern Townships of Quebec. In this role he saw service in 1866 and again in 1870 at the time of Eccles Hill.

On 25 December 1871, while in his office at Fort Garry, he sent a detailed letter to the Adjutant-General in Ottawa. It was a report on the state of the Canadian military forces in the new Military District 10 in Winnipeg.[1] The authorized strength of the militia in the province included one half battery of field artillery, two troops of cavalry and nine companies of infantry. According to Colonel Smith, of all the militia units, the artillery was in the best condition. The gunners possessed two bronze mountain guns, left behind by Colonel Wolseley, and showed signs of becoming "a useful and efficient corps." Of the nine infantry companies, four were fully organized and about to commence their preliminary drills; the remaining five were still in the early stages; the recruits, as yet, had no uniforms. However, the clothing had just arrived and would, of course, be distributed to the organized corps, and to the others when complete. The two troops of cavalry had not even been formed. In fact, Colonel Smith saw their future as that of mounted rifles, rather than cavalry. Considering the fact that the population of the province, not including the Indians and "scattered settlers," was no more than ten thousand, Osborne Smith considered that the proposed establishment was as good as could be expected. Here is how he described the area for which he was responsible:

> From the parallel of forty-nine [the boundary line of the U.S.], the chief settlements extend due north, along the Red River for about ninety miles [144 km]; this line of settlement is crossed by another running nearly east and west, from Point de Chêne, on the River Seine to the eastward, to Prairie Portage to the westward, on the Assiniboine River; both these rivers converge at Winnipeg [Fort Garry] falling into the Red River. The settled country thus forms a cross, of which Fort Garry may be considered the centre, sixty miles [96 km] north of the boundary line at Pembina with Point de Chêne and Prairie Portage distance thirty and seventy miles [48 and 113 km] respectively, to the east and west.[2]

Obviously, in the absence of natural physical obstacles, fixed fortifications would be less important for the defence of these two thin lines of settlement, than the ability to move men quickly from one threatened area to another, and mobility demanded a mounted force rather than foot soldiers. This did not mean traditional cavalry, armed with lances or sabres; it meant mounted infantry equipped with rifles. The American Civil War had taught this lesson. Colonel Smith was intelligent enough to see that impetuosity or stubbornness by itself would not be enough. The combination of these qualities in a single force was the way of the future, especially in Canada's prairie country. Colonel Smith was, therefore, thinking in terms of mounted infantry when he wrote to Ottawa, emphasizing that "The force best adapted to the physical geography of the country and to the habits of the people, is that of Mounted Rifles."[3]

II

Following the arrival of the 1871 reinforcements, the troops in Manitoba were, to all intents and purposes, Canadian regular infantry. They were given the designation of "The Provisional Battalion of Rifles," subsequently changed to "The Provisional Battalion of Infantry." The Battalion was under the command of Major Acheson G. Irvine. He was assisted by Captains Allan McDonald, William Herchmer, Thomas Scott (who had commanded the 1871 draft) and John Fletcher. The Lieutenants included William Kennedy, Oscar Prevost, Hayter Reed and Georges Simard, and Ensigns E. Nash and Herman Martineau. Surgeon Alfred Codd, Captain and Paymaster J. B. Morice, Captain and Adjutant C.F.D. Gagnier and Quartermaster Armstrong made up the rest of the officer establishment.[4]

During the spring and summer of 1872, the Provisional Battalion found life in Manitoba marked more by routine than by excitement. The Fenians had vanished and the only threats imposed upon the new province appeared to be those resulting from excesses of political excitement, usually stimulated by over-indulgence in the lethal combination of raw whisky and a frustrated desire for revenge. Old grudges were not forgotten simply because they had not yet been forgiven. On 19 September 1872 the provincial magistrates were obliged to ask for the assistance of Major Irvine's men in maintaining order during the provincial election. Seventy-five soldiers, with a due complement of officers, were paraded through Winnipeg to ensure that the electoral machinery could function more or less peacefully. According to the Regimental Journal, the presence of these 75 armed and uniformed men had "the desired effect of restoring order and quiet, the men behaving in an extremely soldierly manner, notwithstanding the taunting speeches uttered by some on the hustings and the cheers of others endeavoring thereby to receive a response."[5] The civilians in the streets were apparently intimidated, or at least impressed. It seemed fairly obvious that these soldiers would act if and when ordered to do so. During the same evening the mob, with some reinforcements from the neighbourhood taverns, moved towards the local bank. However, the troops were ahead of them; and, according to reports, "in time to prevent the ransacking and demolition of the Dominion Savings Bank." Deprived of their objective, members of the crowd directed their destructive energies on several local printing houses in town. The "depredators," it may be noted, were not "members of the movement," but more recent arrivals from outside the province. On the reappearance of the troops at dusk, amid cries of "Here come the soldiers," "the hoodlums and troublemakers took to their heels," and remained "at a respectable distance."[6] A guard was posted at the bank and at other buildings in Winnipeg and various detachments of troops patrolled the streets during the remainder of the night. "But nothing happened," noted the regimental diarist, "more than the firing of a number of shots in the air in the neighbourhood of the guards, evidently for the purpose of intimidation."[7] During the next few days the troops, although in reduced numbers, remained on the alert. The Regimental Journal records that the sound of the command "Fix Bayonets" proved to be an effective means of cooling public tempers.

The soldiers in Winnipeg were not restricted to intimidating troublemakers. The Regimental Journal of the Provisional Battalion describes their role as firemen during the destruction of the Parliament Buildings by fire on 3 December 1873. The Journal states that the troops were employed in various ways, preventing the fire spreading, protecting other property, and operating the fire engine.[8] The night was "bitterly cold and so soon as the troops arrived on the scene, the citizens apparently possessed of the idea that nothing further in the shape of work was required of them, therefore the whole devolved upon the soldiers." After the fire was extinguished, a guard of 25 men under an officer was retained the balance of the night to protect the rescued property from thieves and otherwise to have due care for the place."[9] Several weeks later the same thing was repeated when fire broke out in Fort Garry. Here the civilians, rather than assisting the troops in their fire-fighting efforts, actively hindered them, oblivious to the fact that there was more than enough gunpowder in the fort to blow up all of Winnipeg.[10] What credit the troops received, came from the Deputy Adjutant-General commanding the District, who in District Orders on 21 January 1874 expressed his pleasure

> . . . in informing the Troops in Garrison that he has received a communication from the Factor of the Honble Hudson's Bay Company here, in which in the most handsome terms he requests that the sincere thanks of the Company may be conveyed to the officers and men of the Dominion Forces for the services rendered by them on the occasion of the late fire in Fort Garry. Lieut. Colonel Osborne Smith at the same time takes the opportunity of expressing to the Troops his high appreciation of the willing and steady manner in which

they worked through a long and cold winter's night, and by their active exertions were mainly instrumental in saving the whole of Fort Garry from destruction. . ... The conduct of the Officers, Non-Comd Officers and men on the occasion has been brought to the notice of the authorities at Headquarters by the Officer Commanding here.[11]

Later in the same year, 1874, the troops in Winnipeg marched to Qu'Appelle to accompany the new Lieutenant-Governor, the Hon. Alexander Morris, who, with David Laird, negotiated a treaty with the Cree and Ojibway Indians. This was the furthest point into the interior of the Canadian North West yet reached by "any of Her Majesty's Forces." This exercise demonstrated the ability of Canadian infantry to march "with facility and rapidity" over the plains, "without any large supporting bodies of cavalry, or heavy baggage trains" such as the Americans were accustomed to employ. The expedition was led by Osborne Smith, supported by Surgeon Codd, Lieutenant W. H. Cotton of the Dominion Artillery, Ensign Street of the Provisional Battalion as Acting Adjutant, and Captains A. McDonald and W. M. Herchmer, Lieutenant John Allan and Ensign P. de Cazes of the same battalion. The troops were divided into two companies. With them they carried a seven-pounder mountain howitzer, dismantled and stowed in a cart. Other transport was required for the heavy ammunition and for the camp equipage and provisions required for the march to Qu'Appelle, the halt there and the return as far as Fort Ellice at the junction of the Qu'Appelle and Assiniboine Rivers. A small drove of beef cattle accompanied the party, cutting down on transport and providing the troops with fresh meat. Only a small supply of oats was carried for the horses; they were expected to survive on the nutritious prairie grasses. Each man carried his rifle, waist belt, cartridge bags, canteen, bayonet and haversack.

The route followed by the troops ran south of the Assiniboine, southward of Fort Ellice, striking the Qu'Appelle valley about 90 kilometres east of Fort Qu'Appelle. Setting out on 17 August, Osborne Smith's command arrived at Fort Qu'Appelle on 5 September. Here they met the two commissioners representing the federal government in the treaty negotiations. On 8 September they arrived at the place where they were to confer with the Indians. Ten days later, on 18 September, it was all over, and the troops set out on the return journey to Winnipeg, reaching their destination on 5 October. On foot, they covered 536 kilometres in sixteen and a half days. To his great satisfaction, Lieutenant-Colonel Osborne Smith reported to Ottawa that no men or horses had been lost or injured on the march, no accident had occurred and crime and irregularities were entirely absent. Lessons had, of course, been learned from the exercises; marching on the prairies had proved to be "exceptionally difficult" owing to the "adhesive nature of the soil" when it was wet, and to the polishing effect the grass had upon the soles of boots when the weather was dry; the soldiers' boots should be capped "with a fine sheet of copper;" moosehide moccasins should also be available; "the largest ration that can be carried", should be allowed to the men; "no spirits should be taken, but a large ration of tea should be given;" and a keg of water should be carried "in every cart or waggon." Officers not on duty ought to be encouraged to ride ahead and hunt grouse, geese and wild ducks, to supplement rations, and military powers of punishment should be extended, even to "corporal punishment," in cases of "grossly mutinous conduct" on the part of hired teamsters "wilfully destroying wheeled transport, or driving off horses to a distance from camp." A large proportion of the officers should be mounted to enable them to ride well ahead to locate suitable camp-sites; salt should be carried in sufficient quantities to preserve meat killed *en route*; and bacon and smoked shoulders should be carried rather than pork, if only because of the added weight imposed by the barrels of brine required to preserve the latter.

These were all practical and sensible recommendations. And all very obvious. Perhaps less obvious, at first sight, was the suggestion that drums and fifes or bugles be taken, since "nothing is so monotonous or fatiguing as a wide expanse of plain unbroken either by tree or shrub to march over;" when men and horses are "fading down," a cheery tune from the band "lifts them along surprisingly." Osborne Smith added in his report, "It is well worth while to devote transport for band instruments, and to let the bandsmen occasionally exchange their arms for them."[12]

III

When the two rifle battalions were recruited in the spring months of 1870 for special service in the North West, the federal government had not contemplated the possibility of their becoming a permanent military fixture in the new province of Manitoba. A year or two at the most was all that was anticipated. It was the threat, implied rather than real, posed by the activities of William O'Donoghue and his Fenian friends, that led to the reinforcing of the Canadian troops already in Manitoba in 1871; and alarm at the deteriorating conditions in the northwestern territories beyond the western border of Manitoba that led to subsequent reinforcements during the next few years.

Unlike the two previous contingents in 1870 and 1871, the men who enlisted in 1872 for the Third Red River Force agreed to serve for "one year, or three years if required."[13] Ontario recruits were joined at Toronto by those from Quebec on 19 September. From Toronto the soldiers moved by train to Collingwood where they received their uniforms and equipment, and embarked on the steamer *Frances Smith*. The officer in command was former Captain (now Lieutenant-Colonel) F. Villiers. Among the officers assigned to help him were Ensigns John Allan, George W. Street and Joseph Taillefer, Lieutenants Bruce Harman and Ernest Taschereau, the last-named being in command of a detachment of 25 non-commissioned officers and gunners from "A" and "B" Batteries from Kingston and Quebec.[14]

Time had not improved accommodations on *Frances Smith* and the men, for the most part, bunked wherever they could find space not already taken up with boxes of freight, "some spreading their blankets on boxes or barrels." According to one of the soldiers, who published a short account of his experiences in the Winnipeg publication, the *Manitoban*, the recruits were "a motley mixture, Ontario farmers' sons, genteel city youths, old soldiers formerly in British regiments, French habitants." Among them was a strange character by the name of Vigneau, who had fought in the ranks of the "Commune" in Paris, during the terrible outbreak in France following the Franco-Prussian War. He had escaped from France after the defeat of the Commune,[15] ultimately reaching Canada in time to enter the service of Great Britain's Queen! He was, apparently, good company, "singing French songs in an exceedingly forcible and excitable strain."[16] There was another entertainer on board, a ventriloquist who, while singing "Listen to the Mocking Bird," was able to imitate the sound of the wings and the peculiar whistle of the bird so effectively that it seemed to many soldiers that the bird itself was actually on board.

On 22 September the vessel reached Prince Arthur's Landing, and after unloading their stores and provisions, the troops set off at once, climbing the steep hill behind the town. They camped near the bridge over the Kamistikwia. Heavy rains had fallen a short time before and the ground was very wet and muddy. As the men sang the familiar song, "Tenting To-night," they altered the refrain to match the circumstances: "the old camp ground" became the "cold, damp ground."[17] After a breakfast of "the hardest of Christie Brown's hardtack, beef and tea," they continued on the journey to Shebandowan Lake. The boats, now somewhat battered after being used and abused by soldiers and civilians for over two years, were not in the best condition; but at least the oars were new, perhaps too new, as they were roughly hewn out of young saplings. With as many men crowded into each boat as it would carry — about 40, with a proportion of the provisions — each boat, under the command of a sergeant, was tied to a watercraft fitted with a small steam engine. The snake-like fleet of the Third Red River Expedition was then ready to depart for Lake of the Woods, following the same route as that used by Colonel Wolseley. According to one of the men who travelled with the expedition:

> The sight was weird in the extreme, the only lights visible being that from the sparks of the little steamer. We were in the midst of a lake in an uninhabited country, unknown to anyone except the voyageurs in charge. Our hearts however, were light; we knew we were on our way to that far away place — Fort Garry. The time was wiled away by songs, each boat vying with the others in rolling out the choruses.[18]

When they stepped into their various boats at Shebandowan Lake the soldiers invariably congratulated themselves that, unlike Wolseley's men, they would escape the toils of rowing. There was nothing like machine power to take the place of muscle power. But, after a few hours' confinement in the various boats, cramped between their broad-beamed companions and the barrels and boxes of provisions and equipment, they began to wish for a little activity, such as rowing. Finally, about 0100 hrs they came to their first portage. Here they had an opportunity to stretch their cramped bodies. It was easier work than their predecessors had experienced, if only because the third contingent had the aid of "a rickety old wagon and a team apparently reduced to the veritable 'straw a day.' "[19] By daylight the first portage was passed and after a breakfast of hardtack, they embarked on Lake Kashaboiwe. Here there was no steam tug, and the weather being cool, the troops were glad of the chance to handle their clumsy oars — even if their progress was slow. They camped for the night on the shores of Lac des Mille Lacs.

The journey of 1872 over lake and portage followed much the same pattern as those of 1870 and 1871. Crossing Baril Lake, Windigostigwan Portage, Pickerel Lake and the various other portages, the troops finally reached Sturgeon Lake where they encountered a severe gale. The boat occupied by the diarist was commanded by a Sergeant Brodie from Elora, who insisted that they should take refuge on shore. With them was another Sergeant named MacPherson, an old regular soldier who had served with the 100th Regiment. MacPherson saw no need for such delay. But, because Brodie was in command, MacPherson was compelled by army discipline to comply with Brodie's orders, all the while muttering his concern about the quality of Brodie's courage. The next day, MacPherson again insisted upon taking to the water. Despite Brodie's opposition, MacPherson and the men launched their boat, leaving poor Brodie "standing on a rock, wildly gesticulating and threatening" everybody concerned "with arrest and court-martial for disobedience of orders and insubordination." According to the diarist, "we did not quail, however, and as we kept on vigorously at the oars we could faintly hear Brodie's wail to leave him some beef."[20] In the end, the crew persuaded the obstinate MacPherson to return and give "our modern Robinson Crusoe an opportunity of joining us."[21] When, eventually, the Brodie-MacPherson boat reached the next portage, they found other members of the expedition anxious about the safety of the missing boat and preparing to go to search for it. This particular episode, incidentally, provided one of the soldiers, Fred Swire, with the subject matter for a piece of doggerel verse, which he composed at Fort Garry, much to the delight of the soldiers who were aware of the episode, although it did not meet with the complete approval of the two sergeants concerned.[22]

In the absence of the strict discipline imposed by Wolseley, there were occasions when the soldiers in Villiers's charge forgot that theirs was a military expedition and not a sporting event. Racing between crews became a popular activity. On one occasion two boats racing towards Sturgeon Lake collided, damaging both boats and breaking several oars. Rivalry between the Quebec and the Ontario contingents was particularly keen. On one occasion, Ensign Taillefer, a former Papal Zouave, after having given strict orders against racing, rather than let an Ontario boat pass him, pushed one of his oarsmen aside and grasped the oar himself. He was, according to the diarist, "a Hercules in strength and size," and he gave the oar such a mighty tug that he broke the thwart pin, and fell backwards with heels in the air. His only remark on recovering his seat was, "Well, boys, you must not think I am a poor rower." The diarist commented, "It was generally remarked that Mr. Taillefer was never known to smile, and it is certain he did not on that occasion, though his crew did."[23] Fortunately, the Third Expedition, like its predecessors, carried Indian voyageurs on strength, and the running of the rapids in the Maligne River and on the Rainy River above Fort Frances, was their responsibility. Sometimes there were accidents and sometimes narrow escapes, but most of the boats and all of the men completed the journey unscathed.

As the first boat approached Fort Frances, it was greeted by Lieutenant-Colonel Osborne Smith, who, like Captain William Butler in 1870, had made his way westwards through the United States and then travelled by canoe to Fort Frances to meet Lieutenant-Colonel Villiers, who was due to return to Canada. Smith was a strict disciplinarian, much more so than Villiers, who handed over his command and departed. At once Smith called a battalion parade. It being Sunday, the troops imagined it would be a church parade. However, it was not in the language of the Book of Common Prayer that Smith addressed the troops. Instead, with more than faint irritation in his voice, he berated them for wasting "God's precious food," concluding his remarks by stating that "if any man in future saw another wasting provisions, he was to hit him over the head with his rifle," adding "I will justify him in doing so,"[24] The fact was that the Expedition was low on food, and Smith was obliged to obtain additional supplies from the Hudson's Bay Company at Fort Frances. The soldier-diarist's comment was:

> It did not seem to us that there was any waste, as some 300 men, exposed to the exhilarating ozone of the October breezes of the Dawson Route and rowing heavy boats, had perfectly legitimate means of getting away with food without "casting their bread upon the waters."[25]

Bidding "a regretful goodbye to our popular leader, Lieutenant-Colonel de Villiers, who had brought us safely to that point," the men of the Expedition resumed their journey down Rainy River. Generally, the soldiers regretted Villiers's departure, if only because the new commander was a tougher disciplinarian than he was. Moreover, fresh meat had been available at Fort Frances, but now they were back on the old diet of salt pork and hardtack. After laying in further supplies of flour, the Expedition's boats moved on, [26] past Hungry

Hall, and then into Lake of the Woods, where a strong wind was blowing. At this point, the Expedition's diarist returned again to the question of rations, expending his literary talent on further criticisms of the daily bill-of-fare, "slapjacks ":

> The recipe for the preparation of which is — mix flour with rainy River water to the consistency of dough, spread it by hand into cakes of a suitable size and bake on sheet iron frying-pans over an open fire, built on a sandy beach. In order that the slapjacks be properly seasoned, it is necessary that the wind should be blowing at the rate of about ten miles [16 km] an hour, sufficient to incorporate enough sand in them to make them palatable. No other seasoning should be used.[27]

The Expedition cooks, apparently, followed this recipe to the letter. Given the circumstances, they could hardly have done otherwise.

When the wind fell, the troops continued their journey across Lake of the Woods, reaching the North West Angle, where they pushed through "a broad expanse of wild rice bordering the shore at this point."[28] On landing, they were greeted by a cavalcade of Red River carts with Métis drivers ready to carry the heavy stores, some 175 kilometres to Fort Garry. The road proceeded for the first 120 kilometres through stands of tall, dead tamarack and spruce trees, killed by an earlier forest fire. The troops were able to march about 50 kilometres a day, which was respectable, "considering that the road bed was of white sand" in which every man, carrying his rifle, accoutrements and forty rounds of ammunition, sank about five centimetres at every step. It was hardly suitable for those unfortunate beings who had been issued at Collingwood with boots several sizes too large. Some found the answer in throwing the boots into the carts, and filling their socks with hay. At least the socks were more comfortable than ill-fitting boots, but it is questionable if they lasted very long.

On the afternoon of the third day from the North West Angle, the troops finally emerged on the prairie near Pointe de Chêne. Here, for the first time on the march, they encountered snow, 15 centimetres of it. When the muddy snow deteriorated into slush, it was anything but comfortable for the shoeless men. But the troops shambled on. They had no choice, even though fatigue enveloped them like their sodden coats. On 21 October they reached the Seine, where they washed and cleaned up "before entering civilization again."[29] Passing Bishop

Taché's house in St. Boniface, they crossed the Red River by ferry, and then marched over the Assiniboine on a pontoon bridge, and through the south gate of Fort Garry.

The military barracks, enclosed by the walls of the fort, consisted of three buildings, two stories high, built of logs in the Red River fashion, and shingled with heavy oak shingles "fastened to oak sheeting with old-fashioned broad-headed handmade nails." A large door, facing the square, opened into a vestibule, on each side of which was a large barn-like room. From the vestibule a staircase led to two similar rooms on the second floor. Around the rooms were the cots for the men, and in the centre were tables and benches. As the diarist says, "in these homely and primitive quarters we found a home." Each man, having been allotted a cot, proceeded to fill his tick with straw. Then they were free, for the time being, to write letters, renew old acquaintances among those who had re-enlisted and remained with the force, or make their way to a semi-basement room in an adjoining building "to regale themselves with the liquid refreshments provided and for sale to thirsty soldiers."[30]

IV

During the following years a few changes were made in the Canadian military organization in Manitoba. The green uniforms, used since the despatch of the militia rifle battalions by Wolseley in 1870, were replaced in 1873 with the scarlet tunics of the British regular infantry; and a more realistic approach was taken towards the militia establishment as the Adjutant-General struck off corps existing only as paper companies. Meanwhile recruits for the Provisional Battalion continued to be sought in Canada, although in diminishing numbers. In 1874 the reinforcements were drawn from M.D.'s 8 and 9 (Fredericton, N.B. and Halifax, N.S.). The new drafts made their way west during the course of that summer. For the moment there still seemed to be a need for an armed force in the North West, but increasingly, Canadian politicians were returning to John A. Macdonald's original idea of a mounted constabulary rather than developing the mounted infantry urged by Osborne Smith.

Once the decision was taken to go the police route, the Provisional Battalion was simply allowed to dwindle away. By the end of 1875 its enrolment had fallen to: artillery, two officers and 20 non-commissioned officers and men; infantry, nine officers and 89 non-commissioned officers and men with a total strength of 111. Of these, few had served for any length of time. Most of them, as Lieutenant-Colonel Osborne Smith reported, had arrived with the drafts despatched from the Eastern Provinces in August. Of the general conduct and physique of these drafts, Smith reported that they were "all that can be desired, and with few exceptions, reflect credit on the various military districts from which they have been drawn."[31] He also remarked that crime was "rare", that "strictest discipline is observed" and that their military proficiency was "most satisfactory." The British General Officer Commanding the Canadian Militia, Major-General Edward Selby-Smythe, reminded the Minister of Militia in January 1876:

> There has happily been no occasion for calling on the intervention of these troops, except during a Fenian bubble, and though no troops can be maintained without expense, yet the money so expended gives security and is for the most part spent among the tradesmen of the Province . . . since a force has been established . . . regularity and peace have prevailed, with protection to life and property, the presence of the military and their influence on the minds of the people are guarantees of good order.[32]

Despite Selby-Smythe's support of the Provisional Battalion in Manitoba, what remained of that group, the last of the full-time soldiers who had played so important a role in the formative years of the new province, was finally disbanded in 1877. For the next few years, responsibility for western Canada's first line of defence would rest with the several militia companies in Manitoba, supported by the mounted constabulary the government had been talking about since 1870.

Macdonald's ideas of a western Canadian police force, vague as they necessarily had been in late 1869, took on a more precise form on 6 April 1870, when the Canadian government approved an Order-in-Council providing for the organization of a "mixed force" of whites, French and English-speaking Métis, enlisted for three years, at fifty cents per diem and armed with Spencer repeating rifles and revolvers by the Department of Militia. The force was to be a federal force, not one under provincial control.[33] Fifty of the authorized 200 men were to be recruited in central Canada and 15 of them were to be bilingual. The remainder of the force was to be recruited in Red River; "co-mingling the different races," as Macdonald had stated in the House of Commons on 2 May 1870.[34] The police scheme, as originally drafted, had been set aside when the Red River delegates insisted upon provincial status for Manitoba. Under the British North America Act, policing was a matter of provincial and not federal jurisdiction. And so the proposed mounted police did not accompany Wolseley to Red River. Although, let it be noted, the police scheme was never scrapped: it was simply held in abeyance, a point that Macdonald implied in his remarks to the House of Commons on 2 May. A year later Macdonald returned to his idea of a force of mounted police for the west. Writing to Sir George Cartier in June 1871, the Prime Minister suggested that thought might once more be given to a mounted police force for the western territories in view of the possibility of increased immigration to the west.[35]

Meanwhile the situation in the regions west of the province of Manitoba was becoming a threat to peace and good order. As early as October 1870, Captain William Butler, who did not return to central Canada with the regular troops, was commissioned by the Lieutenant-Governor of Manitoba to undertake a journey into the North West Territories. With the minimum of gear and travelling with a Red River Métis guide, Butler made a winter expedition over the western prairies as far as the Rocky Mountains. His instructions were to examine the situation in the Territories "from an independent point of view . . . in reference to the necessity of troops being sent there," to "report upon the whole question of the existing affairs in that territory" and "to ascertain . . . in what places and among what tribes of Indians, and what settlements of whites, the small-pox is now prevailing, including the extent of its ravages and every particular you can ascertain in connexion with the rise and spread of the disease."[36]

Butler had been told to carry out his mission with all possible despatch. This he did. Starting from Fort Garry on 25 October, he journeyed to Fort Ellice, and then on to Fort Carlton on the North Saskatchewan. Passing the Hudson's Bay Company posts at Battle River, Fort Pitt and Victoria, he reached Edmonton on the night of 26 November. From Edmonton he travelled in a southwesterly direction towards Rocky Mountain House, until, on 4 December, he caught sight of the Rocky Mountains "which rose from the westerly extremity of an immense plain and stretched their great snow-clad peaks far away to the northern and southern horizons."[37] Returning to Edmonton he set out for Red River in weather so harsh that his thermometer registered -39 C. on 22 December. "Later in the day a biting wind swept the long reaches of the Saskatchewan River and rendered travelling on the ice almost insupportable."[38] Early in February Butler quit the Saskatchewan River valley at Cedar Lake, crossed the ridge which separated it from Lake Winnipegosis, descending this lake to its outlet at the Waterhen River. Finally, on 18 February, he reached the Pointe de Chêne on the south shore of Lake Manitoba and two days later entered Fort Garry. In this part of his journey, Butler had passed in succession, the Mission of Prince Albert, Fort-à-la-Corne and Fort Cumberland, and the trading posts of The Pas, Moose Lake, Shoal River and Manitoba House. From first to last the journey had taken 119 days and covered a distance of 4345 kilometres. During most of this time Butler experienced the utter loneliness, the intense silence and the vast solitude of the prairie country in winter.

In his report, while commenting on the obvious absence of any means of enforcing the authority of the law, Butler emphasized the fact that "the elements of disorder in the whole territory of Saskatchewan" were "yearly on the increase."[39] This he attributed to the decline in the numbers of the buffalo, "the red man's sole means of subsistence," to the constant "state of hostility" between the Indians and the whites in the United States which was spilling over into British territory, and to the spread of smallpox. In great measure the trouble with the Indians came from the growing threat from free-traders and from the increasing numbers of white immigrants moving into country that the Indians claimed as their traditional hunting grounds. He also detected a growing uneasiness among the Métis, mostly in Red River, a feeling of distrust towards Canada, " and a certain hesitation to accept the Dominion Government."[40] Other disturbing elements were the American miners and the stories of the atrocities they were alleged to have committed in the United States. Butler also reported on the various Indian tribes, and the devastation resulting from smallpox. He commented critically upon the increased sale and consumption of liquor and on the political dangers inherent in the growing numbers of American traders operating out of Fort Benton.

The problems of order and security were of such magnitude, in Butler's view, that he strongly recommended the early appointment of a civil magistrate or commissioner, "after the model of similar appointments in Ireland and in India," who should reside on the Upper Saskatchewan and who should be supported by

> . . . a well-equipped force of from 100 to 150 men, one-third to be mounted, specially recruited and engaged for service in the Saskatchewan; enlisting for two or

three years' service, and at the expiration of that period to become military settlers, receiving grants of land, but still remaining as a reserve force should their services be required.[41]

Butler, who had previously visited American army posts in the west, rejected the idea that soldiers should be employed to police the prairies. This recommendation was most far-reaching in its consequences. Butler was a shrewd observer and his report an eminently readable document.

The federal government did not, however, send the "well-equipped force" that Butler had suggested to the North West in 1872. Instead, it sent reinforcements to the "Provisionals" in Manitoba. Meanwhile, early in 1872, the Adjutant-General of the Militia, Colonel P. Robertson Ross, went himself to take a look at the situation in the North West. By this time Butler had published his book, *The Great Lone Land*, giving a detailed account of his experiences in the far western territories. What he wrote could not be ignored. Ross reported directly to the Prime Minister, pointing out that he found himself in full agreement with Butler. If anything, he believed that the situation was even worse than Butler had described, not because he was more observant than Butler, but because the situation had deteriorated. Ross was appalled at what he saw and heard: rampant lawlessness, American bootleggers importing rotgut alcohol, rifles and revolvers; smugglers making huge profits and showing complete disdain for Canadian sovereignty; Indians demoralized by drunkenness and murder; and when the Hudson's Bay officials protested, they were told by the American interlopers "they would do just as they pleased."[42] Robertson Ross recommended that a force of mounted rifles should be organized and sent to the Canadian North West; that it should number not less than 500 officers and men who should be clothed in the red tunics familiar to the Indians from the days of the 6th Warwickshires at Fort Garry, certainly not in blue like the American troops.[43]

While waiting for action to be taken on the Robertson Ross Report, the new Lieutenant-Governor of Manitoba, Alexander Morris, urged that the Provisional Battalion be retained in Manitoba. News from the North West was becoming steadily more alarming, and when Robertson Ross's Report finally reached the public in March 1873, opinion had moved decidedly in favour of the establishment of the police force Macdonald had been considering for several years. Almost simultaneously with the publication of the Robertson Ross Report in

March 1873, the Prime Minister announced to the House of Commons:

> It is the intention of the Government to ask the House for a moderate grant of money to organize a mounted police force, somewhat similar to the Irish Mounted Constabulary. They would have the advantage of military discipline, would be armed in a simple but effective way, would use the hardy horses of the country, and by being police would be a civil force, each member of which would be a police constable, and therefore a preventive officer.[44]

The government's bill was passed unopposed and received Royal Assent, 23 May 1873. What is surprising is that little or no comment about the bill appeared in the press. It provided for recruiting 300 men, between 18 and 40 years, for three years' service. Departing somewhat from Macdonald's earlier ideas, there was no requirement for bilingualism or for the recruiting of westerners.

The first recruits were enrolled in September, leaving for Manitoba on 2 October. They followed the now familiar route, by train from Toronto to Collingwood, and then by boat to Thunder Bay. The advanced party left Collingwood on 4 October. The officer in charge of the detachment, Major J. M. Walsh, made arrangements for transporting his men by waggon over Dawson's road, now pounded into shape by the feet of hundreds of soldiers and immigrants, from Prince Arthur's Landing to Shebandowan Lake. Here, as one police recruit, No.33, James McKernan, recorded, "our real trip commenced by small government tugs and large open boats, to Rainy Lake and Lake of the

Lower Fort Garry, 1870, from a contemporary print.

Lieutenant-Colonel G.A. French,
first Commissioner of the
North West Mounted Police.

Woods."[45] The Police detachment finally reached Manitoba in a blinding blizzard of snow and rain. Major Walsh led the recruits to Fort Garry, and from there downriver to the Lower Fort, which had been turned over to the Mounted Police by the Militia Department.

This initial contingent, because it was the first, was designated as "A" Troop. Two other troops, "B" and "C" followed. On 3 November 1873, the men of all three Troops were sworn in as members of "The Mounted Police Force of Canada," by Lieutenant-Colonel Osborne Smith, D.A.G. commanding M.D. 10.

The first signature was that of A.H. Griesbach, the second that of Percy R. Neale and the third, that of Samuel Benfield Steele, who after retiring at the end of his year's service with the 1st (Ontario) Rifles, had continued his military training at the School of Artillery at Kingston, Ontario. Taking discharge from the artillery, he enrolled in the Mounted Police as a sergeant-major. For the time being, Lieutenant-Colonel Osborne Smith served as commander of the Police, but only until the arrival of the new Commissioner, Lieutenant-Colonel George A. French, who had formerly commanded "A" Battery and its School of

Gunnery at Kingston, Ontario. In the following year, on 7 June 1874, the Police contingent was officially designated the North West Mounted Police. At the same time it left its first home in the Stone Fort, to establish a new base at Dufferin, not far from North Pembina, the site of O'Donoghue's futile efforts. Here it was joined by reinforcements who had received the necessary authority from the United States government to travel in civilian clothes by train to the Canadian west through American territory. Only the 1873 police recruits used the Dawson route, which had been followed by the soldiers, regular and militia, since 1870.

V

With the disappearance of the "Provisional" force from Manitoba's history, came the end of Canada's first, full-time Canadian infantry battalion. The soldiers who were part of the Canadian expeditions to Red River were more than militia. To all intents and purposes, they were short-term regulars. Until "A" and "D" companies of Princess Patricia's Canadian Light Infantry were domiciled in Winnipeg in 1920, the "provisionals" were the only regular Canadian infantry to serve in Manitoba. One might even go further, and claim for those who went to Manitoba between 1870 and 1876, the distinction of being the Dominion of Canada's first regular infantry soldiers.[46]

CHAPTER TWELVE

Epilogue

I

The Red River Expedition of 1870 and the military expeditions that followed in successive years attracted little attention beyond the territorial limits of Canada, with the exception of a few disappointed people in Minnesota and a few suspicious watch-dogs in the State Department in Washington. Americans generally were disposed to look upon Canada as little more than a British colony. London, rather than Ottawa, was the object of their attention. American concern, in the 1870s, focussed upon how much compensation could be extracted from Great Britain for damages inflicted upon Northern shipping by the Southern commerce raider, *Alabama;* certainly not how much compensation the American government ought to pay Canada for damages inflicted by the Irish-Americans who raided Canada in 1866, 1870 and 1871. When Americans did think of Canada, it was to wonder why Canadians were so slow in accepting the inevitability of annexation, particularly under its new guise of "continentalism." As far as the British were concerned, they were more interested in the aggressiveness of the Germans pounding the armies of Napoleon III with unexpected success just across the English Channel. Red River? Where was it? What was the fuss all about? Few Britons knew. Their newspapers were not highly informative.

From Wolseley's standpoint, the Red River Expedition was a major event in his military career. Perhaps it was *the* major event. He never ceased talking about it for the rest of his days. It brought to his mind "the stories read in boyhood of how wild bands of fierce Norse freebooters set out from some secluded bay in quest of plunder and adventure."[1] Certainly the Expedition meant more to Wolseley than excitement, strange surroundings, or even a knighthood. It brought associations and friendships with a number of officers who, in later years became his close associates, members of "The Wolseley Ring," a group referred to as "the most influential cabal of the late Victorian Army."[2] The Red River Expedition also led to the development of new military techniques; techniques acquired from civilians, Canadian Indians and voyageurs; techniques that Wolseley adopted in later military campaigns. The Red River Expedition was Wolseley's first independent command, and on his record it looked as if he had suppressed a "rebellion" in North West Canada without the loss of a single soldier.[3] A high recommendation, that!

The Red River Expedition is important in Canadian military history, not simply because of the techniques that Wolseley found so fascinating— they were, after all, part of Canadian military tradition from the early days of the French régime — but because it was the last British military operation in North America. The Red River Expedition was carried out at the beginning of the imperial revival in Great Britain, at the time when John Ruskin was telling British undergraduates at Oxford University:

> There is a destiny now possible to us, the highest ever set before a nation to be accepted or refused. . . . Will you youths of England make your country again a royal throne of kings, a sceptered isle, for all the world a source of light, a centre of peace; mistress of learning and of the Arts, faithful guardian of time-honoured principles? This is what England must either do or perish; she must found colonies as fast and as far as she is able, formed of her most energetic and worthiest men; seizing every piece of fruitful waste ground she can set her foot on, and then teaching these her colonists that their chief virtue is to be fidelity to their country, and their first aim is to be to advance the power of England by land and sea. . . .[4]

Yet, even in the midst of this florid rhetoric, the British, like the Romans before them, were beginning to pull back their legions for the defence of the homeland. As the later years of the nineteenth century were to show, there was still glory to be derived from colonial adventures in Asia and in Africa, but not in North America. The new imperially-minded United States had proved its strength during the Civil War. Like other imperially-minded peoples jealous of Great Britain, the Americans were anxious to extend their own concepts of progress, culture and salvation to the less fortunate communities of the western world. Even if Canadians did not quite realize it, Great Britain's role in North America was coming to a close.

Perhaps that was just as well. It is clear that Wolseley, the darling of the imperialists, was too much the British officer to appreciate the delicate nature of his position in Canada. He never seemed quite to grasp the fact that his Canadian troops were an Anglo-French, Protestant-Catholic mix. Emphatically Anglo-Irish, Protestant, anti-Catholic and anti-French, Wolseley saw Louis Riel's actions in Red River only as part of a conspiracy, directed by a clever, cunning, unscrupulous, French Canadian, Roman Catholic bishop in St. Boniface, and an equally cunning, unscrupulous, French Canadian, Roman Catholic Minister of Militia in Ottawa. He listened intently to Colonel G. T. Denison, because he shared Denison's views, views that reinforced his own prejudices. Better by far, for his place in Canadian history, had he kept his thoughts to himself. After all, he knew that a soldier is not expected to be politician or theologian. Admittedly Oliver Cromwell was both. But then he belonged to the 17th, not to the 19th century. It was the soldier's duty to carry out his responsibilities with complete political neutrality.[5] Because Wolseley did not really comprehend the social and political issues in Canada, it would have been better for his historical reputation had he refrained from political comment and simply carried out the military duties assigned to him.

It was particularly unfortunate that Wolseley committed his prejudices to paper. After his return to Great Britain in 1870, he used *Blackwood's Edinburgh Magazine* to display his contempt for the elected officials of Canada's government and the civilian employees of the Canadian Department of Militia. He claimed that, instead of buying superior British products for the Expedition, they insisted upon purchasing "inferior and dearer" military stores and equipment that should have been obtained from British sources. Everything, he deplored, had to pass through the hands of "their own agents" and "their own political friends and supporters." He was inclined to harp on this point, adding, "when money is to be spent in Canada, the opportunity is seldom lost for furthering party objects."[6] He condemned, in unequivocal terms, the employment of civilians in the transport service, calling the drivers:

> . . . a more worthless set . . . it is scarcely possible to imagine. . . . As soon as these men got clear of a station on the road, and out of view of the transport officers, they played all sorts of pranks, and instead of going at a steady walk, chose their own pace, sometimes amusing themselves by racing.[7]

After pointing out that the Minister of Public Works was a French Canadian "known to be heart and soul with the priestly party in Quebec, and therefore most favourably inclined to Riel,"[8] he went on to damn S. J. Dawson with faint praise and to attribute his slow progress with the road to Shebandowan Lake to the "hangers-on" forced on him by the federal Ministers. Some of these workers Wolseley referred to as "broken-down drunkards who, it was thought by their friends might be reclaimed, if they could only be sent on an errand into a country where no whisky was to be had." These civilians, he added, "all more or less belonged to the class known in America as 'loafers' — men who lived no one knew how, spending nearly all their time in bars 'liquoring-up' and smoking."[9] When a number of Indians refused to work for him, Wolseley blamed their defection on "the priesthood of Canada being much opposed to this Expedition."[10] Wolseley also passed harsh judgment on the voyageurs — a judgment he must have overlooked or forgotten several years later, when in 1885 he asked for Canadian voyageurs to be added to his Nile Expedition to help rescue General Gordon at Khartoum.

To express criticism of Wolseley's attitudes towards Canadians, both white and native peoples, is not to suggest that he was an incompetent officer. That he was not. For the success of the initial Red River Expedition, not all but much of the credit must go to him. He was, moreover, impressive in appearance, and possessed good military credentials, the will to succeed, and sufficient arrogance to inspire respect. He had no need to belittle his civilian assistants or to criticize the Minister who employed him.

Acknowledging Wolseley's leadership qualities, it is essential to give credit to the Department of Militia for the successful outcome of the Expedition. The Red River Expedition was, after all, the first major logistical and military exercise undertaken by the Department of Militia after Confederation. And the major credit for mobilizing, equipping and transporting the two militia rifle battalions in 1870 must go to Sir George Cartier and his staff in Ottawa. They, along with the British commanding general, Lieutenant-General, the Honourable James Lindsay, not Colonel Garnet Wolseley, were responsible for finding, outfitting and feeding the troops, and providing them with the means of transport to Prince Arthur's Landing and beyond to Fort Garry. That was no small task for a department less than three years old. Particularly when it is remembered that the same department was faced with the task of fielding another militia force to resist the Irish-American raids directed against Montreal and threats of raids into Ontario, at the very time when the Red River force was being made ready to be sent to the west.

It may have been the Englishman's ingrained assumption of superiority and his tendency to denigrate things colonial, or the professional military officer's impatience with civilian ways of doing things, or even his ill-concealed religious prejudices that led Colonel Garnet Wolseley to quarrel with his civilian engineer, Simon Dawson. Certainly Wolseley was always inclined to argue that Dawson misled him about the state of the road from the head of Lake Superior to Shebandowan Lake, and that the delays in getting the troops under way were the fault of Dawson's workmen.

On the other hand, Simon Dawson, after the Expedition was over, argued, with good reason, that he had given Wolseley an honest statement about the road conditions weeks before any troops had embarked on *Chicora*; and that it was General Lindsay, not Wolseley, who got things moving at Thunder Bay by authorizing the use of "additional companies of troops to aid in opening and improving the road when, up to this time, no aid had been received, except in making a few repairs in the vicinity of Thunder Bay."[11] Wolseley's contribution had been to drag boats up the Kakabeka Falls and to move them over the rough and rocky Kaminstikwia River, at a time when the water level was in its summer decline. The use of this river remained a constant source of argument between the two men. Wolseley took the view that the Kaministikwia experiment had been a success and as a physical achievement, it was; but Dawson argued that it was a waste of men and energy, and productive of damage to the boats; which it was. According to Dawson, it was Wolseley's policy, not the machinations of the "Romish" clergy, that prompted a number of the Indian voyageurs to pack up and go home: that Wolseley's policy entailed the diversion of workmen from building the main road to building access roads to the river, thus wasting time and effort in non-essential tasks. He quoted his voyageurs as asking:

> Why . . . do you keep us dragging boats over rocks where there is no water to float them, when a single waggon could accomplish more in a day than eight of us can in ten? By using waggons you would have your boats in good order; whereas, by exposing them to such usage as this, they are being rendered unfit for the long journey yet before us.[12]

Dawson, who knew the country, also took the view that Wolseley, despite the fact that he had published a statement in Red River that his was a "mission of peace," was, in fact, greatly concerned about a Métis ambush — a military operation that Dawson considered as wholly impractical at any point along the route before reaching Fort Alexander and the flat country of the Red River valley. The Métis, after all, were horsemen accustomed to the prairie, not woodsmen.

Wolseley, and many of the soldiers themselves for that matter, imply in their accounts that they spent long hours working on the road, prior to embarkation at Shebandowan Lake. Dawson's statement shows that between 5 June and 16 November, the total in dollars and cents, paid to the troops as a road work supplement, amounted to $1829.88 of which $736.63 was paid to the Militia and the balance to the regulars: the 60th Rifles, the Royal Artillery and the Royal Engineers. Of this amount, at least one third was spent on work around Thunder Bay, in building an access road from the main road to the Kaministikwia River to "facilitate movements in connection with the scheme of dragging boats by hand;" and in building a stockade at Thunder Bay for the defence of the military encampment. Following General Lindsay's visit in June, the situation improved and, according to Dawson, "new energy seemed infused everywhere," additional companies were sent to work on the roads, and among them the volunteers "from whom, up to this time, no aid had been received, except in making a few repairs in the vicinity of Thunder Bay." The most significant factor in improving road conditions was, as Dawson admitted, an improvement in the weather.[13]

The Dawson Road, it should be noted, remained in constant use in the years that followed. Not only was it followed by the military reinforcements sent to Red River annually and by the first contingent of Mounted Police that arrived in Red River in 1873; it was also the route of many of the civilian immigrants who made their way to the golden west. When spring opened in 1871, Dawson reported that the road built the previous year was in a "primitive condition," but during the summer new portages were constructed and dams built to improve navigation. By August 1872 nine steam launches were in operation, with two "steamers" travelling in the navigable sections of the route. Barges were also under construction for the transportation of horses and waggons. Dawson wrote enthusiastically — perhaps optimistically would be a better word— about the new "comfortable buildings" that were being constructed for the accommodation of immigrants at Shebandowan Lake, at Kashaboiwe, at the Height of

Land and at Fort Frances. Meanwhile stores of lumber were accumulated to erect buildings at the North West Angle and at "convenient intervals" along the North West Angle road. Until the construction of the Canadian Pacific Railway, the Dawson Road remained the principal route for traders and immigrants making their way from Ontario to the Province of Manitoba. But, in its origin, Dawson's road was primarily a military road. And it served adequately as such. Adequately enough to enhance Colonel Wolseley's professional reputation and gain him a knighthood in the Order of St. Michael and St. George.

II

As a military operation, the Red River Expedition was basically a logistical exercise, an exercise in which the determining factors were the shortness of time available to the British troops before their withdrawal, and the nature of the terrain. The 60th Rifles had to be back in Canada, ready to embark for Great Britain by the month of October— and yet the actual authorization of the Red River Expedition was not announced in *General Orders* until 10 May.[14] The problems posed by the terrain involved water transportation from Collingwood on Georgian Bay, to Thunder Bay on the shores of Lake Superior; and the movement of men, arms and supplies overland from Prince Arthur's Landing to the portals of Fort Garry on the Red River. Over 1370 kilometres had to be traversed by lightly constructed wooden boats, and canoes, negotiating hazardous rapids, slippery rocks and marshy ground, at the height of the insect season. Wolseley, even if he was inclined to exaggerate, was expressing the views of the troops, when he wrote, "I doubt whether any British force ever began so serious an undertaking under blacker prophecies of impending disaster, which in some instances seemed meant as threats."[15]

The problem was not just one of moving men. It was one of moving arms, ammunition, rations and other necessary supplies, on the backs of officers and men alike; of manhandling boats, awkward boxes and bundles, even cannon, over the rocky portages; and of loading, unloading and reloading every day.

It could have meant carrying the sick and the injured. Wolseley's expedition was fortunate in that the journeys both ways were remarkably free from injury or disease. The force commander was inclined to attribute his success to the absence of alcoholic beverages. Whatever the explanation, it was a remarkable feature of the Expedition that casualties were minimal: no sick and only two injured personnel who were able subsequently to rejoin their units.

Wolseley always boasted of the high morale of the troops engaged in the Red River Expedition, and the absence of crime — the latter, of course, being the logical sequel of the former. Although neither government did so, both the British and Canadian governments, might well have commented upon the comparatively small cost of the operation, less than 100,000 pounds sterling for moving 1400 troops over half a continent from Toronto to Fort Garry, and for moving the British contingent back again to Toronto. Both Wolseley and the Department of Militia had reason for some self-congratulation. And with no blood shed in battle, no scorched earth, no burnings of homes, no destruction of farmlands.

There is little doubt that Wolseley, and many of his soldiers, British and Canadian alike, despite their commander's talk about a "mission of peace," hoped for, or at least expected, a tussle with the "forces" of Louis Riel's Provisional Government. "After all," they muttered, "isn't that what soldiers are for? To fight?" There was no question that many of the Ontarians did enlist as a result of the emotional excitement whipped up by *Canada First*, in order to avenge the shooting of Thomas Scott. A glance through Wolseley's journal leaves no doubt in the reader's mind that the force commander believed and hoped that Riel would offer resistance. That was because he opened his mind and his ears only to Riel's opponents, the men who had been imprisoned in Fort Garry on the orders of the Provisional Government. His sole intelligence officer at Red River, Captain Butler, likewise drew his information from anti-Riel sources. Given Wolseley's own background and convictions, it was unlikely that he would have listened seriously to any others. However, in all fairness to the force commander, it must be conceded that it was his responsibility to consider all options, all possibilities.

Unfamiliar with the Canadian situation, Wolseley was disposed to see the western problem through the eyes of Colonel George T. Denison, who was one of the most active leaders of *Canada First*. Denison and Wolseley shared similar anti-French and anti-Catholic prejudices, and, probably for those reasons alone, Denison acquired considerable influence over the British officer. Denison was invited to stay at Wolseley's quarters in Montreal and to discuss the political situation in Canada and the West with the British officer. That he influenced Wolseley's thinking is the impression one draws from reading Denison's books. There seems little reason to question the assumption that Wolseley took his cue from Denison on Manitoban affairs. When the Canadian authorities vetoed Denison's appointment to Wolseley's staff, the British commander responded by choosing George Denison's brother, Fred, as one of his aides-de-camp. If we are to believe George Denison, he and his friends were responsible for defeating an alleged "plot" of Cartier to withdraw the Expedition and allow Riel to remain in charge at Fort Garry until Lieutenant-Governor Archibald's arrival.[16]

Even if Wolseley was disappointed at the absence of a fight on 24 August, he and his troops had good reason to be pleased when they discovered that Riel had quietly withdrawn. That meant that the occupation of Red River was effected without a bullet being fired. No one was killed under the guise of justice; there were no field executions; no unpleasant manhunts; no messy internment camps. Broken promises; but no scorched countryside and no genocide. But then, let us also remember that the Red River Expedition took place in the nineteenth century and not in the twentieth. Whether we fully appreciate it or not, the last century was, in many ways, more charitable and less vindictive than that in which we live.

Sic transit gloria — *the remains of Wolseley's transports of 1870.*

APPENDIX A

GENERAL ORDERS[1] Montreal, 10th May, 1870

1. It has been decided that a Force of Regulars and Volunteers shall be sent to the Red River Settlement.

2. Colonel G. J. Wolseley, Deputy Quartermaster-General, has been appointed, with the approval of His Excellency, the Governor-General, to command the Expedition.

3. The following Staff Officers to the Force have been appointed:-
Brevet Lieut.-Col. Bolton R. A., Deputy-Assistant General.
Major McLeod (Active Militia) Assistant to the Dept.-Assist. Adjt.-Gen.
Captain Huyshe R.B.
Lieutenant F.C. Denison (Active Militia) Orderly Officers.

    His Excellency the Governor-General having placed his Military Secretary, Lieutenant Colonel McNeill, at the disposal of the Lieutenant-General, he will be attached to the Staff of the Expedition.

4. The following Control Officers to the Force have been appointed:-

    1. Assistant-Controller M.B. Irving [Irvine] (In charge between Fort William and Fort Garry).
    2. Purveyor Mellish.
    3. Deputy-Assistant Commissary-General Meyer.
    4. Deputy-Assistant Commissary-General Beamish.
    5. Deputy-Assistant Superintendent of Stores Jolly, Captain Money, R.C. Rifles, Acting Deputy Commissary Captain Peebles (Active Militia) Acting Deputy.
    Commissary Lieutenant C.C. Smith, R. C. Rifles, Acting Assistant Commissary.

5. The following Medical Officers to the Force have been appointed:-

    Surgeon-Major Young, M.D., 1st Batt. 60th Rifles, Principal Medical Officer.
    Assistant Surgeon Olliver, M.D. 1st Battalion 60th Rifles.
    Assistant Surgeon Shaw, M.D.
    Assistant Surgeon Robertson, M.D.
    Assistant Surgeon Chatterton, M.D.

6. The force will consist of:-

    A Detachment Royal Artillery, under Lieutenant Alleyne.
    A Detachment Royal Engineers under Lieutenant Heneage.
    7 Companies of the 1st Battalion 60th Rifles under Colonel Fielden.
    A Detachment Army Hospital Corps and Army Service Corps under Assistant Controller Irving [Irvine].
    A Battalion of Militia under Lieutenant-Colonel Jarvis, D.A.G. Militia, 3rd District.
    A Battalion of Militia under Lieutenant-Colonel Casault, D.A.G. Militia, 7th District.

7. The whole of the troops will be held in readiness to move at short notice to Toronto, where the Force will be organized.

8. The Inspector-General of Hospitals will arrange for a careful medical inspection of all men selected for the Expedition.

9. The following daily ration is granted from the date of the Force leaving Toronto, and will be issued free of charge to non-commissioned officers and men. No working pay will be issued, except to men employed by the Public Works Department.

   Daily Ration

   1 lb. Biscuit, or 1 1/2 of Soft Bread
   1 lb. Salt Pork, or 1 1/2 lb. of Fresh Meat
   2 oz. Sugar
   1 oz. Tea
   1/2 oz. Salt (when fresh meat is issued)
   1/3 pint of Beans, or 1/4 lb. Preserved Potatoes
   1.36 oz. Pepper

   Tobacco and soap will be provided by the Control Department for purchase by the Troops.

10. The Secretary of State for War, in consideration of the special nature of the service, has sanctioned the issue of the following necessaries, free of cost, to all non-commissioned officers and privates of the Regular Force. A similar arrangement will be made by the Dominion Government for the Militia:-

    1 Serge Frock   1 Woollen Night Cap
    1 Pair Serge Trousers   1 Cap Cover with peak
    1 pair ox Hide Boots   1 piece Musquito Netting
    2 Pairs Worsted Socks   1 Clasp Knife
    2 Flannel Shirts 1 Tin Cup
    1 Housewife [i.e. sewing kit] 1 Tin Plate

11. Extraordinary field allowance for the months will be issued to all officers herein appointed to take the field.

12. Officers will not be allowed under any circumstances to take civil servants with them.

13. Officers may take a limited amount of mess stores and cooking utensils as far as Fort William. Beyond that place each officer will be allowed 90 lb. [41 kilos] weight only, which will include bedding, and cooking and mess utensils.

    Owing to the peculiar nature of the service upon which this force will be employed, the Lieutenant-General desires that all company officers may be armed with rifles; they will carry 60 rounds of ammunition like the men.

14. Officers of both regulars and militia will be allowed to buy from the military stores any article of equipment they may require. Lists will be sent in by the Commanding Officers to the Senior Control Officer on the spot.

15. The Control arrangement in connection with the Expedition will be made by Lieutenant-Colonel Martindale, Deputy Controller.

    The sub-charge of Assistant Controller Irving [Irvine] will commence at Thunder Bay.

16. With the exceptions of communications on routine business and matters of accounts, the Official Correspondence connected with the Force, after its arrival in Thunder Bay, will pass directly between the Commander of the Expedition, or the Senior Officer Commanding on the spot and the Lieutenant-General.

17. Colonel Wolseley will look to the Lieutenant-General only, for orders and instructions, which he will receive through the Staff or Control.

18. With reference to the General Order No. 5, of the 9th instant, the following officers will also proceed to Toronto:-

    Deputy-Assistant Commissary-General Beamish, from Ottawa.
    Deputy-Assistant Commissary-General Meyer, from Kingston.

By Order

J. E. Thackwell
Deputy Adjutant-General

APPENDIX B

Who Was the Woman Who Accompanied Wolseley's Red River Expedition to Fort Garry in 1870?

In the Hudson's Bay Company magazine *The Beaver* [2] in 1947 in an article entitled "Voyageurs' Artist," the American historian, Grace Lee Nute, drew attention to the voyageur paintings of Frances Ann Beechey Hopkins, an English woman who, in 1858, married Edward Martin Hopkins, the private secretary of Sir George Simpson, the Governor of Rupert's Land. Mrs. Hopkins was a skilful artist who painted several large canvases featuring Canadian voyageurs. It is obvious that the activities of the voyageurs of the Hudson's Bay Company had a special appeal to her. Mrs. Hopkins's sketch books are filled with drawings of voyageurs and canoes, and she depicted various aspects of voyageur life both in watercolours and in oils. One large canvas, in particular, entitled "Expedition to the Red River in 1870" shows what appear to be the Lesser Kakabeka Falls on the Kaministikwia River. In several other paintings a woman is shown in a canoe, modishly dressed, yet obviously at home. These paintings seem to be autobiographical in nature. Largely on the strength of the Kaministikwia River painting and upon the known fact that the Hopkins were on friendly terms with Colonel Garnet Wolseley and presented him with the painting, Miss Nute suggests that Mr. and Mrs. Hopkins accompanied the expedition from Prince Arthur's Landing to Fort Garry. This is given some credibility by the fact that S. J. Dawson, in the *Volunteer Review* refers to a "gentleman who had his wife with him, passed over all the rapids, portages and whirlpools of the Winnipeg without its occurring to its occupants that they were doing anything extraordinary."[3]

The Red River Expedition 1870, from an oil painting by Frances A. Hopkins.

Dr. Nute's conclusion has been challenged by other writers. For instance, in "Frances Ann Hopkins," in *The Lives and Works of Canadian Artists*, Audrey Miller points out that on 1 July 1870,[4] Mrs. Hopkins was in Chicago on her way back to Montreal. Both Mr. and Mrs. Hopkins then departed for England where the former died in 1893. Mrs. Hopkins died in 1918. Alice Johnson, also writing in *The Beaver* in 1971,[5] traces Mrs. Hopkins' movements in 1870, and directs one to the conclusion that the woman referred to by S. J. Dawson was Mrs. Molyneux St. John (née Kate Ranoe) the wife of the *Globe*'s special correspondent. Oddly enough, neither Mrs. Hopkins nor Mrs. St. John was mentioned by Wolseley in his *Narrative*. Personally, I incline strongly towards Miss Johnson's opinion. Unfortunately, when I requested information about the St. Johns from the *Globe and Mail* in Toronto, the reply was to the effect that the newspaper possessed no documentary materials relating to Molyneux or Kate St. John. In 1902 Molyneux St. John became Gentleman Usher of the Black Rod in Ottawa.

For the record, it should be remembered that Frances Ramsay Simpson, cousin and eighteen-year old bride of Sir George Simpson of the Hudson's Bay Company, made the journey from Montreal over the lake and river route to Rupert's Land and down the Hayes River to Fort York on Hudson Bay in 1830. Fort Frances on Rainy Lake was named in her honour. She remained in the West for several years. Lady Simpson was accompanied on the trip from Montreal to Manitoba by Catherine Turner, wife of the Hudson's Bay Company chief factor, John George McTavish.

Mr. and Mrs. St. John running the rapids of the Sturgeon River, 1870, from a watercolour by William Armstrong.

APPENDIX C

The Manitoba Gazette

Winnipeg, Friday, October 13, 1871

TO THE PEOPLE OF THE PROVINCE OF MANITOBA[6]

In the name of the Queen, I thank you, one and all, for the promptitude and spirit with which you have rushed to the defence of the country, when called upon by Her Majesty's Proclamation.

From the moment when the rumours of a Fenian raid assumed a character to be relied upon, my great anxiety was, that our people, irrespectively of past differences, should present a united front to the band of miscreants — the scum of the cities of the United States — who were collecting on our border for purposes of plunder, robbery and murder.

I had the best reason to know that the plans of the marauders were based on the belief that there were divisions in your ranks which would drive a part of the population into their arms.

O'Donoghue, one of the leaders of the gang, assured his companions that, on their arrival at the frontier, they would be joined by a party of our people disaffected to the Crown, and ready to aid any invasion.

The events of the last few days have repelled this slander. At this moment, our whole population has assumed an attitude which affords no encouragement to these dastardly marauders.

On Tuesday, the 3rd inst., information reached me, that left no doubt of a raid being at hand.

On Wednesday, I issued a proclamation, calling upon you to assemble and enroll in your various parishes. Copies were distributed all over the Province, and by the evening of Thursday, the people of every English parish had met, had made up, and sent to me lists, showing 1,000 men, ready at a moment's warning to shoulder their muskets and march to the front.

In the French parishes, meetings were also held, and by the same evening, I was assured, upon unquestionable authority, that my proclamation would meet with a loyal response. I suggested that it should be such as to admit of no misinterpretation, and received the assurance that it would assume a shape entirely satisfactory.

The reports from the front on Thursday left no doubt that the raid was to commence at once, and, the next day, orders were given to advance a body of troops towards the frontier.

Major Irvine detailed, with that view, the bulk of the Service Companies in the Fort, two of those organized at Winnipeg, under Captains Mulvey and Kennedy, and a Company of Canadians and Half-breed French under Captain de Plainval.

In two hours from the issue of the order, two hundred men, with their accoutrements, camp equipage and munitions of war, were across the Assiniboine *en route* for the frontier. The movement was executed in a manner that reflects the highest credit on Major Irvine, the officers of the different corps, and the men.

The march was continued till events occurred to render further advance unnecessary.

On Thursday, about noon, Colonel [*sic*] Wheaton, of the U. S. forces stationed at Pembina, with a loyal discharge of international duties, honorable alike to himself and to his country, attacked and dispersed the raiders as they were crossing the frontier, making prisoners of their self-styled Generals, and a number of the privates.

O'Donoghue escaped to this side of the line, but was arrested in the course of the evening by some French Half-breeds. During the night, under a mistaken view of what was best to be done, he was taken to the frontier and placed in the same custody as the other prisoners, by parties who acted very naturally under the circumstances, but still, in a way to be regretted.

Meanwhile, the French parishes were completing the arrangements which I had been assured were in contemplation. On the afternoon of the 8th inst., about 4 o'clock, Mr. Royal, the Speaker of the Assembly; Mr. Girard, the Provincial Treasurer, and several other of the Representatives of the French parishes, waited on me to say that a body of French Half-breeds were assembled on the East bank of the Red River, and wished to be permitted to assure me personally of their loyalty, and to proffer their services as soldiers. I went over immediately, in company of Capt. Mcdonald, the commander at Fort Garry in Major Irvine's absence. I found assembled on the bank 200 able-bodied French Métis; of these 50 were mounted, and a considerable part of the whole body had firearms.

They received me with a *feu de joie.*

Mr. Girard then, in the name of the men assembled — in the name of the French Métis of all the Parishes — expressed amid loud cheers and much enthusiasm, the loyalty and devotion of the Métis of every origin; and assured me they had rallied to the support of the Crown, and were prepared to do their duty as loyal subjects in repelling any raid that might now, or hereafter, be made on the country.

I thanked the people very cordially for the assurances given in their name, and told them I should take care to make this demonstration of their feelings known to His Excellency the Governor-General.

If among these people there were — and I believe there were — some persons whose exceptional position might have led O'Donoghue to look for their support, it only adds to the value of the demonstration, and removes the last hope of the miscreants who have invaded your soil, that they would receive sympathy or aid from any class of the population.

On Monday the troops returned to the Fort, and the volunteers from Winnipeg were allowed to go to their homes and resume their occupations.

I regret to have to inform you that on the same day, the United States civil authorities at Pembina, to whom Colonel [sic] Wheaton was obliged to hand over his prisoners, discharged these marauders, for reasons which I am unable to comprehend, and that one of them, O'Donoghue, still remains in the neighbourhood of Pembina, awaiting an opportunity of renewing the attack. Nevertheless, the raid for the moment is over. If renewed, it will not be immediately. If the Fenians were men actuated by ordinary reason, it would never be renewed. But they are not. They will trade, while they can, upon the simplicity of their dupes, and hope by excitement to replenish their exhausted exchequer. There is nothing in the wickedness or folly of any scheme to prevent their attempting it.

Rest assured I shall watch over your safety. Should danger come, you will be appealed to again, and you will respond like men of courage — of loyalty — of patriotism.

The Queen relies upon the fidelity of her people of this Province, of every origin.

Adams G. Archibald
Lieutenant-Governor

APPENDIX D

The Canadian General Service Medal 1866, 1870 [7]

In 1897 veterans of the Fenian Raids and the Red River Expedition prepared a petition directed to Her Majesty Queen Victoria, praying that a general service medal might be issued, in her Jubilee Year, to all Canadian volunteers who were called out on active service during the Fenian Raids and who served in the Red River Expedition. This project was initiated by the Veterans' Association of Toronto and the idea was adopted by other groups of veterans in Canada, including those in Winnipeg. The requested medal was not issued in the Queen's Diamond Jubilee Year. But in 1899, twenty-nine years after the Wolseley expedition, a silver medal was struck in Great Britain, commemorating military service in Canada against the Fenians in 1866 and 1870 and for participation in the Red River Expedition of 1870.

The *obverse* bore the head of Queen Victoria, diademed and veiled bust, wearing the Order of the Garter, with the legend *Victoria Regina et Imperatrix*. The *reverse* showed the Canadian Red Ensign surrounded by a wreath of maple leaves surmounted by the word CANADA. The ribbon was red-white-red in three equal stripes. The medals, with bars indicating the place and date of service: Fenian Raid 1866; Fenian Raid 1870; Red River 1870; were issued to Canadian and British troops.

A total of 17,635 medals were issued of which 15,300 went to Canadians. They were distributed as follows:

1866 Fenian Raid	11,221
1870 Fenian Raid	4,510
1866 and 1870 Fenian Raids	1,411
1866 Fenian Raids and Red River	105
1866, 1870 Fenian Raids and Red River	23
1870 Fenian Raid and Red River	15
1870 Red River	350

The Canadian General Service Medal with Bar (obverse).

The Canadian General Service Medal with Bar (reverse).

APPENDIX E

An Episode that Occurred During the Red River Expedition of 1872[*]

This satirical verse was written by Private Fred Swire, one of the Canadian troops who went to Manitoba in 1872. Some 500 copies were printed in the office of the *Liberal* in Winnipeg, edited at that time by Stewart Mulvey. The verse was circulated among the troops at Fort Garry much to the grief and indignation of the two sergeants concerned:

It was on Sturgeon's stormy lake,
    There sailed a martial crew
Provisions they did with them take,
    Both beef and biscuit too;
But when the storm's blast loudly roared,
    And far was port or haven
The leader of this martial band
    Turned out to be a craven.
"What ho!" he cried, "what ho! I say,
    Pray turn the vessel's course,
For much I fear there's danger near
    And keenly stings remorse,
Steer for the shore, I pr'ythee try
    For I am unprepared to die."

"Now out upon thee for a knave!
    I would not lift one toe to save
Nor thee, nor any of thy clan;
    For thou'rt a most egregious ass;
You've not the heart of fowl or pheasant
    So let's proceed boys — are you present?"
'Twas thus spoke Phairson, yet the oar
    Propelled the little bark to shore,
And it would seem that Phairson too
    Was not without a qualm or two.
Arrived at land, ashore they sprang
    Brave Crusoe, and aloud there rang

His voice throughout the forest glade
   "Come on ye divils, whose afraid?"
And Echo, through the sombre shade
   Replied afar, "Crusoe's afraid."

Upon the beach, they camped that night,
   And anxious, waited for the light.
The morning dawned, the tempest roars,
   And hurled the billows from the shores.
No prospect seemed held up to view
   Of launching o'er those waters blue;
But some more bold, were fain to start,
   Save Crusoe of the craven heart;
In vain he begs those few to stay —
   "Not so" says Phairson, "we'll away,
And send for you some other day."
   "What! leave me here with no relief?"

Says Crusoe: "pray then leave the beef;
   And if you venture on that lake,
Upon yourself the blame you take."
   "All right!" cried Phairson, "that I'll do
And now my friend Robinson, Adieu!"
   Out sprang the boat propelled by oars
Manned by a dozen stalwart rowers;
   And, as more distant grew the land,
The voice of Crusoe reached the band.
   Borne by the breeze o'er rock and reef—
"For God's sake 'Phairson, leave the beef."
   "Not so," bawls 'Phairson, "you're astarn,
And that be busted for a yarn."

* * * *

And how the crews were safe at last,
   How dangers numerous they passed
And in the end got safely home,
   Is told in many a book and tome.

And bright ey'd kids, with curly pate
   Will ask their mother to relate
The story o'er and o'er again —
   How Crusoe feared the raging main.
And Rumour says that in his sleep
   Crusoe again is on the deep,
And uttering, "It were not so bad
   If only those spare ribs I had had."
In every breeze that stirs the leaf
   His fancy whispers, "Ribs of beef."
And wavelets breaking on the shore
   Say "Beef ribs come again no more."

NOTES AND BIBLIOGRAPHY

Abbreviations

BEM - Blackwood's Edinburgh Magazine

CHR - Canadian Historical Review

CIN - Canadian Illustrated News

CSP - Canadian Sessional Papers

DCB - Dictionary of Canadian Biography

DND - Department of National Defence

HCD - House of Commons Debates

NAC - National Archives of Canada

PAM - Provincial Archives of Manitoba

VR - Volunteer Review

PROLOGUE - 24 August 1870

1. This regiment was originally formed in North America, as a light infantry unit, with light equipment and modified uniform, and trained along the lines of the American Rangers. Hence the name "Royal Americans". R. M. Barnes, *A History of the Regiments and Uniforms of the British Army* (London, 1930), 66-7.
2. The original letter is in the possession of Queen's University Library. A typescript is available in the Public Archives of Manitoba.
3. Two shillings and sixpence, worth about 65 cents at the exchange rate of $4.86 2/3 to the English pound of that date.
4. The Minister of Militia, Sir George Cartier.
5. The Franco-Prussian War 1870.
6. Personally a brave man, he was awarded the V.C. in the Zulu War, 1878-79. Buller was a close associate of Wolseley and a member of "the Ring," defined by Adrian Preston as an "unofficial improvised general staff for operational purposes" (*In Relief of Gordon*, London, 1967, xix). Wolseley was inclined to gather around himself a group of young officers possessing brains, courage and energy and who could work "in tolerable harmony". The question arises whether these officers were likely to become sycophants. Is a group based on closed membership and favouritism the best kind of staff to cope with the problems of warfare? Buller was, unfortunately, a poor tactician and as a result became known as "Reverse" Buller. Even so, he was always liked by his troops.

CHAPTER ONE - THE SOLDIER EXPLORERS 1685 - 1816

1. See René Chartrand, "From Versailles to Wyoming: French Exploration and Trade in the Eighteenth Century", *Journal of the West*, XXVI, 4 October 1987, 27-33.
2. Gabriel Franchère, *A Voyage to the Northwest Coast of America*, Milo Quaife, ed. (Chicago, 1954), 265-6.
3. Means the same as "salaud" (filthy).
4. J.M. Mauro, *Thunder Bay, A History* (Thunder Bay, 1981), 22.

CHAPTER TWO - THE FIRST RED RIVER EXPEDITION 1816

1. For biographies of Selkirk see J. M. Gray, *Lord Selkirk of Red River* (Toronto, 1963) and Chester Martin, *Lord Selkirk's Work in Canada* (Oxford, 1916). See also Marjorie Wilkins Campbell's *McGillivray, Lord of the Northwest* (Toronto, 1962). This is a biography of the principal Nor'Wester.
2. A second group of settlers followed shortly afterwards under Owen Keveny, who was later murdered after surrendering to a warrant signed by a North West Company partner. For lists of names of Selkirk's settlers, see Chester Martin's report to Dr. A.G. Doughty, *Canadian Archives*, 27 August 1900.
3. The name applied to partners of the North West Company. See W.S. Wallace, *Documents Relating to the North West Company* (Toronto, Champlain Society, 1934), 291. See also Jean Morison, *The North West Company in Rebellion, Simon McGillivray's Fort William Note-book, 1815* (Thunder Bay Historical Museum Society, 1988).
4. *Statement Respecting the Earl of Selkirk's Settlement Upon the Red River . . . with Observations upon a Recent Publication* (London, 1817; Cole's Reprint, Toronto, 1970), 35.
5. Martin, 87.
6. *Statement* etc., 82-3. According to Pritchard, Semple's party numbered twenty-eight, of whom twenty-one were killed and one wounded. The Métis had one man killed and one wounded.
7. *Ibid.*, 84-5. Pritchard stated that "The enemy, I am told, were sixty-two persons, the greater number of whom were contracted servants and clerks of the North-West Company." The leaders, according to the same source, were Cuthbert Grant, Alexander Frazer, Antoine Houle and Bourassa; the first two were North West Company clerks, and the latter interpreters in the service of that company.
8. Margaret Macleod, "Cuthbert Grant of Grantown," *Canadian Historical Review*, March, 1940. Sir George Simpson wrote of Grant in his *Character Book*, "A generous warm hearted Man who would not have been guilty of the Crimes laid to his charge, had he not been drawn into them by designing Men." See Glyndwr Williams, *Hudson's Bay Miscellany* 1670-1870, Hudson's Bay Record Society (Winnipeg, 1975), 210.
9. See the exchange of letters between Selkirk and Drummond, *Statement* etc., 43-53.
10. Guy de Meuron, *Le Régiment Meuron 1781-1816* (Lausanne, 1982), 220-1. The officers included Captain Protais Odet-d'Orsonnens, Captain Frédéric Matthey, and Lieutenants Frédéric de Graffenried and Gaspard Gustave-Adolphe Fauche.
11. *Ibid.*, 222.
12. *Statement* etc., 63.
13. *Ibid.*, 64.
14. Campbell, 234-5.
15. Frédéric von Graffenried, *Sechs Jahre in Canada, 1813-1819* (Bern, 1891), 22-3.
16. de Meuron, 223.
17. *Ibid.*, 224.
18. *Ibid.*
19. Graffenried, 30ff.
20. *Ibid.*
21. *Ibid.*
22. *Ibid.*, 37.
23. *Ibid.*
24. Gray, 239.
25. R. G. MacBeth, *The Romance of Western Canada* (Toronto, 1920), 67.

CHAPTER THREE - THE DEFENCE OF THE RED RIVER SETTLEMENT 1840s-1860s

1. G. F. G. Stanley, *Canada's Soldiers* (Toronto, 1960), 106-17; 117-20.
2. Quoted in H. Faulkner, *American Political and Social History* (New York, 1946), 231.

3. Quoted in M. Curti, R. R. Shyrock, T.C. Cochran, F. H. Harrington, *An American History* (New York, 1950), Vol. 1, 309.

4. G. F. G. Stanley, *The Birth of Western Canada* (London, 1936; Toronto 1960), 37. Americans never thought of themselves as imperialists; instead they wrote of themselves as God's people, specially appointed to bring the virtues of self-determination to North America and the world. Essentially it was a matter of replacing gin and tonic with bourbon on the rocks, as one English writer has expressed it.

5. *DCB* (Toronto, 1976), Vol. IX, 649.

6. A. S. Morton, *A History of the Canadian West to 1870-71* (London, 1939), 808.

7. *Ibid.,* 825.

8. William R. Morrison, *The Sixth Regiment of Foot at Lower Fort Garry* (Canadian Historic Sites: *Occasional Papers in Archeology and History* No. 4), 168.

9. *Ibid.*

10. *Ibid.,* 168-9.

11. *Ibid.,* 169.

12. *Ibid.*

13. Alexander Ross, *The Red River Settlement* (London, 1856), 364.

14. E. E. Rich, *The History of the Hudson's Bay Company 1670-1870,* Vol. II, 1763-1870 (London, 1959), 540.

15. G. F. G. Stanley, "A Soldier at Fort Garry", *The Beaver,* Autumn, 1957, 10.

16. Rich, 544.

17. Ross, 365.

18. Stanley, *Canada's Soldiers,* 208.

19. A. C. Gluek, "Imperial Protection for the Trading interests of the Hudson's Bay Company, 1857-1861", *CHR,* June 1956, 119-40. Gluek argues that the role of the British troops was to defend the monopoly of the Hudson's Bay Company, not to defend the country against the Americans. He does, however, concede that Jefferson Davis, the U. S. Secretary of War stated in his annual report for 1856, that the American troops were sent "for the purpose of acquiring information respecting the region". In other words, to spy out the land.

20. The *VR,* 22 April 1873, 191, published a letter written by a member of The Royal Canadian Rifles outlining some of the problems encountered during the movement of the regiment from Montreal to Fort Garry via Hudson Bay. The letter is dated 9 November 1857. The troops travelled in a wooden sailing ship, *Great Britain,* 572 tons, Dan Wilson, Master. She left Montreal 23 June and arrived at York Factory 1 September.

21. Stanley, "A Soldier at Fort Garry," 14.

22. Rich, Vol. 2, 812.

23. *Ibid.,* 814.

24. James Morris, *Heaven's Command* (London, 1975), 382. The imperialist ethic was expressed in June 1872 in Disraeli's famous Crystal Palace speech. Morris wrote, "Gladstone . . . distrusted the imperialist ethic with fastidious profundity. . . .", 383.

25. Donald Creighton, "Old Tomorrow," *The Beaver,* Winter 1956, 7-8. See also D. Owram, *Promise of Eden: The Canadian Expansionist Movement and the Idea of the West, 1856-1900* (Toronto, 1980).

26. W. P. Morrell, *British Colonial Policy in the Age of Peel and Russell* (Oxford, 1930), 40.

27. Morris, 128.

28. Douglas MacKay, *The Honourable Company, a History of the Hudson's Bay Company* (Toronto, 1936), 273-4.

29. *Ibid.*

30. By Western Canada, he meant what today is called Western Ontario.

31. Joseph Pope, *Memoirs of the Right Honourable Sir John Alexander Macdonald* (Toronto, 1930), 398.

32. The date of transfer was originally to be 1 October, but to give more time to complete financial arrangements, it was postponed two months.

33. D. G. Creighton, "Macdonald and Manitoba," *The Beaver*, Spring, 1957, 16.

34. Pope, *Memoirs*; Macdonald to McDougall, 20 November 1869, 407.

35. For details of the Sayer trial and the intervention of Louis Riel *père*, see W. L. Morton, "Introduction," Hudson's Bay Record Society (London, 1956), LXXXII-LXXXVI. For the role of the R. P. Georges-Antoine Belcourt see G.F.G. Stanley, "Ce prêtre difficile-commentaires sur les activités du Père Georges-Antoine Belcourt," *La Société Historique Acadienne-les Cahiers*, vol. 14, No. 2, juin 1983, 39-58.

36. MacBeth, 101.

37. Stanley, *The Birth of Western Canada*, 43.

CHAPTER FOUR - THE METIS RESISTANCE 1869-1870

1.   W. L. Morton, *Alexander Begg's Red River Journal* (Toronto, Champlain Society, 1956), Introduction, 58.

2.   *Ibid.*, 169-70.

3.   *CSP*, No. 12, Vol. V, 1870, 105. See also G. F. G. Stanley, *The Birth of Western Canada*, 81.

4.   *Ibid.*, 77. The Proclamation was, incidentally, drafted by J. A. N. Provencher, McDougall's secretary.

5.   Stanley, *The Birth of Western Canada*, 78-9.

6.   *Begg's Journal*, 10 December 1869, 226.

7.   MacBeth, *The Romance of Western Canada*, 127.

8.   Pope, *Memoirs*: Macdonald to Rose, 31 December 1869, 414.

9.   Pope, *Correspondence of Sir John Macdonald*: Macdonald to Stephen, 13 December 1920, 412. See also Heather Gilbert, *Awakening Continent, The Life of Lord Mount Stephen, 1829-1891* (Aberdeen, 1965), Vol 1, 20-1.

10. *Begg's Journal*, 303. The irony is that the fireworks let off were those that Dr. Schultz had brought into the Settlement "to commemorate the establishment of McDougall's government."

11. There were a number of Americans in Winnipeg. Some, like O'Lone were there to make money. Others, such as the consuls, Taylor and Malmros, acted as agents for the U.S. State Department and did what they could to promote the idea of American annexation. Henry M. Robinson, another American, used Riel's newspaper, *The New Nation*, for the same purpose. Others, including Joseph Rolette, H. S. Donaldson and Enos Stutsman of Pembina, were engaged in the same activity. Riel was prepared to use them for his own purposes; but he does not appear seriously to have considered American annexation as a viable option for Red River.

12. C. A. Boulton, *Reminiscences of the North-West Rebellions* (Toronto, 1886), 108-9.

13. J. A. Jackson suggests in *The Centennial History of Manitoba* (Winnipeg, 1970), 103, "Riel's execution at Regina on November 16, 1885, was as much vengeance for the shooting of Scott on March 4, 1870, as it was for the treason of the North West Rebellion."

14. *Begg's Journal*, 4 March 1870, 328.

15. *Ibid.*, 25 May 1870, 375.

16. MacBeth, *The Romance of Western Canada*, 159.

17. *Begg's Journal*, 23 July 1870, 392.

18. Alexander Begg, *The Creation of Manitoba* (Toronto, 1871), 385.

19. *Begg's Journal*, 23 July 1870, 394.

20. i.e., 23 August 1870.

21. G. F. G. Stanley et al, *The Collected Writings of Louis Riel* (Edmonton, 1985, vol. 1) "Mémoire ayant trait aux difficultés de la Rivière Rouge," 418-9. This document was also published by A. H. Trémaudan in the *C.H.R.*, June 1924. I have used the Trémaudan translation here. See also Trémaudan, *Histoire de la Nation Métisse dans l'ouest Canadien* (Montréal, 1935), 243-50.

22. The troops were riflemen and wore green, rather than red. J. A. Jackson, *History of Manitoba*, III, is in error when he speaks of "the thin red line."

274

CHAPTER FIVE - MOBILIZATION 1869-1870

1. Joseph Pope, *Memoirs* (Toronto, 1930): Macdonald to McDougall, 20 November 1869, 408.
2. *Ibid.*
3. *Ibid.*: Macdonald to McDougall: 27 November 1869, 410.
4. *Ibid.*: Macdonald to Rose, 31 December 1869, 414.
5. *Ibid.*: Macdonald to Rose, 5 December 1869, 411.
6. *Ibid.*: Macdonald to McDougall, 12 December 1869, 411-2
7. S. W. Horrall, "Sir John A. Macdonald and the Police Force for the Northwest Territories", *CHR*, Vol. LIII, June 1972, 181. The news that McDougall was carrying rifles greatly disturbed the Métis, who believed that McDougall intended to arm the local "Canadian party" dissidents in Red River.
8. *Ibid.*: Macdonald to Cameron, 21 December 1879, 181.
9. NAC, Macdonald Papers, Vol 101, Part I, Minute of Council, 11 February 1870.
10. *Ibid.*
11. *Ibid.*
12. *Ibid.*
13. James Morris, *Heaven's Command An Imperial Progress* (London, 1973), 345.
14. Sir Joseph Pope, *Correspondence of Sir John Macdonald* (Toronto, 1921); Macdonald to Rose, 21 January 1870, 121.
15. *Ibid.*: Macdonald to Rose, 23 February 1870, 127.
16. *Ibid.*, 128.
17. *Globe*, (Toronto), 17 November 1869.
18. *Ibid.*, 9 December 1869.
19. *Ibid.*, 27 January 1870.
20. *Ibid.*, 11 March 1870.
21. *Ibid.*, 13 April 1870.
22. HCD, Canada, Vol. 1, 1870, 1490.
23. Pope, *Correspondence*: Macdonald to Carnarvon, 14 April 1870, 134. In his book, *The Struggle for Imperial Unity, Recollections and Experiences* (Toronto, 1909), 22, G. T. Denison wrote, "Up to this time it had been found difficult to excite any interest in Ontario in the fact that a number of Canadians had been thrown into prison. Foster and I, who had been consulting almost daily, were much depressed at the apathy of the public, but when we heard that Schultz and Mair, as well as Dr. Lynch, were all on the way to Ontario, and that Scott had been murdered, it was seen at once that there was an opportunity, by giving a public reception to the loyal refugees, to draw attention to the matter, and by denouncing the murder of Scott, to arouse the indignation of the people, and foment a public opinion that would force the Government to send up an armed expedition to restore order."
24. Pope, *Correspondence*: Macdonald to Rose, 23 February 1870, 128.
25. *Correspondence Relative to the Recent Expedition to the Red River Settlement* (London, 1871): Colonial Office to War Office, 23 March 1870, 1.
26. *Ibid.*: War Office to Lieutenant-General Lindsay, 5 May 1870, 4.
27. NAC, Macdonald Papers, Vol. 101, part 2: Young to Macdonald, 10 April 1870.
28. *Ibid.*: Young to Macdonald, 11 April 1870.
29. *Correspondence Relative to the Recent Expedition:* Colonial Office to War Office, 23 March 1870.
30. Morris, *Heaven's Command*, 351. Dr. Adrian Preston wrote in the introduction to his *In Relief of Gordon, Lord Wolseley's Campaign Journal of the Khartoum Relief Expedition 1884-1885* (London, 1967), xiii, that Wolseley "was . . . convinced, as were many of his closest admirers, that he was the greatest commander his country had produced since Wellington." Garnet Joseph Wolseley (1833-1913), "the model of a modern Major-General" (to use W. S. Gilbert's words), was Great Britain's most important soldier in the second half of the 19th century. Although he took part in no great war, he established a reputation for success in Britain's

"little wars", in Burma, Crimea, India, China, Red River, Ashanti, Zululand, Egypt and the Sudan. His real importance was as a military reformer and as creator of the "modern" British Army. Drawing upon his knowledge of the Civil War in the United States, he introduced reforms and reorganizations that were of great significance and benefit to the British military organization. He wrote well. His publications included *The Soldier's Pocket Book*, a biography of Marlborough, his own autobiography and his reminiscences of the China Campaign. Wolseley was an obvious figure to be parodied in G. M. Fraser's *Flashman* series, e.g., *Flashman and the Dragon* (Great Britain, 1985). Perhaps Mr. Fraser may discover papers dealing with Flashman's service in the Red River Expedition!

31. R. E. Parkinson, *History of the Grand Lodge of Free and Accepted Masons of Ireland* (Dublin, 1957) II, 221-2. As an ensign in the 91st Regiment, Wolseley was initiated into the military Lodge No. 728, Dublin, in 1858.

32. Queen's University, *Wolseley Papers*: Wolseley to his brother, Dick, 6 April 1870.

33. *Correspondence Relative to the Recent Expedition;* memorandum by Lieutenant-General The Honourable James Lindsay, Ottawa, 11 April 1870, 6-7.

34. R. M. Barnes, *A History of the Regiments and Uniforms of the British Army,* (London, 1950), 67. It is one of the strange quirks of Canadian military history that the Royal American Regiment, later the 60th Rifles, contained not only English, Scots and Americans, but also Swiss soldiers from Bern, Zurich and Basel. The regiment was recruited by Jacques Prévost of Geneva and included among its officers, Henri Bouquet of Rolle and Frédéric Haldimand of Yverdon. Its conversion to light infantry was largely the work of Henri Bouquet. See A. Lätt, *Schweizer Offiziere also Indianerkrieger und Instruktoren der englischen leichten Infanterie* (Zurich, 1933).

35. *Correspondence Relative to the Recent Expedition:* Lindsay to the Secretary of State for War, 15 July 1870, 36.

36. *Ibid.*: Lindsay to the Governor General, 23 April 1870, 14.

37. *Ibid.*

38. The problems encountered by the 6th Warwickshires, when they made the journey to Red River, were well known as a result of Major Crofton's evidence given to the Parliamentary Committee of 1857. He and his men had taken 103 days between the port of embarkation, Cork, Ireland, and the Red River Settlement; 25 June to 6 October, including a sea voyage over the North Atlantic to York Factory, and river and lake to Lower Fort Garry on the Red. And he took with him two three-pounders and one six-pounder cannon, leaving behind him the remainder of his artillery and such impedimenta as "420 iron bedsteads". See *Notes on the route from Lake Superior to Red River and on the Settlement Itself* (London, War Office, 1870), Appendix 20. This particular reference is drawn from William Morrison, *The Sixth Regiment of Foot at Lower Fort Garry* .

39. S. J. Dawson, *Report on the Red River Expedition of 1870* (Ottawa, 1871), 7.

40. *Ibid.*, 11.

41. For details here, see Bell Irvine, *Report on the Red River Expedition of 1870* (London, 1871).

42. *Ibid.*, 5.

43. *Ibid.*

44. *Ibid.*

45. *Ibid.*, 7.

46. *Ibid.* See also H.S.H. Riddell, "The Red River Expedition of 1870," *Transactions of the Literary and Historical Society of Quebec*, Session 1870-71, new series, part 5 (Quebec, 1871), 101-2. Riddell was a lieutenant with the 60th Rifles.

47. *Correspondence Relative to the Recent Expedition:* Adjutant-General to the Minister of Militia, 15 April 1870, 9-10.

48. See DCB, (Toronto, 1972) Vol. X, 152. The 100th Royal Canadian Regiment of Foot was raised initially in Canada in 1858 for service abroad in the Imperial interest. It was subsequently territorialized in Ireland, becoming the Prince of Wales Leincester Regiment (Royal Canadians). It was disbanded in 1922. It is not to be

confused with the Royal Canadian Rifles, raised for garrison purposes and localized in Canada as an "old soldier" corps. See G. F. G. Stanley, *Canada's Soldiers*, 208, 215-6.

49.	J. K. Johnson, *Affectionately Yours, the letters of Sir John A. Macdonald and his family* (Toronto, 1915, 1969), 16-7.

50.	S. B. Steele, *Forty Years in Canada* (Toronto, 1915).

51.	The *Globe*, 11 May 1870.

52.	J. M. Hitsman, *Safeguarding Canada, 1763-1871* (Toronto, 1965), 221. See also F. W. Campbell, *The Fenian Invasions of Canada, 1866 and 1870 and the Operations of the Montreal Militia Brigade in Connection Therewith* (Montreal, 1904). The 1866 events are covered in pp 7 - 32; and those of 1870 (Eccles Hill) in pp 33 - 55.

53.	According to Bruce Harman, a captain in the 1st (Ontario) Rifles, "This building was situated south of the Lunatic Asylum. . . . It afforded the recruits "very suitable quarters". See Harman, *'Twas 26 Years Ago - Narrative of the Red River Expedition 1870* (Toronto, 1869), 7,9. The author was a participant in the events described.

54.	*Globe*, 11 May 1870.

55.	*Ibid*.

56.	Harman, *'Twas 26 Years Ago*, 9.

57.	*Correspondence Relative to the Recent Expedition;* Appendix, Official Journal of the Red River Expedition, 54. See also S. J. Dawson, "Report of the Red River Expedition of 1870", in the VR, 3 July 1871, 420. This is a more complete report than that published in the CSP.

CHAPTER SIX - FROM COLLINGWOOD TO SHEBANDOWAN LAKE MAY-JULY, 1870.

1.	*Globe*, 14 May 1870

2.	*Ibid*.

3.	The vessel *Chicora* was built at Birkenhead to run the northern blockade during the American Civil War. She ran between the Bahamas and Charleston. On one occasion she was pursued for over 14 hours by northern gunboats, *Atlantic* and *Connecticut*, which failed to catch her. This event was commemorated by a member of her crew with the following verse:

> "Chicora, Chicora, hopes rest in thy flight,
> As thou glidest along through dangers tonight;
> While the sound of the guns as the flash lights the foam,
> Brings a thrill to the hearts of the loved ones at home.
> Hark: a hail from aloft, 'There's a cruiser abeam',
> Keep her off, steady so, pass the word for all steam.
> And now, Mr. Yank, if you're sharp you may see
> Our name on the stern - but look out! Let her be."

The vessel then became known as the *Letter B*. After Lee's surrender at Richmond, she was brought to Halifax and sold to Messrs. McDonnell & Co. at Collingwood where she was refitted with cabins, deck saloons and state rooms. She was capable of 17 knots an hour. See Peter O'Leary, *Travels and Experiences in Canada, The Red River Territory and the United States* (London, 1877), 112. See also Joseph Mauro, *Thunder Bay-A History* , 51.

4.	*Globe*, 16 May 1870.

5.	*Ibid*., 17 May 1870. "great indignation" and "curses without stint" were called down on the heads of the "Yankee Government," but they did not serve to release the expedition "from its dilemma," was how the *Globe* reported the episode.

6.	*Ibid*.

7.	Bolton was described as "courteous and affable and while possessing nothing of the martinet, still holds his troops well in hand. He is generally liked." *Globe*, 24 May.

8. *Ibid.*, 19 May 1870.
9. *Ibid.*, 26 May 1870.
10. *Ibid.*, 19 May 1870.
11. *Ibid.*, 26 May 1870.
12. *Ibid.*
13. *Ibid.*
14. *Ibid.*, 28 May 1870. Oddly enough L.B. Shippee virtually ignored this episode at Sault Ste. Marie in his *Canadian-American Relations 1849-1874* (New Haven, Toronto, 1939).
15. *Ibid.*, 23 May 1870.
16. *Ibid.*, 30 May 1870.
17. Bruce Harman, *'Twas 26 Years Ago - Narrative of the Red River Expedition* , 10. According to the CIN,11 June 1870, 6, "the Fenian" was making the sketch for that publication!
18. Joseph F. Tennant, *Rough Times, 1870-1920,* A Souvenir of the 50th Anniversary of the Red River Expedition and the Formation of the Province of Manitoba (Winnipeg, 1920), 25.
19. G. M. Grant, *Ocean to Ocean, Sandford Fleming's Expedition Through Canada in 1872* (Toronto, 1925), 23.
20. Paul Kane, *Wanderings of an Artist* (Toronto, 1925), 32.
21. By an Officer of the Expeditionary Force, "Narrative of the Red River Expedition," Part II, BEM, 1871, 50. The author was Colonel Garnet Wolseley and will henceforth be cited as Wolseley, *Narrative, II.*
22. G. L. Huyshe, *The Red River Expedition* (London, 1871), 48. HRH Prince Arthur, later Duke of Connaught and Strathearn and Governor General of Canada, 1911-1916, spent 1870 in Canada. He was not, however, a member of the Red River Expedition. Prince Arthur's Landing was officially incorporated as Port Arthur in 1884 and, in 1970, amalgamated with Fort William, to become Thunder Bay.
23. S. J. Dawson, "Report on the Red River Expedition of 1870" in the VR, 3 July 1871, 421. This report is the unexpurgated version without the deletions made when it was published by the Canadian government.
24. *Globe*, 30 May 1870. The report was actually written on 14 May. The author was Molyneux St. John who, with his wife, accompanied the Expedition all the way to Fort Garry.
25. *Ibid.*
26. *Ibid.*
27. *Ibid.*
28. *Ibid.*
29. *Ibid.*
30. *Ibid.*
31. Huyshe, 49. See also Mauro, 44-5.
32. Wolseley, *Narrative, II,* 50.
33. Huyshe, 49-50.
34. Wolseley, *Narrative,II,* 51.
35. In his report Dawson wrote, "no action on the part of the Canadian Government could have provided for the arrival of the Troops at an earlier date; when the *Algoma* set out from Collingwood on the 3rd of May, it was not even known that she would get through on account of the ice which generally remains in the straits, above Sault Ste. Marie, till a later time than that at which she would be there, and when the *Chicora* left on the 7th it was well understood that there was at least a probability of her finding the canal shut." S. J. Dawson, *Report on the Red River Expedition 1870* (Ottawa, 1871), 15.
36. Huyshe, 56.
37. *Ibid.*, 55.
38. "Reminiscences of the Red River Expedition by a volunteer of the Ontario Battalion," *CIN*, 26 Aug. 1887, 8.

39. Huyshe, 53.

40. Riddell, *op. cit.*, 104-5. But why eat salt pork? As Wolseley admitted "the men caught immense quantities of lake trout, many of them weighing ten or twelve pounds, those of five or six being considered small." (Wolseley, *Narrative*, II, 60). He called these fish "the most tasteless of the finny tribe." Poor officers! Lucky men!

41. Huyshe, 63.

42. *Globe*, 1 July 1870. The correspondent was quite complimentary. "The camp is becoming prettier" and was losing "the higgledy-piggledy appearance which it wore when the steamers and schooners, laden with stores were daily arriving. . . ."

43. *Ibid.*

44. Huyshe, 64.

45. *Ibid.* There appears to have been remarkably little drunkenness. One might draw the conclusion from Wolseley's account that there were no spirits at Prince Arthur's Landing. This was not the case. J. M. Mauro in his *Thunder Bay*, 49, quotes a letter from Captain Thomas Scott of the 1st (Ontario) Rifles stating: "At the store here everything you can get at a general store in Canada is kept, and the prices are about the same. And the liquor is ahead of everything I ever tasted before. Rum is the favourite with us; real Simon pure article; no headache next morning." That alcoholic drinks were available is also attested to by Hugh John Macdonald who, in a letter to James Coyne on 15 July wrote, "At about 4 o'clock [i.e. 4 July 1870] the start was effected, the delay being caused by a good many of the men and some of the officers being as drunk as the devil. Of course this is private and confidential as I would not like to have it circulated." Macdonald to Coyne, 15 July 1870 in Elizabeth Arthur, *Thunder Bay District* (Champlain Society, Toronto, 1973), 115.

46. Harman, 11. Harman relates that his company, "E" Company (Kingston, Ont.) accepted the challenge of "G" Company (Gananoque, Ont.), to a mile race (6 men to a boat plus a coxwain) and came in "easy winner." They also defeated the Royal Engineers who had been victorious over the 60th Rifles boat.

47. Wolseley, *Narrative*, II, 56-7.

48. *Globe*, 1 July 1870.

49. Harman, 12.

50. *Ibid.*

51. Wolseley to D. D. Van Norman 22 July 1870: Dawson, *Report*, 54-5. There is no evidence that beer or any other alcoholic beverage was taken with the troops when they embarked at Shebandowan Lake. The explanation offered by Dawson seems reasonable: ". . . the reason why Col. Wolseley did not take and maintain a canteen at headquarters, during the march to Red River, was the difficulty in transporting so bulky and weighty an article as beer or spirits, along so difficult a line of march, and such an ever increasing distance from his source of supply." *VR*, 21 Aug. 1871, 557.

52. *CIN*, 26 August 1871, 8.

53. *Ibid.*

54. Quoted in J. F. Bertrand, *Highway of Destiny* (New York, 1959), 173. In his report Dawson wrote, "In the memorandum submitted by me to the military authorities, I had pointed out the fact that the boats and supplies could at once be sent forward as far as the Matawin Bridge, and while this was being done, it was my intention to have set all the available force of workmen and voyageurs to improve and open the unfinished sections of the line, beyond that place, and I may here remark that this was, without any question, as events proved, the proper course to have adopted. It would have . . . enabled the Expedition to reach Shebandowan Lake earlier than it did." S. J. Dawson, *VR*, 4 July 1871, 421. It is pertinent to note that a few days after the arrival of the first detachment of troops, the experiment of sending boats forward on waggons was tried and was successful. The boats were placed bottom upwards on the waggons, the gunwales resting on blocks felled to receive and support them. Actually 20 boats were sent to Matawin Bridge this way, the horses and waggons making the round trip in three days.

55. Huyshe, 67.
56. Kane, 34.
57. S. B. Steele, *Forty Years in Canada* (Toronto, 1914), 17.
58. *Ibid.*, 18.
59. Dawson, *Report*, 18.
60. *Ibid.*
61. *Ibid.*, 19.
62. *Ibid.*, 20.
63. Huyshe, 72.
64. *Ibid.*
65. "By an Officer of the Expeditionary Force, Narrative of the Red River Expedition, Part II," *BEM*, January 1871, 59. This was by written by Colonel Wolseley and will henceforth be cited as Wolseley, *Narrative, II.*
66. Steele, 18.
67. *Ibid.*
68. Dawson, *Report*, 20.
69. *Ibid.*, 21.
70. *Ibid.*
71. Steele, 19.
72. *Ibid.* See also Mauro, 47.
73. Dawson, *Report*, 21.
74. Dawson was sharply critical of Wolseley's action. In his report he wrote, "If all the boats should be exposed to wreck in the channel of a river for which they never were intended, there was reason to apprehend the most serious consequences as to the future progress of the Expedition. We were but at the outset of the journey. . . I therefore urged strongly upon the officer commanding the Field Force, the expediency of sending to Collingwood for waggons, where, as the sowing season was over, any number of farmers could be found ready enough to come forward with their teams. This advice was to a certain extent taken, and a limited number of waggons and horses were brought from that place, but the military teams began to fall off, as their drivers said, from starvation, being allowed but military rations. . . . Seeing therefore that there was nothing for it but the river, I sent voyageurs to improve the portages, and endeavoured to organize some system by which the boats might be in as far as possible saved from damage." Dawson report, VR, 10 July 1871, 444. This paragraph was deleted from the version printed in the CSP.
75. Wolseley, *Narrative, II,* 61.
76. C.K. Sissons, *John Kerr,* (Toronto,1946), 31.
77. Wolseley, *Narrative, II,* 62.
78. Huyshe, 97.
79. *Ibid.*, 28.
80. Arthur; Hugh John Macdonald to Coyne, 15 July 1870, 115.

CHAPTER SEVEN - SHEBANDOWAN TO RAT PORTAGE JULY-AUGUST 1870

1. Wolseley, *Narrative,II,* 62-3.
2. S. J. Dawson, "Report on the Red River Expedition of 1870", VR, 17 July 1871, 460.
3. G. L. Huyshe, *The Red River Expedition* (London, 1871), 98.
4. *Correspondence Relative to the Recent Expedition to the Red River Settlement: with Journal of Operations* (Presented to both Houses of Parliament by Command of Her Majesty, 1871), (London, 1871), 78.
5. Huyshe, 99.
6. *Ibid.*, 99-100.
7. Wolseley, *Narrative, II,* 63.
8. *Ibid.*
9. The term "brigade" is used here in the sense of an organized military group.

10.   H.S.H. Riddell, "The Red River Expedition of 1870", *Transactions of the Literary and Historical Society of Quebec*, Session 1870-71, new series, part 5, Quebec, 1871, 109.

11.   *Ibid.*, 111.

12.   *Ibid.*

13.   There were two sizes of canoes, the large "canots du maître" and the smaller "canots du nord." These were the common names used in the fur trade.

14.   And they were not even unionized! See *Journal of Operations*, 17 July, 78.

15.   *Ibid.*, 78-9.

16.   C. K. Sissons, *John Kerr* , 33 quotes John Kerr's diary on 24 July, "Colonel Wolseley passed us today in a bark canoe paddled by thirteen Indians."

17.   S. B. Harman, *'Twas 26 Years Ago-Narrative of the Red River Expedition 1870* (Toronto, 1896), 18.

18.   S.B. Steele, *Forty Years in Canada* (Toronto, 1915), 22. See also *John Kerr*, 32 and Sherrill Maclaren, 111.

19.   Maclaren, 114.

20.   Riddell, 113.

21.   *Ibid.*

22.   Harman, 19.

23.   *Ibid.*

24.   *Journal of Operations*, 24 July, 82.

25.   *John Kerr*, 35.

26.   Riddell, 114.

27.   *Journal of Operations*, 25 July, 82.

28.   Peter O'Leary, *Travels and Experiences in Canada, The Red River Territory and The United States* (London, 1877), 125.

29.   Wolseley, *Narrative*, II ,66.

30.   Harman, 21.

31.   Steele, 24.

32.   *John Kerr*, 35.

33.   *Ibid.*

34.   John F. Tennant, *Rough Times 1870-1920* (Winnipeg, 1920), 40-1.

35.   *John Kerr*, 34.

36.   *Ibid.*, 35.

37.   *Journal of Operations*, 26 July, 83.

38.   *Ibid.*

39.   *Ibid.*, 29 July, 84.

40.   *Ibid.*

41.   Riddell, 117.

42.   *Ibid.*

43.   *Ibid.*, 118.

44.   *John Kerr*, 37.

45.   *Ibid.*

46.   *Harman*, 21.

47.   *Ibid.*

48.   *Ibid.*, 22.

49.   *Journal of Operations*, 29 July, 84.

50.   *Ibid.*, 84-5.

51.   Harman, 22.

52.   *Ibid.*

53.   It is suggested that the name Rainy River and Rainy Lake were derived from the words *La Reine*. However, general opinion does not support the "Queen" theory. Early maps give the name of the lake as *Lac la Pluie*. Rainy Lake, therefore, is simply a translation of the earlier French name.

54.   *Journal of Operations*, 31 July, 85.

55.   *Ibid.*

56.   *Ibid.*

57. Huyshe, 133.
58. *Ibid.*, 134.
59. *Ibid.*
60. *Journal of Operations*, 2 August, 86.
61. Huyshe, 138. Fort Frances was named after Frances Simpson, wife of Sir George Simpson, who visited the locality on a trip with her husband, from Montreal to Fort York, Manitoba, over the inland waterways in 1830.
62. *Ibid.*
63. *Ibid.*
64. *Ibid.*, 145; *Journal of Operations*, 4 August, 86.
65. Huyshe, 155.
66. Steele, 24-5.
67. Kerr wrote in his diary on 19 August, "A big meeting of the Indians today. They had a war-dance after which they were presented with a few trinkets, tobacco, hard-tack, pork, and so forth. At twelve or one o'clock we were awakened by the guards, ordered to put on our accoutrements, and lie down again with our rifles ready for instant action. A raid on the Fort was expected. The savages had been beating the tom-tom for a couple of days, and the factor scented trouble. We saw signals of some sort being made by the Indians across the river. Arrows with little balls of fire attached were shot into the air - why, we never knew. However, there was no real disturbance.", *John Kerr*, 46.
68. W. F. Butler, *The Great Lone Land; A Narrative of Travel and Adventure in the North-West of America*, 5th edition (London, 1873), 168.
69. *Ibid.*, 48.
70. *Ibid.*, 77.
71. *Ibid.*
72. *Ibid.*, 78.
73. *Ibid.*, 83.
74. *Ibid.*, 91.
75. *Ibid.*, 103-4.
76. *Ibid.*, 104.
77. *Ibid.*, 113.
78. *Ibid.*
79. It was much more likely that they were bringing Riel word that Willie Drever, one of the local inhabitants of Red River Settlement, and a well known opponent of Riel, was on board. See also Maclaren, *Braehead*, 111-3.
80. The vessel swung around in the current below Fort Garry and then steamed slowly to the wharf, her bow facing the current. For his arrangement with Drever see Butler, 116-8.
81. Alexander Begg, *Begg's Red River Journal and other papers 1869-70*, W. L. Morton, ed. Champlain Society Publication (Toronto, 1956), 391. Drever was taken prisoner by Riel and detained for a short time in Fort Garry.
82. Butler, 127-8.
83. *Ibid.*, 130.
84. Begg, 23 July 1870, 392-3.
85. Butler, 132.
86. *Ibid.*, 133.
87. *Ibid.*, 134.
88. *Ibid.*, 136.
89. Begg, *Red River Journal*, 393.
90. Wolseley, *Journal*, 9 August, 87.
91. *Ibid.*, 13 August, 88.
92. *Ibid.*, 14 August.
93. Huyshe, 169.
94. Wolseley, *Narrative*, II, 167.
95. Wolseley, *Journal*, 16 August, 89.

96. *Ibid.*, 15 August, 89.
97. *Ibid.*
98. This had nothing to do with the brown or black rat. Muskrat is the name usually applied to the Musquash (ondatra zibethicus), an aquatic animal whose fur has long been in demand for export. Its flesh, at those times of the year when it is fat, is not unpalatable. It was frequently used for food by native people.
99. Butler, 171-2.

CHAPTER EIGHT - RAT PORTAGE TO FORT GARRY, AUGUST 1870

1. G. F. G. Stanley and L. C. C. Stanley, "The Brothers Hind," *Collections of the Nova Scotia Historical Society* (Kentville, 1980), 111-2. Hind's pertinent work was his *Narrative of the Canadian Red River Exploring Expedition of 1857 and of the Assiniboine and Saskatchewan Expedition of 1858* (London, 1860) 2 Vols. reprinted Edmonton, 1971.
2. S. J. Dawson was disposed to look upon the reports of the difficulties of navigating the Winnipeg River as exaggerated. In his account published in the *VR*, 31 July 1871, 493, he wrote:
     "In former times, the whole trade of the northern parts of the continent passed up by the Winnipeg. The French first used it as a highway; succeeding them came the great North-West Company of Canada, who also followed it, and at a later day, when the Hudson Bay Company had its Head Quarters on the Albany, the route to the Saskatchewan was by way of Lac Seul and the Winnipeg. Whatever may be said of other parts of the route, the Winnipeg was at least a well known and long travelled highway presenting remarkable facilities for boats.
     As a case in point, I may draw attention to the fact, that at the very time the Expeditionary Force was passing, two frail, and poorly manned canoes, the one occupied by a very fat newspaper editor, and the other by a gentleman who had his wife with him, passed over all the rapids, portages and whirlpools of the Winnipeg without its occurring to their occupants that they were doing anything extraordinary."
3. Hind, *Narrative*, 106-7.
4. Wolseley, *Narrative, Conclusion, BEM*, February 1871, 170.
5. Steele, 26-7.
6. *Ibid.*, 26.
7. Butler, 151.
8. Huyshe, 175.
9. *Ibid.*, 175-6.
10. Wolseley, *Journal*, 18 August, 90.
11. Riddell, 123. For the story of the Sioux captives, see Huyshe, 182.
12. Huyshe, 181.
13. Wolseley, *Journal*, 18 August, 90.
14. Harman, 26.
15. A term familiar in the 19th century in Canada and elsewhere to indicate that everything was "according to the book," all spit and polish and correct.
16. Dawson *Report, VR*, 25 July 1871, 477.
17. Huyshe, 184.
18. *Ibid.*, 185.
19. Wolseley, *Journal*, 21 August, 91.
20. Riddell, 126.
21. Huyshe, 190.
22. *Ibid.*, 191.
23. Butler, 187.
24. Quoted in Riddell, 127.
25. *Ibid.*
26. Wolseley, *Journals*, 23 August, 91.

27. *Ibid.*, 24 August, 92.
28. Riddell, 127-8.
29. Huyshe, 192.
30. Riddell, 128.
31. Wolseley, *Narrative, Conclusion*, 176.
32. Begg, *Creation of Manitoba*, 391.
33. Butler, 192.
34. MacLaren, *Braehead*, 114.
35. *Ibid.*
36. *John Kerr*, 46. Kerr noted in his diary, "The Governor came out and thanked us handsomely. He regretted, he said, that he had nothing in the way of drink, such as raspberry vinegar, currant wine, or cold water, but nevertheless was highly pleased with the singing performance."
37. Wolseley, *Journal*: Archibald to Wolseley, 2 September, 95.
38. *Ibid.*: 25 August 1870, 93.
39. Butler, 193.
40. *Ibid.*, 193-4.
41. *Correspondence Relative to the Recent Expedition to the Red River Settlement* (London, 1871): Lindsay to the Secretary of State for War, 18 October 1870, 52.
42. Edward McCourt, *Remember Butler, The Story of Sir William Butler* (London, 1967), 56.
43. C. P. Stacey, *Canada and the British Army* (London, 1936): Campbell's Report to the Governor-General, 10 September 1870, 245.
44. *Weekly Globe*, 8 July 1870: quoted in Stacey, 243.
45. *Ibid.*, 241.
46. *Ibid.*: Kimberley to Young, Confidential, 30 August 1870, 241. My explanation of the British withdrawal was the anxiety of the British government to avoid any possibility of hostilities with the United States, particularly after the Americans had demonstrated the strength of their armies in gaining victory over the Confederate States when many people in Great Britain were backing the Confederates to win the Civil War. This, combined with the rising power of Germany (demonstrated by the Franco-Prussian War, 1870), was sufficient inducement for the British to make a virtue of necessity, and give up any idea of defending Canada against a hostile United States.

CHAPTER NINE - MANITOBA'S FIRST YEAR, 1870-1871

1. Wolseley, *BEM*, January 1871, *Narrative, II*, 64.
2. *Ibid.*
3. The Saulteaux were a branch of the Ojibwa or Chippewa Indians. As among other Algonkian Indians, the majority of their bands were small, largely owing to their limited reserves of food. Their bands seldom exceeded 300 to 400 individuals. See Diamond Jenness, *The Indians of Canada* (Ottawa, 1934, Bulletin 65, Anthropological Series No. 15), 277. See also Douglas Leechman, *Native Tribes of Canada* (Toronto, n.d.), Ch. 2.
4. *Report of the Select Committee On the Causes of the Difficulties in the North-West Territory in 1869* (Ottawa, 1874): McTavish to Taché, 31 July 1870, "Whatever you may hear from others to the contrary, I feel quite confident that the Provisional Government are determined *coute que coute* to hand everything over quietly to the proper authorities, and in no case do I apprehend any rising on the part of the English or Indians."36. This report will henceforth be cited as *1974 Report*.
5. *Ibid.*: Macdonald to Taché, 16 February 1870, 19.
6. Dom Benoit, *Vie de Mgr Taché, Archevêque de St. Boniface* (Montreal, 1904), Vol. 2, 59.
7. *1874 Report*: Taché to Howe, 9 June 1870, 32-3.
8. *Ibid.*: Howe to Taché, 4 July 1870, 34-5.

9. G. F. G. Stanley, "The Journal of J-J Ritchot, March 24 to May 28, 1870" in W. L. Morton, ed., *Manitoba, the Birth of a Province* (Altona, 1965), 136ff, 145-6, 154-5.
10. *Ibid.*, 156.
11. G. T. Denison, *The Struggle for Imperial Unity, Recollections and Experiences* (Toronto, 1909), 37-8.
12. *1874 Report;* Taché Deposition, 40-1.
13. G. F. G. Stanley et al, *The Collected Writings of Louis Riel* (Edmonton, 1985): Riel to Taché, 24 July 1870, Vol. 1,94.
14. *1874 Report*: Ritchot Deposition, 77. It may be recalled that the Fenians were active during the spring and summer of 1870.
15. One staunch "loyalist" in Winnipeg when asked by the reporter of the Toronto *Telegraph* what kind of government he expected, replied "Anything, anything but the Hudson's Bay rule - and in fact we must agitate for another revolution." Toronto *Telegraph*, 10 Sept. 1870 quoted in N.E. Allen Ronaghan, "The Archibald Administration in Manitoba, 1870-1872" (unpublished doctoral thesis, University of Manitoba, 1987), 347.
16. *John Kerr*, 53.
17. *1874 Report*: Archibald Deposition, Memorandum Connected with Fenian Invasion of Manitoba in October 1871, 140.
18. *Ibid.*
19. R. G. MacBeth, *The Romance of Western Canada* (Toronto, 1920), 163-4.
20. Alexander Begg, *History of the North-West*, 3 Vols. (Toronto, 1894), Vol. 2, 31.
21. Toronto *Telegraph*, 22 Sept. 1870, quoted in Ronaghan thesis, 360.
22. CSP, No. 20, Vol. V, 1871: Archibald to the Secretary of State for the Provinces, 10 September 1870, 10.
23. Gerald Friesen, *The Canadian Prairies, A History* (Toronto, 1984), 195-6.
24. Steele, 34.
25. *Ibid.*
26. *Ibid.*
27. *Ibid.*
28. *Ibid.*, 35.
29. Tennant, 66-7.
30. *Ibid.*, 67.
31. *Ibid.*
32. CSP, No. 20, Vol. V: Archibald to the Secretary of State for the Provinces, 17 September 1870, 15.
33. They included John Sutherland as Sheriff, Dr. Curtis Bird as Coroner, and Alfred Boyd, Marc Girard, Donald A. Smith, Donald Gunn, Robert McBeath, Solomon Hamelin, John Fraser, Andrew McDermott, Roger Goulet, William Henderson, Pierre Delorme, Thomas Sinclair, James McKay, Charles Nolin, William Dease, J-B Desautels dit Lapointe, Thomas Traithwaite, Pascal Breland, Charles Begg, Alban Fisher, John Bruce, Patrice Breland, John James Setter, George Klyne, George Gunn, Maxime Genthon, William Hall, Narcisse Marion, William Watt and James Meagher as Justices of the Peace. The appointments were dated 30 September, 1871. *Ibid.*, 21.
34. CSP, No. 20, Vol. V, 1871: McConville to Archibald 27 September 1870, 53.
35. *Ibid.*
36. *Ibid.*: Copy of evidence at a Coroner's Inquest on the body of James Tanner, 2 December 1870, at Poplar Point, Manitoba, 57.
37. *1874 Report;* excerpt from the *Manitoban,* "The History of a Year," 158.
38. R. G. MacBeth, *The Romance of Western Canada,* 165.
39. *John Kerr*, 72.
40. CSP, No. 20, Vol. V, 1875: Boyd to the Gentlemen Residents. . . , no date, but obviously October 1870, 49.
41. *Ibid.*
42. *John Kerr*, 71.

43. *1874 Report*; excerpt from *Manitoban*, 58.
44. *Ibid.*, 159.
45. Alexander Begg, *History of the North-West*, Vol. 2, 29.
46. CSP, No. 20, Vol. V, 1871: Abstract Statement of the Census for the Province of Manitoba, November 1870, 92.
47. Begg, *History of the North-West*, Vol. 2, 27.
48. Steele, 39-40.
49. *Ibid.*, 40.
50. Manitoba adopted the ballot in 1875.
51. Steele, 45.
52. D. Owram, *Province of Eden, The Canadian Expansionist Movement and the Idea of the West, 1856-1900* (Toronto, 1980), 98.
53. Tennant, 72-3.
54. *Ibid.*, 77-8.
55. *Ibid.*, 82.
56. For a discussion of the administration of the Manitoba Land Claims see D. N. Sprague, "Government Lawlessness in the Administration of Manitoba Land Claims, 1870-1887," *Manitoba Law Journal*, 10 (1980), 415-41.
57. CSP, No. 64, Vol. VII, 1972, 8. At the same time, 12 officers of the 2nd (Quebec) Rifles and 103 non-commissioned officers and men of the same battalion returned over the route from Fort Garry to Thunder Bay. Tennant, who remained in Manitoba to become a Customs' Department officer, gives an incomplete list of the names of those who remained in the west, most of them in Manitoba. Tennant also gives a nominal roll for No. 2 Company 2 (Quebec) Rifles.
58. A steam tug had been placed in operation late in 1870.
59. Steele, 40.

CHAPTER TEN - THE FENIAN RAID IN MANITOBA   1871

1. G. F. G. Stanley, "William Bernard O'Donoghue," *DCB*, (Toronto, 1972), Vol. X, 556-7.
2. G. F. G. Stanley et al, *The Collected Writings of Louis Riel*, Vol. 1, 117-8. For the story of O'Donoghue's alteration of the text of the original, see J. P. Pritchett, "The Origin of the so-called Fenian Raid in Manitoba in 1871," *Canadian Historical Review*, 1929, 23-42; see also G. F. G. Stanley, "Riel's Petition to the President of the United States," *CHR*, 1939, 422.
3. LeCaron, whose real name was T. M. Beach, had served with O'Neill during the U.S. Civil War. See his book, *Twenty-Five Years in the Secret Service: The Recollections of a Spy* (London, 1892), Vol. 11, 166; also J.A. Cole, *Prince of Spies, Henri Le Caron* (London, 1984), and Hereward Senior, *The Fenians and Canada* (Toronto, 1978).
4. Dom Benoit, *Vie de Mgr. Taché* (Montreal, 1904) vol. II, 166.
5. *Ibid.*, 164-5.
6. *Ibid.*, 165. The French language newspaper, *Le Métis*, 19 octobre 1871, stated that O'Donoghue had been seen on "la route de Georgetown chevauchant, en excellent cavalier qu'il est, sur un magnifique cheval et portant éperons dorés. Quatre militaires féniens, accompagnaient M. O'Donoghue . . . la rumeur portait l'armée d'invasion de cent à quinze cents féniens, et indiquait les endroits où les chefs avaient fait tout l'été dernier des *caches* énormes d'armes et d'ammunitions."
7. *1874 Report*: Archibald Deposition, 142-3.
8. Ernest J. Chambers, *The 90th Regiment, Winnipeg Rifles* (n.p., 1906), 26.
9. CSP, No. 26, Vol. VII, 1872: Archibald to Howe, 27 Oct. 1871, 4.
10. *Ibid.*
11. *1874 Report*: Archibald Deposition, 141.
12. *Collected Writings of Louis Riel*, Vol. 1: "Compte rendu de réunions ayant trait aux Féniens", St. Vital, 28 sept - 7 octobre 1871, 146.
13. CSP, No. 26, Vol. VII, 1872: Archibald To the People of the Province of Manitoba, Friday, 13 October 1871, 11.

14.   *Collected Writings of Louis Riel*, Vol. 1; Riel à Archibald, 7 octobre 1871, 157.

15.   *1874 Report*: Ritchot to Archibald, 4 Oct. 1871, 90.

16.   *Ibid.*: Archibald to Ritchot, 5 Oct. 1871, 91. Archibald wrote, "Should Mr. Riel come forward as suggested, he need be under no apprehension that his liberty shall be interfered with in any way; to use your own language, 'Pour la circonstance actuelle.' "

17.   CSP, No. 26, Vol. VII, 1872, 12. See also *1874 Report*: Archibald Deposition, 148.

18.   G. F. G. Stanley, "L'invasion fénienne au Manitoba-un journal contemporain", *Revue d'Histoire de l'Amérique française*, Sept. 1963, XVII, No. 2, 263-4.

19.   A good Irish word meaning "bullies".

20.   DND, *Historical Section*, Report No. 2, August 1965, "Canadian-American Defence Relations, 1867-1914." See also *U.S. National Archives*, AGO 3343/1871: Taylor to A/Sec State Davis, 11 Sept. 1871.

21.   *Ibid.*, AGO 3504/1871; Taylor to Gen. Sherman, 2 October 1871.

22.   CSP, No. 26, Vol. VII, 1872: Wheaton to Irvine, 8 October 1871, 9. The Hudson's Bay Company fort was located south of what the United States regarded as the legitimate boundary and General Sheridan who commanded all U.S. troops in the Missouri District forwarded Wheaton's report to the Secretary of War with the observation that, having saved Manitoba for the Dominion, the Canadians were now trying to rob the United States "of the justification of our actions." The Secretary of State, however, refused to press for a British withdrawal, on the grounds that, although it was known that the exact location of the frontier was uncertain, it would be premature to call the British occupation a "willful trespass". *U.S. National Archives*, AGO 60/1872: Fish to Belknap, 5 Jan. 1872.

23.   The official reports from M.D. 10 by Major Irvine, 23 Oct. 1871; Capt. Joseph Royal, 17 Oct. 1871; Lieut. Col. W. Osborne Smith, 23 Oct. 1871 and Capt. Thomas Scott's report and diary, 23 Oct. 1871 will be found in CSP, No. 8, Vol. V, 1872, 77-85.

24.   *1874 Report*: Douglas to Archibald, 7 Oct. 1871, 144.

25.   *Ibid.*, 145.

26.   *Ibid.*: Riel, Lépine and Parenteau to Archibald, 7 October 1871, 147.

27.   *Le Métis*, 26 October 1871, Vol. 1, No. 21, gives the following strength of the force mustered against the Fenians in Manitoba in October 1871:

Major Irvine's command

Two companies of Active Militia	80 men	
Captain Kennedy's company	50	
Captain Mulvey's company	70	
Captain de Plainval's company	42	
Captain Royal's and Mr. Breland's company	50	
	292	292

volunteers - Métis under Riel and Lépine	100	
volunteers - Métis scouts from White Horse Plains	50	
volunteers - Métis from Baie St. Paul	25	
volunteers - Métis from St. Charles	25	
	200	200
TOTAL		492 men

28.   CSP, No. 26, Vol. VII, 1872: Archibald To the People of the Province of Manitoba, 13 Oct. 1871, 11-2. See Appendix C.

29.   *Ibid.*: Kimberley to Lisgar, 7 December 1871, 13.

30.   *Ibid.*: Howe to Archibald, 2 Jan. 1872, 14.

31. *Le Métis*, 10 octobre 1871, "Histoire des quinze derniers jours," 1-2.
32. CSP, No. 26, Vol. VII, 1872: Archibald to Howe, 3 Oct. 1871, 1-2.
33. *Ibid.*: Archibald to Howe, 13 October, 10-1.
34. CSP, No. 8, Vol. V, 1872, 40.
35. "Journal of a trip from London, Ont. to Fort Garry, October 17, 1871 - November 18, 1871," *PAM*. The author was George Adshead, subsequently accountant at Stony Mountain Penitentiary under Mr. Bedson. Henceforth cited as "Adshead Journal."
36. *Ibid.*, 20 Oct. 1871.
37. *From Toronto to Fort Garry-An Account of the Second Expedition to Red River, Diary of a Private Soldier* (Hamilton, n.d.) 5. The authorship is attributed to Justin A. Griffin. Henceforth cited as Griffin, *Diary*.
38. "Adshead Journal," 23 Oct. 1871.
39. Griffin, *Diary*, 7.
40. "Adshead Journal," 23 Oct.
41. Griffin, *Diary*, 8.
42. "Adshead Journal," 24 Oct.; Griffin, *Diary*, 11. Griffin saw a great future for Prince Arthur's Landing which he described as "a village containing about forty houses."
43. "Adshead Journal," 25 Oct.
44. *Ibid.*, 26 Oct.
45. Griffin, *Diary*, 13.
46. *Ibid.*, 16.
47. *Ibid.*, 19.
48. "Adshead Journal," 28 Oct.
49. *Ibid.*, 30 Oct.
50. Griffin, *Diary*, 19.
51. "Adshead Journal" 3 Nov. On 4 Nov. Adshead recorded "box of Medical Comforts in my charge, broken open during the night & all the Brandy & Port Wine stolen." Because "all hands, had been obliged to take to the water and haul the boats . . . bitter cold work" according to Adshead, perhaps one might be inclined to sympathize with the thieves!
52. Griffin, *Diary*, 25.
53. *Ibid.*, 26-7.
54. *Ibid.*, 25.
55. *Ibid.*, 26.
56. *Ibid.*, 35-6.
57. *Ibid.*, 36.
58. *Ibid.*, 38.
59. *Ibid.*, 40.
60. "Adshead Journal," 10 Nov.
61. Griffin, *Diary*, 42.
62. "Adshead Journal," 12 Nov.
63. Griffin, *Diary*, 43
64. "Adshead Journal," 13 Nov.
65. Griffin, *Diary*, 49.
66. "Adshead Journal," 17 Nov.
67. *Ibid.*, 18 Nov.

CHAPTER ELEVEN - THE PROVISIONAL BATTALION AND THE ESTABLISHMENT OF M.D. 10

1. CSP, No. 8, vol. V, 1872, 75.
2. *Ibid.*, 76.
3. *Ibid.*
4. PAM, "Journal of the Provisional Battalion of Rifles at Fort Garry," 1871, 1.
5. *Ibid.*

6. *Ibid.*

7. *Ibid.*, 1-2.

8. *Ibid.*, 3 December 1873, 6.

9. *Ibid.*

10. *Ibid.*

11. *Ibid.*, 7-8.

12. *Ibid.*, 15-6. See also CSP, No. 6, Vol. 1875: Osborne Smith to Deputy Adjutant-General, 20 Dec. 1874, 51-5.

13. This account of the 1872 expedition to Red River is taken from "Dawson Route Military Expedition" by "A Private in the Force," published in the *Manitoban*, March 1892. The reference here is to p.116.

14. *Ibid.* See also "Journal of the Provisional Battalion," 3.

15. The Communists, or rather "communards" of 1870, should not be confused with the later Marxist variety in Russia. Before the details of peace were arranged between France and Germany following the Franco-Prussian War, Paris was taken over by a revolutionary group who established a "commune" or autonomous government independent of the government of France. The rising began in March 1871 and was suppressed only after bloody fighting between the Communists, i.e. the supporters of the commune, and the government of France.

16. *Manitoban*, March 1892, 116.

17. *Ibid.*, 117.

18. *Ibid.*

19. *Ibid.*

20. *Ibid.*, 118.

21. *Ibid.*

22. See Appendix E.

23. *Ibid.*, June 1892, 226.

24. *Ibid.*, 227.

25. *Ibid.*

26. *Ibid.* At Fort Frances the troops bound for Manitoba passed a detachment of 90 NCO's and men on their return from Fort Garry "to their several places of enlistment on completion of service, being under the command of Capt. J.P. Fletcher, assisted by Lieut. Hayter Reed and Ensign Constantine, which last named had received a commission in the spring previously after having done faithful duty as Sergeant Major." "Journal of the Provisional Battalion of Rifles," 3.

27. *Manitoban*, June 1892, 227.

28. *Ibid.*, 228.

29. *Ibid.*, 229.

30. *Ibid.*

31. CSP, No. 7, Vol. VI, 1876: Report by Lt. Col. W. Osborne Smith, Winnipeg, 14 Dec. 1875, 66.

32. *Ibid.*: Annual report of Major-General E. Selby-Smythe, 1 Jan. 1876, 4.

33. Order in Council, 6 April 1870, No. 1335.

34. HCD, 3rd Session, First Parliament, 33 Vict. 1870; 2 May 1870, 1310.

35. Macdonald to Cartier, 16 June 1871 quoted in S. W. Horrall, "Sir John A. Macdonald and the Police Force for the Northwest Territories," CHR, No. 2, June 1972, 186. See also HCD, 4th Session, Vol. 3, 34 Vict., 1872, 1142.

36. Butler, *The Great Lone Land*, Governor Archibald's Instructions, 10 Oct. 1870, Appendix, 354.

37. *Ibid.*: Butler's report to Archibald, 10 March, 1871, Appendix, 355-6.

38. *Ibid.*, 356.

39. *Ibid.*, 358.

40. *Ibid.*, 358-60, 363.

41. *Ibid.*, 378-9.

42. R. S. Allen, "A Witness to Murder," in A. L. Getty and Antoine Lussier, *As Long as the Sun Shines and the Water Flows* (Vancouver, 1983), 232.

43. J. P. Turner, *The North-West Mounted Police 1873-1893* (Ottawa, 1950), Vol. 1, 80-1, 92. This suggestion of red tunics was based on the fact that the British regular infantry wore red tunics. The Indians would readily recognize the significance of the red. So, too, would the Americans. The red implied "friends" to the Indians and "enemy" to the Americans.
44. HCD, March 1873.
45. Ex-constable James McKernan, "Expeditions Made in 1873," *Scarlet and Gold Annual*, R.N.W.M.P. Veterans' Association (Vancouver), No. 2, 1920, 84.
46. R. C. Fetherstonhaugh ignores the Provisional Battalion in Manitoba in claiming seniority for the Infantry School Corps in *The Royal Canadian Regiment, 1883-1933* (1936, reprinted Fredericton, 1981), 6ff.

CHAPTER TWELVE - EPILOGUE

1. Morris, *Heaven's Command*, 353.
2. *Ibid.*
3. Gilbert and Sullivan caricatured Wolseley in the *Pirates of Penzance*. Disraeli's judgement of him was, "Wolseley is an egotist and a braggart. So was Nelson." And that was not an unfair assessment of a leader who never played a role in a "great war," and won his distinction in "little wars." I wonder how he would have shaped up in 1914-1918?
4. Morris, 380. This has a 20th century American ring to it!
5. This doctrine may appear to run counter to that advanced at the war trials following World War Two. The soldier's lot is not a happy one. He may be damned if he does and damned if he doesn't, if not by his own generation, then by those that follow.
6. Wolseley, *Narrative,II*, BEM, January 1871, 56-7.
7. *Ibid.*, 57.
8. *Ibid.*, 52.
9. *Ibid.*, 61-2.
10. *Ibid.*, 65. By way of contrast, Dawson blamed the defection of some of the Indians on Wolseley's insistence on using the Kaministikwia route rather than concentrating on the highway to Shebandowan Lake. See VR, 10 July 1871, 444.
11. S. J. Dawson, *Official Report on the Red River Expedition of 1870* (Ottawa, 1871), 23.
12. *Ibid.*, 21.
13. *Ibid.*, 22-3.
14. *Correspondence Relative to the Recent Expedition to the Red River Settlement* (London, 1871); "General Orders" issued over the signature of J. E. Thackwell, Deputy Adjutant-General, 10 May 1870, 16.
15. Roger Willock, "Green Jackets on the Red River," *Canadian Army Journal*, January 1959, XIII, No. 1, 35.
16. I have never found positive evidence supporting Denison's statement that there was a "plot" to cancel the Red River Expedition. If Denison was responsible, as he claimed, for delaying Archibald's arrival at Fort Garry, he did a great disservice to the country to which he was unquestionably devoted. It is interesting to note that when Wolseley returned to Ontario, en route to Great Britain, he did not stop at Toronto, although he did telegraph Denison to meet him at the railway station. Denison did not receive the telegram in time and had to be content with a letter praising Fred Denison as "the best of aides-de-camp, and a most zealous, hardworking soldier." G. T. Denison, *Soldiering in Canada* (Toronto, 1909), 180.

APPENDICES

1. *Correspondence Relative to the Recent Expedition to the Red River Settlement* (London, 1871); General Orders, 10 May 1870, 16-7.
2. Grace Lee Nute, "Voyageurs' Artist",*The Beaver*, June 1947, 32-6.
3. *The VR*, 31 July 1871, 493.

4.   Audrey Miller, "Frances Ann Hopkins 1838-1919" in R. H. Stacey ed., *Lives and Works of Canadian Artists*, No. 6 (Toronto, Dundurn Press, n.d.)

5.   Alice M. Johnson, "Edward and Frances Hopkins of Montreal, *The Beaver*, Autumn, 1971, 14-9. Other articles on Frances Hopkins include John W. Chalmers, "Frances Ann Hopkins: the lady who painted canoes," in the *Canadian Geographical Journal*, Vol. LXXXIII, July 1971, 18-27; Nancy Tousley, "Visual Arts," *Calgary Herald*, 6 July 1978; and Catherine Sinclair, "A strangely forgotten frontier artist, Frances Ann Hopkins," *Chatelaine*, December 1961. Perhaps some enterprising student of women's history will look further into the career of Frances Ann Hopkins, and into that of Kate St. John.

6.   CSP, No. 26, Vol. VII, 1872, 11-2.

7.   F. J. Blatherwick, *Canadian Orders, Decorations and Medals* (Toronto, 1985), 47. See also G. H. Neale and Ross W. Irwin, *The Medal Roll of the Red River Campaign of 1870 in Canada* (Toronto, 1982).

8.   The *Manitoban*, March 1892, 118.

BIBLIOGRAPHY

While preparing this book, I relied, for the most part, upon printed sources, although in several instances I used photocopied materials from the National Archives of Canada, the Public Archives of Manitoba and the Library of Queen's University in Kingston, Ontario. There are also items relating to Wolseley in the library of the Alberta-Glenbow Museum in Calgary. As far as printed materials relating to Louis Riel are concerned, Volume 5 of *The Collected Writings of Louis Riel/ Les Ecrits Complets de Louis Riel*, Edmonton, 1985, contains over four hundred items. There is no point in listing all of them here. The printed collections of documents, books, pamphlets and articles noted below are those I have consulted. They bear more directly upon the military events than upon the political career of Riel.

I have also examined files of the *Globe, The Canadian Illustrated News, L'Opinion Publique* and *Le Métis*.

I. PRIMARY SOURCES (Printed)

A. BRITISH GOVERNMENT DOCUMENTS

British Parliamentary Papers - *Reports, Correspondence and other Papers relating to Canada, 1867-1874* (Irish University Press Series, Shannon, Ireland, 1970).

Correspondence Relative to the Recent Expedition to the Red River Settlement: With Journal of Operations (London, 1871).

Report on the Red River Expedition of 1870 by Assistant Controller Irvine (London, 1871).

B. CANADIAN GOVERNMENT DOCUMENTS

Debates of the House of Commons, 1870, 1871, 1872, 1873.

Report of the Select Committee on the Causes of the difficulties in the North West Territory in 1869 (Ottawa, 1874).

Canada Sessional Papers, Nos. 8, 12, 20, Vol. V, 1870.

Canada Sessional Papers, Nos. 8, 20, Vol. V, 1871.

Canada Sessional Papers, No. 20, Vol. VIII, 1871.

Canada Sessional Papers, Nos. 26, 64, Vol. VII, 1872.

Canada Sessional Papers, No. 7, Vol. V, 1874.

Canada Sessional Papers, No. 5, Vol. VI, 1875.

Canada Sessional Papers, No. 7, Vol. VI, 1876.

S. J. Dawson, *Report on the Red River Expedition of 1870* (Ottawa, 1871).

C. CORRESPONDENCE

Arthur, Elizabeth, *Thunder Bay District 1821-1892 - A Collection of Documents* (Toronto, 1973).

Johnson, J.K., *Affectionately Yours, the letters of Sir John A. Macdonald and his family* (Toronto, 1969).

Pope, Sir Joseph, *Correspondence of Sir John Macdonald* (Toronto, 1921).

-----, ed. *Memoirs of the Right Honourable Sir John Alexander Macdonald* (Toronto, 1930).

Stanley, G. F. G., *et al*, *The Collected Writings of Louis Riel / Les Ecrits Complets de Louis Riel* (Edmonton, 1985), 5 vols.

Statement Respecting the Earl of Selkirk's Settlement upon the Red River (London, 1817; Cole's Reprint, Toronto, 1970).

D. ACCOUNTS BY PARTICIPANTS

Adshead, George, "Journal of a trip from London, Ont. to Fort Garry, October 17, 1871-November 18, 1871", PAM.

Begg, Alexander, *The Creation of Manitoba, a History of the Red River Troubles* (Toronto, 1871).

-----. *History of the North-West*, Vol. 2 (Toronto, 1894).

Boulton, C. A., *Reminiscences of the North-West Rebellion* (Toronto, 1886).

Butler, William, *The Great Lone Land, A Narrative of Travel and Adventure in the North-West of America* (London, 1873).

Dawson, S. J., "Report on the Red River Expedition," the *VR*, 26 June, 3 July, 10 July, 17 July, 24 July, 7 August, 14 August, 21 August, 1871. This is an unexpurgated edition of his *Report* published by the Canadian Government.

Denison, G. L., *Soldiering in Canada, Recollections and Experiences* (Toronto, 1900).

-----. *The Struggle for Imperial Unity, Recollections and Experiences,* (Toronto, 1909).

Franchère, Gabriel, *A Voyage to the Northwest Coast of America,* ed. Milo Quaife (Chicago, 1954).

Graffenried, Friederich von, *Sechs Jahre in Canada, 1813-1819* (Bern, 1891).

Grant, G. M., *Ocean to Ocean, Sanford Fleming's Expedition Through Canada in 1872* (Toronto, 1925).

Griffin, Justin A., *From Toronto to Fort Garry, An Account of the Second Expedition - Diary of a Private Soldier* (Hamilton, 1872).

Hargrave, J., *Red River* (Montreal, 1871).

Harman, *'Twas 26 Years Ago - Narrative of the Red River Expedition 1870* (Toronto, 1896).

Hind, H. Y., *Narrative of the Canadian Red River Exploring Expedition of 1857 and of the Assiniboine and Saskatchewan Expedition of 1858*, 2 vols. (London, 1860; Toronto, 1971).

Huyshe, George L., *The Red River Expedition* (London, 1871).

Kane, Paul, *Wanderings of an Artist* (Toronto, 1925).

McKernan, James, "Expeditions made in 1873," *Scarlet and Gold*, No. 2 (Royal North-West Mounted Police Association, 1920).

Morison, Jean, *The North West Company in Rebellion, Simon McGillivray's Fort William Notebook 1815* (Thunder Bay Historical Museum Society, 1988).

Morton, W. L., *Alexander Begg's Red River Journal and Other Papers* (Champlain Society, Toronto, 1956).

O'Leary, Peter, *Travels and Experiences in Canada, the Red River Territory and the United States* (London, 1877).

Riddell, H. S. H., "The Red River Expedition of 1870", *Literary and Historical Society of Quebec*, Session 1870-71 (Quebec, 1871).

Ross, Alexander, *The Red River Settlement: Its Rise, Progress and Present State with Some Account of the Native Races, and its General History to the Present Day* (London, 1856).

Stanley, G. F. G., ed., "Le Journal de L'Abbé J-J Ritchot," *La Revue d'Histoire de l'Amérique française*, Vol. XVII, mars 1964. For an English version see

-----. "The Journal of J-J Ritchot, March 24 - May 28, 1870" in W. L. Morton, *The Birth of a Province*, Manitoba Record Society, Vol. 1, 1965.

-----. "L'Invasion fénienne au Manitoba - un journal contemporain," *La Revue d'Histoire de l'Amérique française*, Vol. xvii, septembre 1963.

-----. "Riel's petition to the President of the United States 1870," CHR, September 1939.

-----. "A Soldier at Fort Garry," *The Beaver*, Autumn, 1957.

Steele, S.B., *Forty Years in Canada* (Toronto, 1915).

Tennant, Joseph F., *Rough Times 1870-1920*, a souvenir of the 50th Anniversary of the Red River Expedition and the Formation of the Province of Manitoba (Winnipeg, 1920).

Trémaudan, A. H., de, "Louis Riel and the Fenian Raid of 1871", CHR, June, 1935.

Wallace, N.B., *The Rebellion in the Red River Settlement 1869-70, its causes and suppression:* a lecture delivered at Clifton, Quebec, 1871, by Captain N. Willoughby Wallace, 60th Rifles (Barnstaple, 1872).

Wallace, W.S., *Documents Relating to the North West Company* (Champlain Society, Toronto, 1934).

Wolseley, Field Marshal Viscount, *The Story of a Soldier's Life* (London, 1903), Vol. 2.

-----. "Narrative of the Red River Expedition by an Officer of the Expeditionary Force," *BEM*, December, January, February 1871. The unnamed author was Colonel Wolseley. See also the anonymous and critical review of Wolseley's "Narrative" in the *VR*, 16 January, 5 February, 13 February, 20 February, 17 April, 22 April, Vol. V, 1871. Was this author S. J. Dawson?

Young, George, *Manitoba Memories, Leaves from my Life in the Prairie Provinces 1868-1884* (Toronto, 1897).

II. SECONDARY SOURCES

A. BOOKS

Barnes, R.M., *A History of the Regiments and Uniforms of the British Army* (London, 1950).

Benoit, Dom, *Vie de Mgr. Taché Archevêque de St. Boniface,* 2 vols., (Montreal, 1904).

Bertrand, J. F., *Highway of Destiny* (New York, 1959).

Blatherwick, F. J., *Canadian Orders, Decorations and Medals* (Toronto, 1985).

Bumsted, J. M., *The People's Clearances 1770-1815* (Edinburgh, 1982).

Campbell, M. W., *McGillivray, Lord of the Northwest* (Toronto, 1962).

The Canadian Militia, a History of the Origin and Development of the Force (Montreal, 1907).

Chambers, E. J., *The 90th Regiment, Winnipeg Rifles* (n.p., 1906).

Cole, J.A., *Prince of Spies, Henri Le Caron* (London, 1984).

Cooke, O. A. *The Canadian Military Experience* (Ottawa, 1984).

Cox, Ross, *Adventures on the Columbia River* (New York, 1822).

Friesen, Gerald, *The Canadian Prairies, A History* (Toronto, 1984).

Gibson, D., Gibson, L., and Harvey, C., *Attorney for the Frontier: Enos Stutsman* (Winnipeg, 1983).

Giraud, Marcel, *Le Métis Canadien, son rôle dans l'histoire des provinces de l'ouest* (Paris, 1945).

Gray, J.M. *Lord Selkirk of Red River* (Toronto, 1963).

Hill, R. B., *Manitoba History of the Early Settlement, Development and Resources* (Toronto, 1880).

Hitsman, J. M., *Safeguarding Canada 1763-1871* (Toronto, 1968).

Howard, J. K., *Strange Empire* (New York, 1952).

Jackson, James A., *The Centennial History of Manitoba* (Toronto, 1970).

Jenkins, Brian, *Fenians and Anglo-American Relations during Reconstruction* (Ithaca, 1969).

Jenness, D., *The Indians of Canada* (Ottawa, 1934, Bulletin 65, Anthropological Series, No. 15).

Kingsford, C. L., *The Story of the Royal Warwickshire Regiment* (London, 1921).

Lamb, R. E., *Thunder in the North, Conflict over the Riel Risings, 1870-1885* (New York, 1957).

MacBeth, R. G., *The Romance of Western Canada* (Toronto, 1920).

McCourt, Edward, *Remember Butler* (Toronto, 1967).

MacKay, Douglas, *The Honourable Company, a History of the Hudson's Bay Company* (Toronto, 1936).

Maclaren, Sherrill, *Braehead, Three Founding Families in Nineteenth Century Canada* (Toronto, 1986).

Macleod, R. C., *The North West Mounted Police and Law Enforcement, 1873-1905* (Toronto, 1976).

Martin, Chester, *Lord Selkirk's Work in Canada* (Oxford, 1916).

Mauro, Joseph, *Thunder Bay, A History* (Thunder Bay, 1981).

Meuron, Guy, de *Le Régiment Meuron 1781-1816* (Lausanne, 1982).

Mitchell, G. D., *R. C. H. A., Right of the Line* (Ottawa, 1986).

Morice, A. G., *A Critical History of the Red River Insurrection after Official Documents and Non-Catholic Sources* (Winnipeg, 1935).

Morris, James, *Heaven's Command, An Imperial Progress* (London, 1973).

Morrison, W. R., *The Sixth Regiment of Foot at Lower Fort Garry*, Canadian Historic Sites, Occasional Papers in Archaeology and History, No. 4, National Historic Sites Service (National and Historic Sites Branch, Department of Indian Affairs and Northern Development, Ottawa, 1970)

-----. *The Second Battalion, Quebec Rifles at Lower Fort Garry*, Canadian Historic Sites, Occasional Papers in Archaeology and History, No. 4 (National Historic Sites Service, National and Historic Sites Branch, Department of Indian Affairs and Northern Development, Ottawa, 1970).

Morton, A. S., *A History of the Canadian West to 1870-71* (Toronto, 1939).

Morton, W. L., *The Critical Years, the Union of British North America 1857-1873* (Toronto, 1964).

-----. *Manitoba, a History* (Toronto, 1957).

Neale, G. H. and Irwin, Ross W., *The Medal Roll of the Red River Campaign of 1870 in Canada* (Toronto, 1982).

Nute, Grace Lee, *Rainy River Country* (St. Paul, 1950).

Owram, D., *Province of Eden, The Canadian Expansionist Movement and the Idea of the West 1856-1900* (Toronto, 1980).

Parsons, J. E., *West on the 49th Parallel, Red River to the Rockies 1872-1876* (New York, 1963).

Preston, R. A., *Canada and Imperial Defense* (Toronto, 1986).

Prud'homme, L. A., *Monseigneur Noel-Joseph Ritchot* (Winnipeg, 1928).

Racette, Calvin, *Flags of the Métis* (Regina, 1987).

Rich, E. E., *The History of the Hudson's Bay Company, 1763-1879* (London, 1959).

Senior, Hereward, *The Fenians and Canada* (Toronto, 1978).

Shippee, L. B., *Canadian-American Relations, 1849-1874* (New Haven-Toronto, 1939).

Sissons, Constance Kerr, *John Kerr* (Toronto, 1946).

Sprague, D. N., *Canada and the Métis 1869-1885* (Waterloo, 1988).

Stacey, C. P., *Canada and the British Army, 1846-1871* (London, 1936).

Stanley, G. F. G., *The Birth of Western Canada* (London, 1936; Toronto, 1960).

-----. *Canada's Soldiers* (Toronto, 1974).

-----. *Louis Riel* (Toronto, 1963).

Sulte, Benjamin, *L'Expédition Militaire au Manitoba*, (Montreal, 1871).

Sweeny, Alistair, *George Etienne Cartier, a Biography* (Toronto, 1976).

Trémaudan, A. H., de, *Histoire de la Nation Métisse* (Montreal, 1935).

Turner, J. P., *The North West Mounted Police, 1873-1893* (Ottawa, 1950).

Van Kirk, Sylvia, *Many Tender Ties* (Winnipeg, 1980).

Warner, Donald, *The Idea of Continental Union, Agitation for the Annexation of Canada to the United States 1849-1893* (University of Kentucky Press, 1960).

Watson, Robert, *Lower Fort Garry: A History of the Stone Fort* (Winnipeg, 1928).

Willson, Beckles, *The Life of Lord Strathcona* (London, 1915).

Winks, R. W., *Canada and the United States - The Civil War Years* (Baltimore, 1960).

B. PAMPHLETS AND ARTICLES

Allen, R. S., "A Witness to Murder" in A. L. Getty and Antoine Lussier, *As Long as the Sun Shines and the Water Flows* (Vancouver, 1983).

Chalmers, J. W., "Frances Ann Hopkins: the lady who painted canoes", *Canadian Geographical Journal*, July 1971.

Chartrand, René, "From Versailles to Wyoming: French Exploration and Trade in the Eighteenth Century", *The Journal of the West*, October, 1987.

Creighton, Donald G., "Old Tomorrow", *The Beaver*, Winter, 1956.

----. "Macdonald and Manitoba", *The Beaver*, Spring, 1957.

Gluek, A. C., "Imperial Protection for the Trading Interests of the Hudson's Bay Company, 1857-1861", CHR, June, 1956.

Horrall, S. W., "Sir John Macdonald and the Police Force for the Northwest Territories,", CHR, June 1972.

Ingersoll, W. E., "Red Coats at Fort Garry", *The Beaver*, December, 1945.

Johnson, Alice M., "Edward and Frances Hopkins of Montreal", *The Beaver*, Autumn, 1971.

Kemp, D., "Land Grants Under the Manitoba Act", a paper presented at Brandon University: Métis Historical Conference, 6,7 May 1971, mimeographed.

MacKay, D. S. C., "The Red River Expedition 1870", *Military Collector and Historian*, Fall, 1977.

Macleod, Margaret Annett, "Cuthbert Grant of Grantown", CHR, March, 1940.

Macleod, R. C., *The Northwest Mounted Police, 1873-1919, Canadian Historical Association Historical Booklet No. 31*, (Ottawa, 1978).

Nute, Grace Lee, "Voyageur Artist", *The Beaver*, June, 1947.

Pritchett, J. P., "The Origin of the so-called Fenian Raid in Manitoba in 1871", CHR, 1929.

Spankie, Donald F., "The Canadian Connection", *Journal of the Society for Army Historical Research*, Winter, 1987.

Sprague, D. N., "Government Lawlessness in the Administration of Manitoba Land Claims, 1870-1887", *Manitoba Law Journal*, 10, (1980).

Stacey, C. P., "The Second Red River Expedition", *Canadian Defence Quarterly, Vol. VIII, No. 2, January, 1931*.

----. "The Undefended Border, the Myth and the Reality," *Canadian Historical Association Booklet No. 1*, Ottawa, 1953.

----. "The Military Aspect of Canada's Winning of the West, 1870-1885", March, 1940.

Stanley, G. F. G., "French Settlement West of Lake Superior",*Transactions of the Royal Society of Canada*, June 1954.

-----. "Louis Riel, Patriot or Rebel?", *Canadian Historical Association Booklet No. 2*, Ottawa, 1954.

-----. "A Soldier at Fort Garry", *The Beaver*, Autumn, 1957.

Stanley, G. F. G., and L. C. C. Stanley, "The Brothers Hind", *Collections of the Nova Scotia Historical Society*, 1980.

Van Kirk, Sylvia, "Women of the Trade", *The Beaver*, Winter, 1972.

Willock, Roger, "Green Jackets on the Red River", *Canadian Army Journal*, January, 1959.

C. UNPUBLISHED THESES

Best, Henry B. M., "George-Etienne Cartier" (Université Laval, 1969).

Ronaghan, N. E. Allen, "The Archibald Administration in Manitoba, 1870-1872", (University of Manitoba, 1987).

Illustration Credits

Archives of Ontario: 97, 103.

Canadian Illustrated News: 54, 60, 93 (left).

Canadian Parks Service: 24.

Glenbow Archives: 20 (left), 61, 63, 94, 106 (upper), 110, 144, 166, 171, 190.

Glenbow Museum: 42, 106 (lower), 227.

Hudson Bay Company Archives, Provincial Archives of Manitoba: 64.

Library of Congress: 99.

Metropolitan Toronto Library: 102, 112, 131.

Musée des Armes et d'Histoire, Colombier (Switzerland): 26.

National Archives of Canada: cover, 14, 29, 33, 39, 43, 50, 71, 80, 82, 87, 93 (right), 116 (upper and lower), 117, 120, 122, 124, 126, 128, 137 (upper and lower), 138 (upper and lower), 141, 147, 148, 157, 158, 182 (right), 185, 187, 205, 214-5, 228, 246, 261, 268 (upper and lower).

National Museums of Canada: 152, 213 (upper).

National Portrait Gallery: 13, 57.

Office of the Sheriff, York County, Ontario: 20 (right).

Provincial Archives of Manitoba: 22, 59, 66, 169, 173, 179, 194, 197, 203, 208, 212, 213 (lower), 218, 230.

Royal Canadian Mounted Police Museum (Regina): 114, 247.

Royal Ontario Museum: 262.

Société Historique de Saint-Boniface: 182 (left).

State Historical Society (Bismarck, North Dakota): 200.

Thomas Fisher Rare Book Library, University of Toronto: 27.

Thunder Bay Public Library: 17, 111, 118, 257.

William Constable: 41, 56, 139, 164, 211, endpapers.

INDEX

Numbers in **boldface** indicate an illustration.